William Adams (1594-1661) of Ipswich, Massachusetts

and Some of His Descendants

A History of the
Ancestral Adams Lineage of
Madeline (Adams) Whitehead and
Descendants of John Quincy Adams of
Mound City, Kansas

with
Details of Related Families
Including: Dickinson, Knowlton, Leach, Locke, Burnap,
Wilson, Mapes, Cochran, Whitehead, and Eaton

Revised and Expanded Second Edition

Kenneth L. Bosworth

HERITAGE BOOKS
2007

HERITAGE BOOKS
AN IMPRINT OF HERITAGE BOOKS, INC.

Books, CDs, and more—Worldwide

For our listing of thousands of titles see our website
at
www.HeritageBooks.com

Published 2007 by
HERITAGE BOOKS, INC.
Publishing Division
65 East Main Street
Westminster, Maryland 21157-5026

Other Heritage Books by the author:
*Edward Colborne of Ipswich, Massachusetts, 1618-1712,
and Five Generations of His Descendants*

International Standard Book Number: 978-0-7884-0528-0

DEDICATED TO:
JANE ANN (WHITEHEAD) BOSWORTH
D.A.R. No. 733444

Jane is a daughter of Madeline (Adams) Whitehead and a direct descendant of the patriot Ephraim Adams who served his country before, during, and after the Revolution. Jane is the wife of the author. Her patience, assistance, and understanding made this book possible.

APPLICATION FOR MEMBERSHIP TO THE NATIONAL SOCIETY

OF THE

DAUGHTERS OF THE AMERICAN REVOLUTION

WASHINGTON, D.C.

State _____CALIFORNIA_____

City_____MISSION VIEJO_____

Name of Chapter _____MISSION VIEJO_____

Computer Code Number _____8-181-CA_____

National Number _____

~~Miss~~ or Mrs.) ____Jane Ann Whitehead Bosworth____
    (First name) (Middle and Maiden name) (Last name)

Wife ☒ Widow ☐ Divorced ☐ __Kenneth Lloyd Bosworth__
         (Husband)

Residence____24702 Pallas Way, Mission Viejo, CA 92691____
  Number Street City State Zip Code

DESCENDANT OF

EPHRAIM ADAMS

The undersigned have investigated and approved the applicant and her application.

Judy A. Deeter
         Chapter Regent.

Kathleen Maurey
         Chapter Registrar.

August 6 , 19_90_

Application, duplicate, and Fees received by Treasurer General _____

Application and duplicate received by Organizing Secretary General _____

Application and duplicate received by Registrar General _____

Application verified and approved _____

         Registrar General.

Accepted by the National Board of Management _____, 19____

         Recording Secretary General.

Endorsement for membership at large:

_____
  State Regent.

Nominated and recommended by the two undersigned members of the Society in good standing, to whom the applicant is personally known. Endorsers must be of same Chapter; if joining At Large, of the same State.

ENDORSED IN HANDWRITING BY

DAR National Number *0709284* DAR National Number *0728101*

Name *Beverly Salus* Name *Suzanne Perry*

Residence *28275 Felicia Mission Viejo* Residence *30682 Sea Island Dr. Monarch Beach*

Chapter *Mission Viejo* Chapter *Mission Viejo*

1

THE APPLICATION FOR MEMBERSHIP IN THE D.A.R.
FOR JANE ANN (WHITEHEAD) BOSWORTH
Membership was possible because of the service of
Ephraim Adams in the Revolution

LINEAGE

_____ JANE ANN WHITEHEAD BOSWORTH _____ being duly sworn

(Full name of applicant)

1. I was born on __30 Jan 1945__ at ~~Los Angeles, Los Angeles,~~ CA

married on __8 Feb 1964__ at _Las Vegas, Clark Co. NV_

to_Kenneth Lloyd Bosworth____ born on __2 Apr 1942__ at _Pomona, Los Angeles Co., CA_

I am the daughter by blood line of

2. _Charles Edward Whitehead_ born __11 Aug 1909__ at _____ Carroll Co. Missouri

died at _____ on _____ and his (first ~~or~~) wife

____Madeline Adams____ born __22 Oct 1913__ at _Paris, Linn Co. Kansas_

died at _____ on _____ married_26 Jul 1936, Kansas City_ MO

date and place

3. The said ___Madeline Adams___ was the child by blood line of

___Robert Clyde Adams___ born __16 Mar 1885__ at _____ Linn Co., Kansas

died at _Corvallis, Benton Co. OR_ on __17 Oct 1955__ and his (first ~~or~~) wife

___Hattie Mapes___ born __8 Apr 1885__ at _____ Kansas

died at _Paris, Linn Co., Kansas_ on __6 Dec 1918__ married_16 Sep 1909, Allen Co Kansas_

date and place

4. The said _Robert Clyde Adams_ was the child by blood line of

___John Quincy Adams___ born _9 Mar 1830_ at _Boston, Suffolk Co. Mass._

died at _Linn Co., Kansas_ on _13 Oct 1893_ and his (first ~~or~~) wife

___Sarah Jane Wilson___ born _24 Jun 1838_ at _Decatur Co. Indiana_

died at _Linn Co. Kansas_ on _15 Dec 1920_ married_22 Jan 1856, Decatur Co. IN_

date and place

5. The said _John Quincy Adams_ was the child by blood line of

___John Quincy Adams___ born _19 Dec 1800_ at _New Ipswich, Hillsborough Co. NH_

died at _Keen, Coshocton Co. OH_ on _12 Nov 1873_ and his (first ~~or~~) wife

___Lovina Walker___ born _22 Nov 1807_ at _Maine_

died at _Keene, Coshocton Co. OH_ on _7 Feb 1890_ married _16 Mar 1828, Boston, Mass._

date and place

6. The said _John Quincy Adams_ was the child by blood line of

___Quincy Adams___ born _29 Sep 1775_ at _New Ipswich, NH_

died at _Temple, Hillsborough, NH_ on _abt 1815_ and his (first ~~or~~) wife

___Dolly Elliot___ born _____ at _____

died at _____ on _____ married_____

date and place

7. The said _Quincy Adams_ was the child by blood line of

___Ephraim Adams___ born _abt 1724_ at _Mass_

died at _New Ipswich, NH_ on _26 Mar 1797_ and his ~~first or~~ 2nd wife

Rebecca Locke born _13 May 1735_ at _Hopington, NH_

died at _____ on _____ married_18 Nov 1761 New Ipswich NH_

date and place

8. The said _____ was the child by blood line of

_____ born _____ at _____

died at _____ on _____ and his (first or) wife

_____ born _____ at _____

died at _____ on _____ married_____

date and place

9. The said _____ was the child by blood line of

_____ born _____ at _____

died at _____ on _____ and his (first or) wife

_____ born _____ at _____

died at _____ on _____ married_____

date and place

10. The said _____ was the child by blood line of

_____ born _____ at _____

died at _____ on _____ and his (first or) wife

_____ born _____ at _____

died at _____ on _____ married_____

date and place

11. The said _____ was the child by blood line of

_____ born _____ at _____

died at _____ on _____ and his (first or) wife

_____ born _____ at _____

died at _____ on _____ married_____

date and place

12. The said _____ _____ was the child by blood line of
_____ _____ born _____ at _____
died at _____ _____ on _____ and his (first or   ) wife
_____ _____ born _____ at _____
died at _____ _____ on _____ married_____
                                                                date and place

REFERENCES FOR LINEAGE

Give below authorities for EACH statement of Birth, Marriage, Death dates and places and connections between generations from the applicant through the generation of the Revolutionary ancestor. Published authorities should be cited by title, author, date of publication, volume and page. Send one certified, attested copy or photocopy of each piece of unpublished data. Proofs for line of descent comprise wills, administrations, deeds, church, town and court records, Bible, census and pension records, tombstone inscriptions, genealogies and such other records. TRADITION is not acceptable. Give National Numbers and relationships of any close relatives credited with this ancestor.

1st Gen Birth Certificates for Jane Ann Whitehead and Kenneth Lloyd Bosworth.
Marriage Cert. for above.

2nd Gen. Birth certificates for Charles Edward Whitehead and Madeline Adams
          Marriage Certificate for above. Birth Cert. for Madeline lists parents

3rd Gen. Marriage cert for Robert Clyde Adams and Hattie Mapes - 1910 Census
Death Certificates for Hattie Mapes Adams and Robert Clyde Adams - lists parents
4th Gen. Estate paper of John Q. Adams listing Robert Clyde Adams.   Marriage cert. of John Q. Adams
and Sarah Jane Wilson. Death of Sarah Jane Wilson Adams.

5th Gen. 1850 census showing John Q.Adams as son of John Q. and Lovina Adams.
Birth Cert for John Quincy Adams 19 Dec 1800. Court record showing Lovina as widow.

6th Gen. Birth Cert for John Quincy Adams showing parents Quincy and Dolly.
Probate of Quincy Adams showing Dolly as widow.. History of New Ipswich NH 1735-1914
7th Gen. Ibid p. 178/179   by Charles Chandler, pg183.
Birth Cert of Quincy Adams as son of Ephraim Adams.   Will of Ephraim Adams.

8th Gen. _____

9th Gen. _____

10th Gen. _____

11th Gen. _____

Give, if possible, the following data: My Revolutionary ancestor was married
(1) to Lydia Kinsman _____ at _____ abt 1728 _____ , 1 _____
(2) to _ Rebecca Locke _____ at _____ Nov. 18 _____ , 1 761
(3) to _____ at _____ , 1 _____

CHILDREN OF REVOLUTIONARY ANCESTOR
(By each marriage, if married more than once.)

Names	Dates of Birth	To Whom Married, noting if Married more than once
Ephraim	26 Dec 1749	
Thomas	12 Sep 1751	
Stephen	6 Nov 1753	
Daniel	24 Aug 1755	
Lydia	16 Jul 1757	
John	10 Nov 1762	
John	29 Feb 1764	
Ebenezer	2 Oct 1765	
Rebecca	27 Jul 1767	
James	20 May 1769	
Betsey	13 Mar 1772	
Quincy	29 Sep 1775	Rebecca Locke

3

ANCESTOR'S SERVICES

The said _____ Ephraim Adams _____ who resided during the American

Revolution at _____ New Ipswich, New Hampshire _____ assisted in establishing

American Independence, while acting in the capacity of _____ Private in Col. Daniel Moore's

_____ Regiment of New Hampshire Volunteers _____

My ancestors's services during the Revolutionary War were as follows:

Joined the Cotinental Army at Saratoga in 1777.

Served in Capt. Smith's company at the battle of White Plains.

Represented New Ipswich, NH in the Provincial Congress.

Give references by volume and page to the documentary or other authorities for—MILITARY RECORD: *Where reference is made to unpublished or inaccessible records of service, the applicant must file the official copy.*

ELIGIBILITY CLAUSE

"Any woman is eligible for membership in the National Society of the Daughters of the American Revolution who is not less than eighteen years of age, and who is descended from a man or woman who, with unfailing loyalty to the cause of American Independence, served as a sailor, or as a soldier or civil officer in one of the several Colonies or States, or in the United Colonies or States, or as a recognized patriot, or rendered material aid thereto; provided the applicant is personally acceptable to the Society." (Constitution, Article III, Section 1.)

Marriage in every instance means legal and lawful marriage. Date of marriage may be substituted for dates of birth and death where such date proves the soldier to have been living during the Revolution and of a suitable age for service.

The following form of acknowledgement is required:

Applicant further says that the said _____ Ephriam Adams _____ (name of ancestor from whom eligibility is derived) is the ancestor mentioned in the foregoing application, and that the statements hereinbefore set forth are true to the best of her knowledge and belief.

The applicant also pledges allegiance to the United States of America and agrees to support its Constitution. This applies to applicants for membership within the United States of America and its territories.

(Signature of Applicant) _Jane_ _ann_ _whitehead_ _Bosworth_
                              (First name)   (Middle and Maiden name)   (Last name)

Print or type name exactly as you wish it to appear on DAR Certificate

_____ Jane Ann Whitehead Bosworth _____

Subscribed and sworn to before me at _____ Mission Viejo _____ California _____
                                       (City)   (State)

this _____ 10th _____ day of _____ August _____ A.D. _____ 1990 _____

[SEAL] _____ Dog S. SC _____
                                                     Signature of Notary.

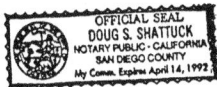

OFFICIAL SEAL
DOUG S. SHATTUCK
NOTARY PUBLIC - CALIFORNIA
SAN DIEGO COUNTY
My Comm. Expires April 14, 1992

My Commission Expires: _____ April 14 1992 _____

4

June 1983

TABLE OF CONTENTS

INTRODUCTION

William Addams came to New England from his family home at Wem, Shropshire, England, about 1628. While he and a couple of generations of his descendants after him spelled their names "Addams", this work uses the modern spelling, Adams. The original spelling is Welsh. The town of Wem is in England, not too far from the Welsh border.

William Adams settled first at Cambridge, then at Ipswich. Historians have consistently referred to this William Adams as "William of Ipswich" to distinguish him from others of the same name. Being a very early settler and a man of some influence, his early history has been studied frequently and many articles have been written describing his families growth and activities up until the late 1700's. After that time, only family and legal documents and items written by family members are available to help one piece together the family history. This work attempts to consolidate that material into a modern history of the family.

This work traces the direct lineage of Madeline Adams ten generations back from the present to the arrival of William Adams in New England. The first seven generations, from William to his fourth great-grandson, John Quincy Adams, deal primarily with the lineage of interest. Although an attempt has been made to identify all children of each ancestor, no effort has been made to trace each line to the present.

Starting with the eighth generation, also John Quincy Adams, an attempt has been made to identify all descendants. This John Quincy Adams, born in 1830, had ten children. The attempt to identify every descendant of all ten children has not been completely successful. Most of the descendants, however, have been identified. So have many of the descendants of the connected families. Without tremendous help from many of the present family members, this work would not have been possible. Particular thanks are extended to Mable Brownback, Margery Donald, and Delphine Chase. Their work in compiling data was monumental.

In the more than 350 years the Adams family has been in what is now the United States of America, it has grown and spread over the entire country. The descendants of William Adams have been among the earliest pioneers to settle in parts of Massachusetts, New Hampshire, Illinois, and Kansas. They include many who were involved in the early indian wars of New England and some who were patriots of the Revolution. John Quincy and Sarah Jane Adams made the trek from Indiana to Kansas by covered wagon in 1859.

The research conducted to prepare this work resulted in sufficient proof of lineage for the wife of the author to join the Daughters of the American Revolution. A copy of the successful application is included as part of the dedication in this book. It is hoped that other descendants of the patriot Ephraim Adams will be able to use the information contained herein to also join this prestigious organization.

ABOUT THE AUTHOR

Kenneth L. Bosworth

Kenneth is married to Jane Ann (Whitehead) Bosworth, a daughter of Madeline (Adams) Whitehead. This book is a history of the ancestral Adams lineage of Madeline Adams.

Kenneth was born in Pomona, California, April 2, 1942. He is the son of Lloyd Omer and Carol Rose (Colburn) Bosworth, and is a first generation Californian. Lloyd was born near Mishawaka, Indiana, and Carol was born in Valley City, North Dakota.

Although born in Pomona, Kenneth never lived there. His mother was staying with her parents in Pomona in order to be near a hospital. Lloyd and Carol lived on a ranch near Glennville, California, about 30 miles from the nearest hospital. Much of the road was unpaved. As roads and vehicles improved, it was possible for Kenneth's sister, Nancy, and brother, Richard, to be delivered at the local hospital. They were born in Bakersfield.

In January 1951, Lloyd and Carol moved from the ranch to Taft, California, where Lloyd worked for the Standard Oil Company. Kenneth completed school thru junior college in Taft. He transferred to Long Beach State College (now the California State University at Long Beach), where he graduated in February 1965 with a Bachelor of Science Degree in Mechanical Engineering. He had started working as a student engineer for the Los Angeles Department of Water and Power before graduation and continued as an engineer after graduation. Kenneth has been promoted to various positions leading to his present position as Superintendent of the Haynes Generating Station in Long Beach.

While at college, Kenneth met and married Jane Ann Whitehead. Jane is the daughter of Madeline (Adams) Whitehead, one of the primary subjects of this work. Jane also graduated from the same college and started her working career as a teacher.

Jane and Kenneth moved to Laguna Hills, California, in 1970. In 1972 their twin sons, Thomas Lloyd and Charles Floyd were born. This makes Thomas and Charles twelfth generation American descendants of William Adams.

Kenneth and Jane relocated to Huntington Beach in 1973, and to Mission Viejo in 1980. Jane retired from teaching when her sons were born and enjoyed success writing short mysteries for Ellery Queen Mystery Magazine. She stopped writing to pursue her interest in assisting learning disabled students and continues to operate a private tutoring service.

While raising their children, Kenneth and Jane worked actively with the Boy Scouts of America and the American Youth Soccer Organization. Since both sons are now away from home attending college, Kenneth spends much of his spare time doing genealogical research and writing family histories.

THE CALENDAR CHANGE AND ITS EFFECTS ON DATES
IN GENEALOGICAL RESEARCH

In 1752 a calendar change took place which now causes researchers a great deal of difficulty.

From early medieval times, most Christian countries observed New Years Day to be March 25 (Lady Day or Annunciation Day). Even though the first day of the new year was on the 25th of the month, the entire month of March was considered the to be first month. April was the second month, May was the third month, and so on. Since Norman times, the historical year was considered to start on January 1. Herein existed one of the many disagreements between the church and the government. A result of this was that between January 1 and March 25, a double dating system was used.

For example: George Washington was born on 11 February 1731/32. This shows he was born on the 11th day of February in the year 1731 under the Julian Calendar. It translates to the year 1732 under the Gregorian Calendar, the calendar now used. The following chart using the years 1731/32 will explain:

Julian Calendar Used Prior to 1752	Gregorian Calendar Used After 1752	Numbering of Months Prior to 1752
February 1730/31	February 1731	12
March 25, 1731	March 1731	1
April 1731	April 1731	2
May 1731	May 1731	3
June 1731	June 1731	4
July 1731	July 1731	5
August 1731	August 1731	6
September 1731	September 1731	7
October 1731	October 1731	8
November 1731	November 1731	9
December 1731	December 1731	10
January 1731/32	January 1732	11
February 1731/32	February 1732	12
March 24, 1731/32	March 1732	1

The change in dates is just a little more confusing than just the renumbering of the months. When one is converting from the Julian to the Gregorian Calendar, 11 days must be added. The example is continued using George Washington's birthday.

George was born 11 February 1731/32. We know now he was born in February 1732 according to the present, Gregorian Calendar. To correct the day, we must add 11 days, thus giving us the correct birth date of February 22, 1732.

If someone is born during the last eleven days of any month using the old dates, the birth month will change too. Thus a recorded birth date of November 28, 1620, under the old system would yield a date of December 8, 1620, using the new system. It's probably best to just leave the dates alone and to remind the reader of the potential confusion. So be it.

ADAMS LINEAGE

WILLIAM ADAMS
(1594 - 1661)

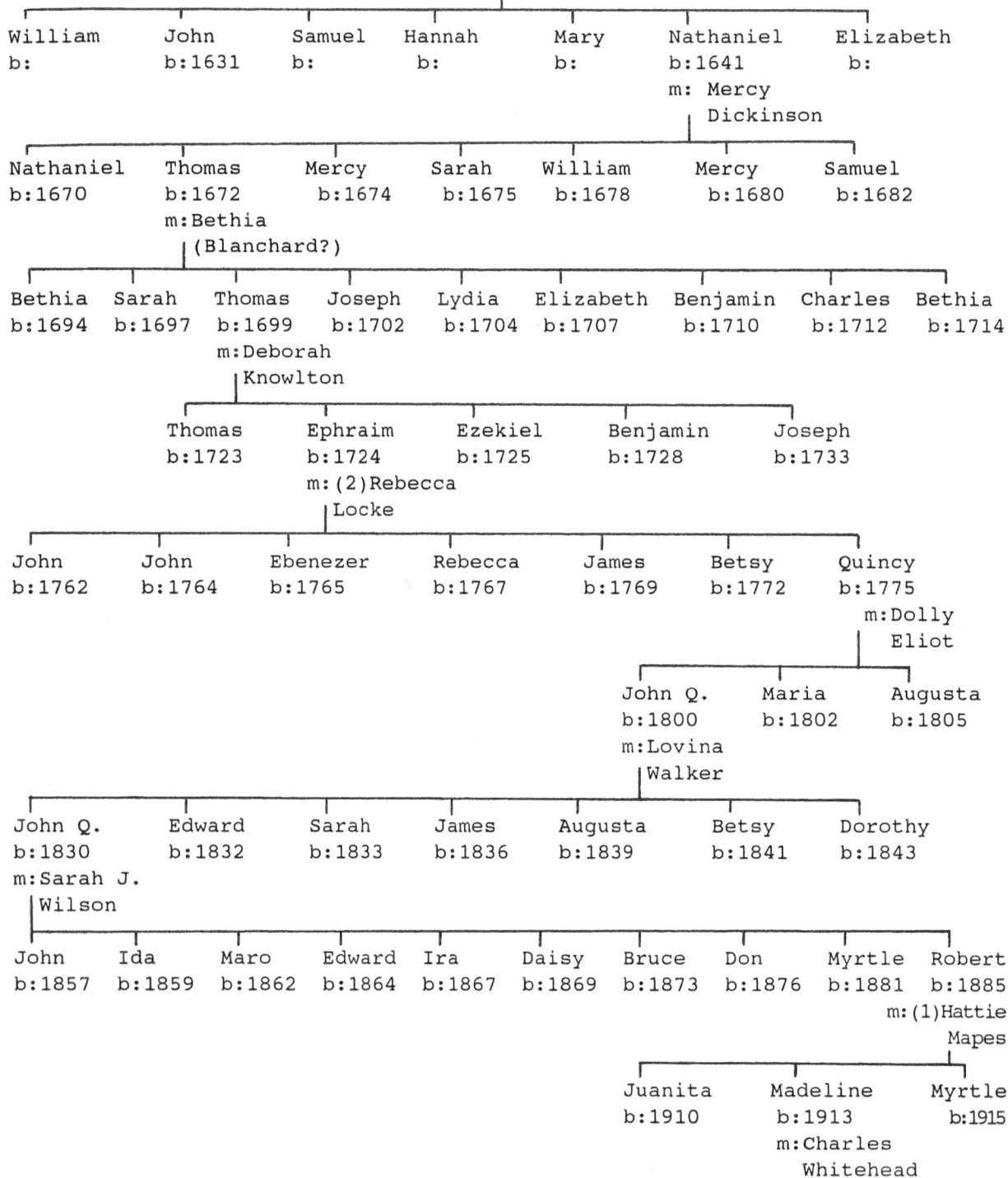

William	John	Samuel	Hannah	Mary	Nathaniel	Elizabeth
b:	b:1631	b:	b:	b:	b:1641 m: Mercy Dickinson	b:

Nathaniel	Thomas	Mercy	Sarah	William	Mercy	Samuel
b:1670	b:1672 m:Bethia (Blanchard?)	b:1674	b:1675	b:1678	b:1680	b:1682

Bethia	Sarah	Thomas	Joseph	Lydia	Elizabeth	Benjamin	Charles	Bethia
b:1694	b:1697	b:1699 m:Deborah Knowlton	b:1702	b:1704	b:1707	b:1710	b:1712	b:1714

Thomas	Ephraim	Ezekiel	Benjamin	Joseph
b:1723	b:1724 m:(2)Rebecca Locke	b:1725	b:1728	b:1733

John	John	Ebenezer	Rebecca	James	Betsy	Quincy
b:1762	b:1764	b:1765	b:1767	b:1769	b:1772	b:1775 m:Dolly Eliot

John Q.	Maria	Augusta
b:1800 m:Lovina Walker	b:1802	b:1805

John Q.	Edward	Sarah	James	Augusta	Betsy	Dorothy
b:1830 m:Sarah J. Wilson	b:1832	b:1833	b:1836	b:1839	b:1841	b:1843

John	Ida	Maro	Edward	Ira	Daisy	Bruce	Don	Myrtle	Robert
b:1857	b:1859	b:1862	b:1864	b:1867	b:1869	b:1873	b:1876	b:1881	b:1885 m:(1)Hattie Mapes

Juanita	Madeline	Myrtle
b:1910	b:1913 m:Charles Whitehead	b:1915

FIRST GENERATION

WILLIAM[1] ADAMS

William Adams is said to be descended from Randall Adams of an old Saxon family at Norwood, town of Wem, Shropshire, England. It is believed he was born in Shropshire, England, on February 3, 1594. It is also believed he arrived in America in the spring of 1628. All official departures from England were carefully documented in England. Emigrants from England were required to sign oaths of loyalty to the Crown. Since no departure records for William have been found, it is supposed he was a man of independent action, and left without the necessary papers.

William settled at Cambridge, Massachusetts, before 1635. He was admitted a freeman at Cambridge on May 22, 1638. Cambridge was the original shire town of Middlesex County in the Commonwealth of Massachusetts. It was originally founded as a fortified place, very small in extent, and apparently without definite bounds. Charlestown and Watertown, on the northerly side of the Charles River, had already been settled. About six months after the arrival of Governor John Winthrop with the fleet of emigrants in 1630, a spot between the two towns was selected in which a fortified town could be constructed. This was to be Cambridge. Houses were first constructed in 1631. Cambridge was first called "The New Town," and afterwards New Town or Newtown. On May 2, 1638, the General Court ordered that "Newetowne shall henceforward be called Cambridge." Mass. Col. Rec., i. 102.

It is important here to offer a little information concerning the reference to the arrival of Governor John Winthrop. John Winthrop was born to a prominent family in England. He was a deeply religious man and was extremely troubled by what he considered the immorality of contemporary England and the religious laxity of the established church. He associated himself with a segment of the Puritan movement which was determined to leave England to establish a Holy Commonwealth in America as a sanctuary for what they considered the true church. The movement was to be made under the auspices of the newly chartered Massachusetts Bay Company, the government of which was to be transferred to the projected colony. In 1629, no doubt with the influence of his father, John Winthrop was elected governor of the company. The next year, 1630, he led nine hundred people across the Atlantic to settle what was to become Massachusetts. Seven towns were founded the first year, including Boston, where John was to live during the last nineteen years of his life. John Winthrop continued to bring colonists to New England thru 1638.

Sometime before 1642, William Adams removed to Ipswich where he was a farmer. He served as a member of the grand jury in 1642. He was a selectman in 1646. He lived in the part of Ipswich which is now known as Hamilton.

No record has been found to identify the name of William Adams' wife, or when they married. Although he died in 1661, she is known to have still been living in 1681. No record of her death has been found.

William Adams was the father of seven children. They are listed below in the order in which they are believed to have been born. From the dates known, it appears the first born, William, was born in England. All of the other children were most likely born in Cambridge. Much of the information about the descendants of William Adams of Ipswich was provided in The Essex Antiquarian, Vol. II, No. 6, Salem, Massachusetts, June 1898.

(1) **WILLIAM**[2]: born about 1620; died in Ipswich, January 18, 1658/59; married Elizabeth Stacey (daughter of Simon Stacey) of Ipswich. Elizabeth died in 1655, probably shortly after the birth of her third son. William and Elizabeth had three sons, all born in Ipswich.

> (1) **William**[3]: born May 27, 1650; married, first, Mary Manning on October 21, 1674. She died June 24, 1679. He married, second, Alice Bradford of Plymouth on March 27, 1680. William died in Dedham on August 17, 1685. William and Mary (Manning) Adams had three children.
>
>> (1) **Mary**[4]: born at Dedham, November 12, 1675; died April 13, 1676.
>> (2) **Eliphalet**[4]: born at Dedham on March 26, 1677; married, first, Lydia Pygan on December 15, 1709, and second, Elizabeth (Bradstreet) (Slaughter) Wass on September 21, 1751; died October 4, 1753.
>> (3) **William**[4]: born at Dedham on January 17, 1679; died August 15, 1679.
>
> (2) **John**[3]: was a minor in 1658/59.
> (3) **Simon**[3]: was born about the time of his mother's death. He was a soldier in the Narrangansett campaign, was a weaver, and lived in Ipswich. Simon married Hannah _____ . He died at Ipswich on October 17, 1723. His widow died there May 6, 1727. Simon and Hannah Adams had four children.
>
>> (1) **Sarah**[4]:
>> (2) **Hannah**[4]: born at Ipswich on January 18, 1692; married John Grammage of Ipswich on May 23, 1728; died March 10, 1753.
>> (3) **Simon**[4]: born October 20, 1694; died December 24, 1721.
>> (4) **Daniel**[4]: born November 26, 1697; died November 26, 1773.

The estate of William[2] Adams was distributed as reported in the Ipswich Quarterly Court Records, vol. 1, page 74. "Administration on the estate of William Addams, jr. of Ipswich, granted Mar. 29, 1659, to William Addams, his father, and John Addams, his brother. The inventory amounted to 218li. The estate was distributed to eldest son William, one half, and one fourth to each of the other two children, when they were of the age of twenty-one years. Elder John Whipple and Thomas Stace, overseers."

The distribution was aided by an extensive inventory taken November 24, 1658, by John Appleton and Robert Lord.

(2) **JOHN**[2]: born about 1631; died in 1703. The most reliable records indicate he married three times. First to Rebecca _____, who died December 31, 1666; second to Sarah Woodman, who died May 31, 1676; and last to Dorcas (Watson) Dwight, on May 8, 1677, who survived him and died November 9, 1707. Dorcas was the daughter of John Watson of Roxbury. She was first married to Timothy Dwight. Sarah Woodman was the widow of John Brocklebank. John[2] Adams was the father of at least six children.

> (1) (unnamed): died 31:10:1666. This is also the date of the death of John's first wife.
> (2) **John**[3]: born March 11, 1667/68; was a miller; lived in Ipswich; married Hannah Tredwell of Ipswich on May 22, 1690; died March 1717/18. She died in Ipswich on October 23, 1733. John and Hannah had six children, all born in Ipswich.
>> (1) **Hannah**[4]: born April 25, 1691; married Jonadab Waite of Ipswich, intentions published September 11, 1725.
>> (2) **Sarah**[4]: married Samuel Gardner of Salem, intentions published March 21, 1719.
>> (3) **John**[4]: born about 1700; married Phebe Burnham, intentions published May 1, 1725; had two children; died November 28, 1729.
>> (4) **Abigail**[4]: married Thomas Brown of Wenham, intentions published June 25, 1727.
>> (5) **Mary**[4]: married Daniel Choate of Ipswich on February 26, 1727/28.
>> (6) **Priscilla**[4]: born 23:9:1712; married Nathan Chapman of Ipswich on December 26, 1734.
> (3) **Mary**[3]: born December 26, 1670; married Joseph Whipple about 1688; died June 16, 1734. Jospeh and Mary Whipple had six children, all born in Ipswich.
>> (1) **Mary Whipple**: born February 15, 1689; married Increase Howe, intentions published April 23, 1709; died in August 1721.
>> (2) **Archelaus Whipple**: born March 26, 1692; died young.
>> (3) **Sarah Whipple**: born May 14, 1693; died in 1695.
>> (4) **Elizabeth Whipple**: born December 9, 1696; married Nathaniel Emerson on November 19, 1715.
>> (5) **Susannah Whipple**: born February 22, 1699; died the same day.

(6) **Priscilla Whipple**: born March 6, 1700; died young.

(4) **Archelaus^3**: born in Ipswich. He was a soldier at York, Maine in 1695. He kept inns in both Newbury and Salisbury. He married, first, Sarah (Coker) March, widow of Hugh March, on March 18, 1697/98; second, widow Sarah Green on March 4, 1718/19; third, twice widowed Dorothy (Carr) (Frees) Clement; and fourth, Mary, widow of James Pearson, on April 20, 1742. Archelaus Adams died in 1753. He made his will May 24, 1753, and it was proved September 27, 1753. Archelaus was the father of eight children, all born to his first wife, Sarah.

> (1) **Sarah^4**: born January 22, 1698/99; married Ephraim Wadleigh of Salisbury on June 28, 1720.
> (2) **Mary^4**: born October 29, 1701; married Israel Morrill of Salisbury on April 19, 1720.
> (3) **John^4**: born October 11, 1704; he was a joiner; married, first, Alice Piper, intentions published August 1725, and second, Lydia ____; died at Chelmsford, Massachusetts, and was buried there May 21, 1759.
> (4) **Elizabeth^4**: born May 29, 1707; married Samuel Swett, Jr. on August 5, 1730; probably died before 1753 as she is not mentioned in her father's will.
> (5) **Samuel^4**: born April 29, 1710; was a joiner until about 1750 when he became a shipwright; married Elizabeth Bagley of Amesbury on June 27, 1734; died in Salisbury on May 16, 1767. Samuel had nine children, all born in Salisbury.
> (6) **Stephen^4**: born March 14, 1712; married Mary ____; lived in Newbury. Administration was granted on his estate on July 9, 1753. Stephen had two children, both born in Newbury.
> (7) **Archelaus^4**: born November 21, 1714; lived in Salisbury; was a joiner and shipwright; married Mercy Dow on April 28, 1737; died in Salisbury on January 1, 1783. Archelaus and Mercy Adams had twelve children, all born in Salisbury.
> (8) **Nathaniel^4**: born June 29, 1717; died September 1, 1717.

(5) (unnamed son): born May 1676; died June 24, 1676.

(6) **Dorcas^3**: born March 16, 1677/78; married Daniel Warner of Ipswich in 1703; died May 13, 1749.

(3) **SAMUEL^2**: born in 1635; died ____; was living in Ipswich, perhaps as late as 1730; married Mehitable Norton on December 20, 1664. Samuel and Mehitable had five children.

> (1) **Mehitable^3**: born October 27, 1665; married John Osborne of Ipswich on October 11, 1685.
> (2) **Mary^3**: born October 20, 1667.
> (3) **Samuel^3**: born December 26, 1670; was living in Ipswich in 1743.

(4) **William**[3]: born January 26, 1672/73; was living in Ipswich in 1720.
(5) **Sarah**[3]: born June 12, 1676.

(4) **HANNAH**[2]: born about 1637; died ____; married, first, Francis Muncey on December 6, 1659, at Ipswich, Massachusetts, second, John Ramsden of Newtown, New York, in about June 1677, and third, Thomas Wickingham of Newtown on October 12, 1687. After Hannah married Francis Muncey, they relocated from Ipswich, Massachusetts, to Brookhaven, New York. It is believed that Hannah and Francis Muncey had at least two sons.
    (1) **John Muncey**:
    (2) **Samuel Muncey**:

(5) **MARY**[2]: born about 1639; died ____; married Thomas French on February 29, 1659/60, at Ipswich, Massachusetts. Thomas French is the son of Ensign Thomas and Mary French. Mary and Thomas French had eight children, all born at Ipswich.
    (1) **Thomas French**: born November 30, 1661; died December 14, 1661.
    (2) **Mary French**: born March 9, 1663.
    (3) **Thomas French**: born May 21, 1666.
    (4) **Abigail French**: born June 27, 1668; died October 17, 1703.
    (5) **Hannah French**: born January 30, 1670.
    (6) **William French**: born November 30, 1673.
    (7) **Hester French**: born January 2, 1676.
    (8) **John French**:

(6) **NATHANIEL[2]: born about 1641; died April 11, 1715; married Mercy Dickinson, daughter of Thomas and Jennet (Jeanette) Dickinson of Roxbury, on June 30, 1668. Nathaniel and Mercy had seven children.
    (1) **Nathaniel**[3]: born July 11, 1670.
  (2) **Thomas[3]: born June 14, 1672; died October 24, 1729; married Bethia (Blanchard ?) in early 1694.
    (3) **Mercy**[3]: born April 1, 1674; died June 13, 1674.
    (4) **Sarah**[3]: born July 19, 1675; married Walter Fairfield of Wenham before 1707; died between 1717 and 1719.
    (5) **William**[3]: born June 22, 1678.
    (6) **Mercy**[3]: born May 18, 1679/80.
    (7) **Samuel**[3]: born June 29, 1682.

(7) **ELIZABETH**[2]: married James Moulton on February 10, 1662, at Wenham, Massachusetts. James Moulton was born February 10, 1662, at Salem, Massachusetts. Elizabeth and James Moulton had five children.
    (1) **James Moulton**: born March 8, 1666, at Wenham.
    (2) **John Moulton**: born October 4, 1668, at Wenham; married Sarah Conant.
    (3) **Jonathan Moulton**: born in 1670 at Wenham; married Jane Conant.

(4) **William Moulton**: born in 1672 at Wenham.
(5) **Elizabeth Moulton**: born in 1673 at Wenham.

The estate of William[1] Adams of Ipswich was distributed as transcribed from the Ipswich Quarterly Court Records, vol. 1, page 104.

"The will of William Addams proved Mar. 25, 1662, and inventory received."

"An agreement made Apr. 24, 1668, between Nathaniell Addams of Ipswich and Samuell Addams his brother; that all the lands and goods which William Addams their father had bequeathed to them should be equally divided between them according to the true meaning of the will, allowing convenient maintenance unto his wife during her life, and paying such portions as their father had bequeathed unto his daughters. The house and barn and the land about the house wherein the said Nathaniell now dwelleth containing about 16 acres, also another division of land lying between the land of Samuell Addams, brother to Nathaniell and the land of Thomas Stace, bounded by a long hill running down from the thick woods to a piece of meadow appertaining to John Addams, our brother, that he bought of Anthony Potter, also another peice of meadow being upon the Black brooke, bounded northwest by a point of upland running down to the borrk & southeast by the land of Symon Stacy, shall belong unto Nathaniell and his heirs forever. All the land that is now in the occupation Samuell Adams, being an entire parcell of land joining to Mr. Saltonstall's farm shall belong to him and his heirs forever. And all the goods and chattells that are at present in the possession of either of them shall so continue to them and their heirs. Signed and sealed Apr. 24, 1668 by Samuell Addams. Wineess: William White, Thomas Waite.
Acknowledged June 30, 1668 by Samuell Addams." Ipswich Deeds, vol. 3, page 79.

THE ADAMS HOUSE AT HAMILTON

Sketch by Charles Bosworth from a photograph
ca. 1890

The Adams house remained in the immediate
family for over 250 years

SECOND GENERATION

NATHANIEL^2 ADAMS

Nathaniel Adams was the youngest son of William^1 Adams. He was born about 1641, either at Cambridge or Ipswich, Massachusetts. Nathaniel's father relocated his family to Ipswich from Cambridge before 1642. Nathaniel spent his entire youth and adult life at Ipswich, where he was made a freeman on May 27, 1674. He inherited his father's house and part of the family farm when his father died in 1661. Nathaniel died at Ipswich, Massachusetts, on April 11, 1715.

Nathaniel married Mercy Dickinson, daughter of Thomas and Jennet (Jeanette) Dickinson, on June 30, 1668, at Ipswich. Mercy was born at Rowley, Massachusetts, in October 1646. Nathaniel and Mercy had seven children.

(1) **NATHANIEL^3**: born July 11, 1670; died August 31, 1736; married Abigail Kimball, daughter of Caleb and Anne Kimball, in January 1693/94. Abigail was born in July 1668. Nathaniel and Abigail had nine children.
    (1) **Nathaniel^4**: born March 1, 1694/95; died October 25, 1712.
    (2) **William^4**: born November 26, 1696, in Ipswich; married Mary Warner of Ipswich, intentions published December 31, 1715. William and Mary had six children.
        (1) **Mary^5**: born 19:3:1717; married William Whipple April 11, 1738.
        (2) **Abigail^5**: born 28:12:1719; married Joseph Bolles of Ipswich, intentions published June 23, 1744,
        (3) **William^5**: baptized March 25, 1722; married Mary _____; died in Hamilton December 17, 1797.
        (4) **Nathaniel^5**: baptized May 21, 1727; married Ruth Bolles, intentions published December 2, 1757; had seven children; died August 27, 1779.
        (5) **Sarah^5**: baptized July 20 1729; married Jacob Low of Windham, intentions published June 22, 1750.
        (6) **John^5**: born July 1731; married Mary Lamson, intentions published July 20, 1754.
    (3) **Abigail^4**: born December 6, 1699; married William Goodhue, intentions published November 28, 1718; died September 10, 1764.
    (4) **Caleb^4**: born February 13, 1701/02; married Ester Brown of Ipswich February 3, 1730/31; died at Hamlet parish, Ipswich, on October 21, 1783. Caleb and Ester had six children.
        (1) **Caleb^5**: baptized February 27, 1731/32; married, first, Hannah Lamson, intentions published March 2, 1754. She died soon after the marriage. Caleb married, second, Margaret Davison of Wenham,

intentions published December 24, 1757. Caleb and Margaret had two children.

    (2) **Ester**[5]: baptized July 15, 1733; married Moses Cummings of Ispwich, intentions published November 2, 1754.

    (3) **George**[5]: baptized February 9, 1734/35; married Elizabeth Rogers of Ipswich June 27, 1757; George and Elizabeth had two children.

    (4) _____: baptized December 5, 1736.

    (5) **Mary**[5]: baptized March 4, 1738/39.

    (6) **Nathaniel**[5]: lived in Ipswich in 1771.

(5) **Mercy**[4]: born February 25, 1703/04; married Thomas Savory, intentions published August 10, 1723.

(6) **Robert**[4]: born October 14, 1705.

(7) **Anna**[4]: born March 25, 1707/08; married John Woodman of Newbury, intentions published November 7, 1725.

(8) **Eliphalet**[4]: born in Ipswich; married Anna Morse of Newbury on April 16, 1730; had six children, all born in Hamlet parish, Ipswich.

    (1) **Sarah**[5]: baptized April 30, 1732.

    (2) **Anna**[5]: baptized January 27, 1733/34.

    (3) **Moses**[5]: baptized December 21, 1735.

    (4) **Aaron**[5]: baptized March 19, 1737/38.

    (5) _____: baptized March 1739/40.

    (6) **John**[5]: baptized February 1741/42.

(9) **Mary**[4]: born 8:6:1714; married Thomas Lamson, Jr. of Ipswich, intentions published August 11, 1732.

(2) THOMAS[3]: born June 14, 1672; died October 24, 1729; married Bethia (Blanchard ?) in early 1694. Thomas and Bethia had nine children.

    (1) **Bethia**[4]: born October 21, 1694; died June 26, 1710.

    (2) **Sarah**[4]: born April 29, 1697; married Josiah Bishop on February 7, 1717.

    (3) Thomas[4]: born August 31, 1699; died 1765; married Deborah Knowlton on April 17, 1722.

    (4) **Joseph**[4]: born November 12, 1702; married first, Priscilla Warner on January 10, 1727/28, and second, Dorothy Merriam on November 4, 1736; died May 10, 1790. Priscilla (Warner) Adams died January 6, 1734, at Concord, Massachusetts. Joseph and Priscilla Adams had three children.

        (1) **Priscilla**[5]: born January 3, 1729, at Ipswich; died February 19, 1791, at New Ipswich, New Hampshire. Priscilla married Benjamin Adams on April 18, 1751. Benjamin Adams, Priscilla's first cousin, is a son of Thomas Adams and Deborah Knowlton.

        (2) **Lydia**[5]: born October 16, 1730, at Ipswich; died July 3, 1731, at Ipswich.

        (3) **Mary**[5]: born May 5, 1733, at Concord; died at Concord, September 9, 1733.

Joseph and Dorothy (Merriam) Adams had six children.
  (1) **Dorothy**[5]: born August 26, 1737; died April 10, 1766.
  (2) **Ruth**[5]: born January 14, 1739, at Concord; married Peter Fletcher on September 8, 1761; died April 28, 1816.
  (3) **Mary**[5]: born March 14, 1742; married Isaac Appleton on April 24, 1760; died May 22, 1827.
  (4) **Bethia**[5]: born June 3, 1744; died September 30, 1753.
  (5) **Mercy**[5]: born January 14, 1747; married, first, Benjamin Pollard on April 21, 1768, and second, Jonas Whiting; died August 12, 1815, at Norway, Maine.
  (6) **Lydia**[5]: born August 22, 1750; married Joseph Chandler of Concord on April 28, 1774; died December 10, 1829.
(5) **Lydia**[4]: born December 16, 1704; married, first, Benjamin Woodbury on January 12, 1722/23, and second, Rice Knowlton, Jr. on December 12, 1727.
(6) **Elizabeth**[4]: born June 22, 1707; married Peter Lamson on April 18, 1728.
(7) **Benjamin**[4]: born April 22, 1710; married Persis Potter; died September 15, 1785. Benjamin and Persis Adams had fifteen children.
  (1) **Persis**[5]: born November 13, 1732; died before 1742.
  (2) **Silas**[5]: born November 17, 1733, at Marlboro, Massachusetts.
  (3) **Rebecca**[5]: born February 29, 1736; married Obediah Bartlett.
  (4) **Silas**[5]: born September 14, 1738, at Brookfield, Massachusetts.
  (5) **Lucy**[5]: born March 20, 1740.
  (6) **Persis**[5]: born April 16, 1742; married Silas Stevens on November 21, 1782.
  (7) **Mary**[5]: born March 3, 1744, at Brookfield, Massachusetts; married Emerson Woolcott on December 2, 1776.
  (8) **Sarah**[5]: born March 30, 1746, at Brookfield, Massachusetts; married Joseph Stow on May 22, 1765.
  (9) **Benjamin**[5]: born April 20, 1748, at Brookfield, Massachusetts; married Eunice Hale on December 16, 1773; died February 23, 1829.
  (10) **Ephraim**[5]: born May 12, 1750, at Brookfield, Massachusetts; married, first, Eunice Moulton on May 19, 1774, and second, Sybil Bemis on May 14, 1785; died January 3, 1822.
  (11) **Joel**[5]: born April 19, 1752, at Brookfield, Massachusetts; married Joanna Hale on July 14, 1776.
  (12) **Charles**[5]: born April 23, 1754, at Brookfield, Massachusetts.

(13) **Lydia**[5]: born March 11, 1756, at Brookfield, Massachusetts.
(14) **Darius**[5]: born June 27, 1758, at Brookfield, Massachusetts.
(15) **Lemuel**[5]: born November 22, 1760, at Brookfield, Massachusetts.
(8) **Charles**[4]: born 29:4:1712; married Mary Perkins of Wenham on October 30, 1733; died September 17, 1786.
(9) **Bethiah**[4]: baptized 8:6:1714; died young.

(3) **MERCY**[3]: born April 1, 1674; died June 13, 1674.

(4) **SARAH**[3]: born July 19, 1675; married Walter Fairfield of Wenham in 1696 at Ipswich; died between 1717 and 1719. Sarah and Walter Fairfield had six children.
   (1) **Samuel Fairfield**: born February 22, 1696. died October 28. 1733.
   (2) **Benjamin Fairfield**: born February 1, 1697; died February 9, 1698.
   (3) **Sarah Fairfield**: born October 7, 1699; died before April 18, 1711.
   (4) **Daniel Fairfield**: born April 30, 1702, at Ipswich; married Remember Stevens on September 11, 1723.
   (5) **Nathaniel Fairfield**: born April 30, 1704; died before January 25, 1745.
   (6) **Tabitha Fairfield**: born October 7, 1699.

(5) **WILLIAM**[3]: born June 22, 1678; died after December 26, 1742. William removed from Ipswich, Massachusetts, to Milford, Connecticut in 1699. In that same year he married Abigail Oviatt, daughter of Thomas and Frances (Bryan) Oviatt. William Adams was a farmer and a lawyer. He was admitted to the Milford Church on November 5, 1699. Abigail (Oviatt) Adams died in 1711. In about 1713, William married Mary _____. William and Abigail Adams had six children, all born at Milford.
   (1) **Abigail**[4]: baptized on November 5, 1699; married Isaac Stiles on February 25, 1719, at Stratford, Connecticut.
   (2) **Mehitabel**[4]: baptized on February 18, 1700; married Ebenezer Blackman in about 1725.
   (3) **Esther**[4]: baptized December 7, 1701.
   (4) **Elizabeth**[4]: born March 3, 1704.
   (5) **Samuel**[4]: born April 28, 1706; married Mary Fairchild, daughter of Samuel and Ruth (Beach) Fairchild, on March 7, 1729; died November 12, 1788, at Litchfield, Connecticut. Samuel Adams moved from Milford to Stratford, Connecticut about 1728 or 1729. He was a lawyer and became judge of the Court of Common Pleas of Fairfield County. In 1745 he served as one of five captains of the Connecticut Troupe. Samuel Adams sired a child out of wedlock when he was about 20 years of age.

That child, Samuel Adams, was born in 1726 according to New Haven County court records. The mother, Jemima Plumb, married William Wheeler, whom the young Samuel Adams chose as his guardian after his mother's death. Samuel and Mary (Fairchild) Adams had six children.

(1) **Samuel**[5]: born January 2, 1730, at Stratford, Connecticut; married, first, Martha Curtis, and second, Mrs. Hopkins; died in January 1810, at Johnstown, Ontario, Canada. Dr. Samuel Adams was a physician and surgeon.

(2) **Elijah**[5]: born December 19, 1731.

(3) **Lemuel**[5]: born September 15, 1734; died September 25, 1734.

(4) **Andrew**[5]: born December 11, 1736, at Stratford, Connecticut; married Eunice Booth; died November 27, 1797, at Litchfield, Connecticut. Andrew Adams received a Doctor of Laws degree from Yale College in 1760.

(5) **Mary**[5]: born October 28, 1745; married Hezekiah De Forest.

(6) **Lemuel**[5]: born September 19, 1751; married Ann Blackman in 1782.

(6) **MERCY**[3] (Marcy): born May 18, 1679/80; died September 11, 1733; married first, John Smith, son of Richard and Hannah Smith of Ipswich on February 4, 1702/03. John Smith was born in 1677 and died May 20, 1713. They had four children. Second, Mercy married Arthur Abbott, son of Arthur and Mary Abbott, on September 18, 1716. This husband was born in Ipswich on February 3, 1694, and died June 16, 1767.

(7) **SAMUEL**[3]: born June 29, 1682; married Mary Burley, daughter of Andrew Burley, intentions published April 28, 1706; died at Ipswich August 13, 1747. Mary (Burley) Adams died at Worchester March 5, 1772, aged 84. Samuel and Mary had eleven children, all born at Ipswich.

(1) **Mary**[4]: born July 27, 1708, at Ipswich, Massachusetts; married Abner Stow June 27, 1733.

(2) **Sarah**[4]: born March 2, 1709/10, at Ipswich, Massachusetts; married James Whipple, Jr. of Ipswich on January 9, 1728/29, at Hamilton, Massachusetts; died November 22, 1759.

(3) **Samuel**[4]: born January 19, 1710/11, at Ipswich, Massachusetts; married Sarah Treadwell, intentions published March 25, 1738; died August 26, 1757, at Ipswich. Samuel and Sarah Adams had two children.

(1) **Sarah**[5]: baptized September 23, 1739; married John Whipple, the 3rd, intentions published April 23, 1767.

(2) **Samuel**[5]: baptized May 16, 1742 at Ipswich, Massachusetts; married Jemima Whipple on December 12, 1766; died November 18, 1835.

(4) **Nathaniel**[4]: born November 16, 1712 (16:9:1712), at Ipswich, Massachusetts; married Martha Emerson on February 1, 1746/47.

(5) **Andrew**[4]: born May 29, 1715; married, first Elizabeth Hunt on October 15, 1741, and, second, Mrs. Sarah Torrey of Mendon on May 30, 1771. Andrew and Elizabeth (Hunt) Adams had seven children, all born at Grafton.

    (1) **Elizabeth**[5]: born March 4, 1744.

    (2) **Ruth**[5]: born April 25, 1746; married John Whipple on June 20, 1765.

    (3) **Mary**[5]: born December 28, 1748; married Daniel Grout.

    (4) **Andrew**[5]: born October 21, 1751; married Lucy Merriam; died August 25, 1841.

    (5) **Sarah**[5]: born April 30, 1754; married Solomon Rand on June 22, 1774.

    (6) **Nathaniel**[5]: born January 1, 1756; married Mary Harrington; died January 24, 1829.

    (7) **Martha**[5]: born December 23, 1759; married Daniel Whipple, probably on April 17, 1776; died December 8, 1844.

(6) **James**[4]: baptized April 14, 1717, at Ipswich, Massachusetts; married Elizabeth Dane on April 6, 1742; died at Sutton August 4, 1804.

    (1) **James**[5]: died young

    (2) **Nathaniel**[5]: born at Sutton, Massachusetts; married Lucy Woods.

    (3) **Francis**[5]: born at Sutton, Massachusetts; married Abigail Taft on April 11, 1780.

    (4) **Elizabeth**[5]: born at Sutton, Massachusetts; married David Temple.

    (5) **Samuel**[5]: born at Sutton, Massachusetts; married Olive Jones.

    (6) **Israel**[5]: (twin) born at Sutton, Massachusetts; married Joanna Dodge on January 10, 1787; died May 11, 1811.

    (7) **Anna**[5]: (twin) born in Sutton, Massachusetts; married Ezekiel Goldthwait on December 3, 1772.

    (8) **Lydia**[5]:

    (9) **Moses**[5]: born in 1760 in Sutton, Massachusetts; married Elizabeth Whipple on March 29, 1786; died May 2, 1839.

    (10) **James**[5]: born in Sutton, Massachusetts; married Hannah Potter on November 29, 1787.

(7) **John**[4]: baptized September 13, 1719 at Hamlet parish, Ipswich; died young.

(8) **John**[4]: (twin) baptized June 1722; married Mary Hunt of Concord on October 31, 1745; died April 24, 1796, at Northbridge, Massachusetts. John and Mary (Hunt) Adams had one son.

    (1) **Andrew**[5]: born November 7, 1759; died June 30, 1822.

(9) **Elizabeth**[4]: (twin) baptized June 1722; married _____
Dane before 1747.
(10) **Jonathan**[4]: born in 1722.
(11) **Eunice**[4]: baptized November 1, 1724; married George
Andrews of Ipswich, intentions published March 28, 1747.

Mr. NATHANIEL ADDAMS
DIED: APRIL Y 11, 1715
IN Y 74 YEAR OF
HIS AGE:
NOW HE'S GON TO ETER-
NALL REST
GOD WIL HIM SAFLY KEEP
ALLTHOUGH HES BURIED
IN Y DUST
IN JESUS HE DOTH SLEEP
O YOU HIS CHILDREN
THAT ARE LEFT
I PRAY LET SOME BE FOUND
THAT DO ENDEAVOUR
TO MAKE GOOD
YOUR FOREGON LEADERS
GROUND
GRAVE SAINT BEHIND
THAT CANNOT FIND
THY OLD LOVE NIGHT NOR
MORN: PRAY LOOK A
BOVE FOR THARE'S YOUR LOVE
SINGING WITH Y
FIRST BORN

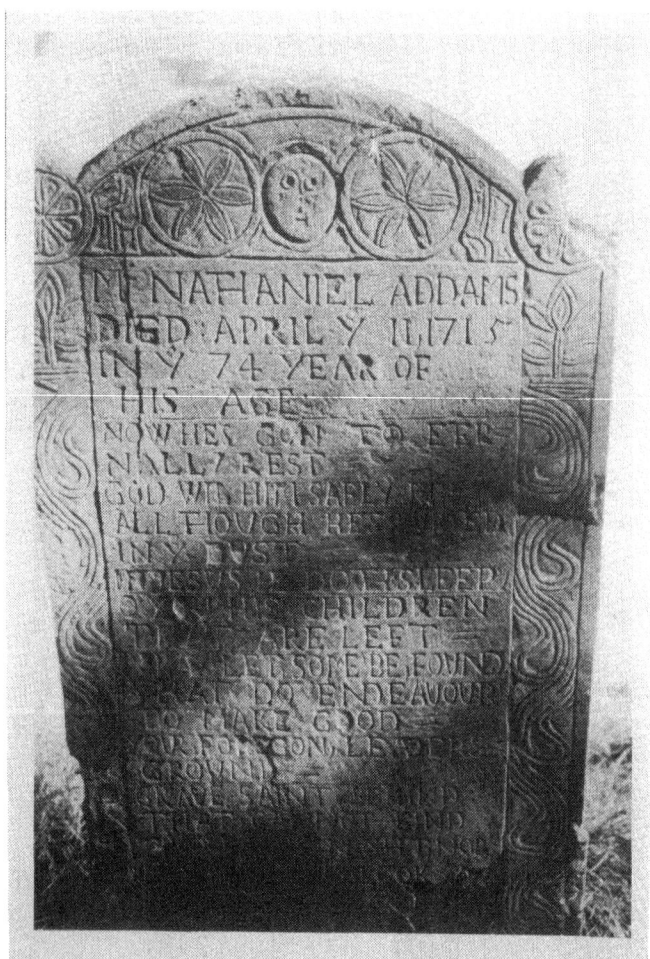

THE GRAVESTONE AND INSCRIPTION AT THE GRAVESITE
OF NATHANIEL ADAMS AT THE OLD BURYING GROUND
IPSWICH, MASSACHUSETTS.
Picture by Marv Adams

DICKINSON FAMILY

Mercy Dickinson married Nathaniel Adams on June 30, 1668. Mercy was a native of Massachusetts, having been born to Thomas and Jennet (Jeanette) Dickinson in Rowley in August 1646.

Although it is not known when the Dickinson family first came to America, it is certain that, like the Adams Family, they were among the early settlers. It is known that Thomas Dickinson, father of Mercy, was one of the original owners of a house and a one and one-half acre lot on Bradford Street in Rowley. Town records indicate that twenty house lots are recorded on Bradford Street in the first survey. Thomas Dickinson's name appears in this survey which was registered in 1643. A sketch showing the location of the Dickinson house is provided on the next page.

Much of the following history of Rowley is extracted from the books Rowley, Massachusetts, by Amos Everett Jewett and Emily Mabel Adams Jewett, and Early settlers of Rowley, Massachusetts, by George Brainard Blodgette and Amos Everett Jewett.

Rowley began as a plantation under the directorship of the church leaders, and especially Mr. Ezekiel Rogers. Ezekiel Rogers arrived in the summer of 1638 aboard the ship John. With about twenty other families, nearly all from Yorkshire, England, he sought to make a new life for himself and his friends where they could practice their religion and work for their common good. They spent the first winter in Salem while they made arrangements for a location in which to establish their homes.

Rogers petitioned the courts at Ipswich and Newbury for land between the two, and was granted the area desired on March 13, 1639. The settlement was began that spring. Although the first mention of the new plantation was in March, it was not incorporated until the following autumn, when in September 1639, the court directed "Mr. Ezechi: Rogers plantation shalbee called Rowley." Some of the land claimed by Rowley had been pre-empted by Ipswich and Newbury and was purchased by the Rowley Company at a cost of 800 pounds. The purchase money was contributed by those who were able and consideration for the money contributed was given in the size of the lots granted and/or in the rights to use the commons.

The Rowley settlers laid out their first house lots on a fairly level plain about equal distance from Ipswich and Newbury, through which flowed a year-round stream appropriately referred to as the Town Brook. This brook and its tributaries governed, to a

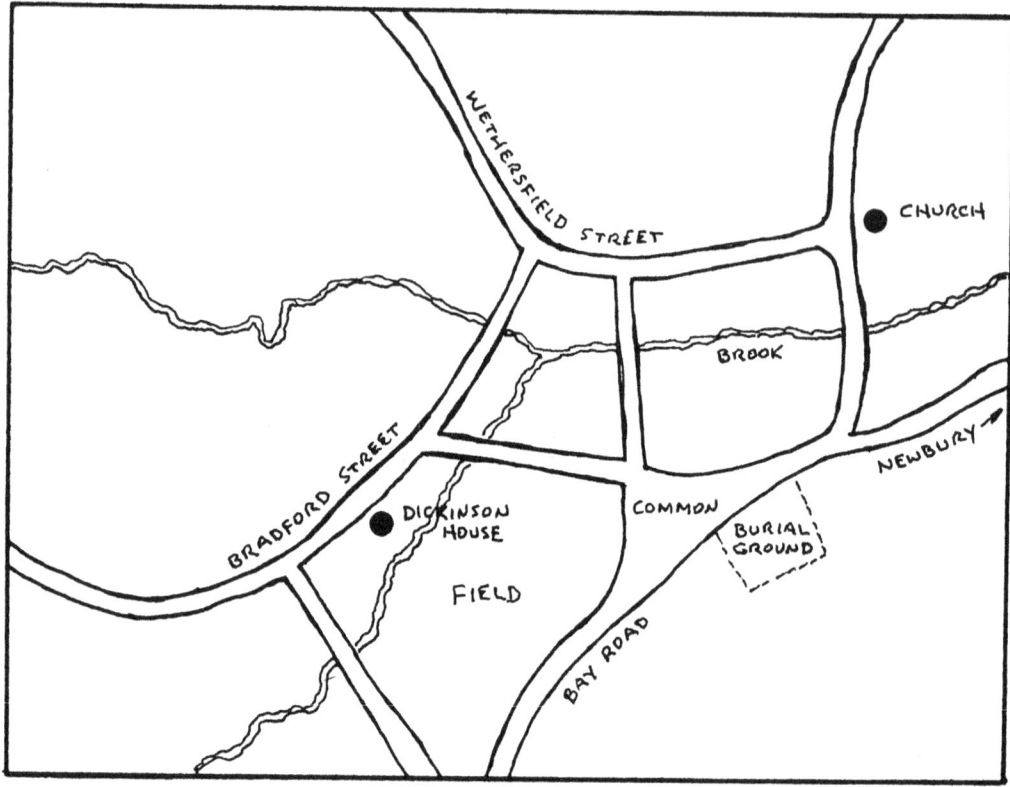

**LOCATION OF THE DICKINSON HOUSE
IN ROWLEY, MASSACHUSETTS**

The first survey of lots in Rowley, Massachusetts was conducted in 1643. In that survey, Thomas Dickinson is identified as the owner of a one and one-half acre lot on Bradford Street, roughly at the location shown in the map above.

large extent, the layout of the town. Nearly every house lot bordered on or had easy access to the brook, assuring all residents a good supply of water.

It is most likely that Thomas Dickinson was among the original members of the company which settled Rowley, based upon his shares in the commons. He most likely arrived in New England with the Rogers party in 1638.

The children of Thomas and Jennet Dickinson, all born in Rowley, are:
   (1) **James:** born July 6, 1640; married Rebecca _____.
   (2) **Mary:** born July 27, 1642; married Abel Langley.
   (3) **Sarah:** born October 18, 1644; married Jeremiah Jewett.
  (4) **Mercy: born August 1646; married Nathaniel Adams of Ipswich on June 30, 1668.
   (5) **Martha:** born December 9, 1648; married William Quarles of Ipswich on December 9, 1669.
   (6) **Thomas:** born August 26, 1655; buried March 30, 1659.

DICKINSON HOUSE, BRADFORD STREET, GEORGETOWN
Believed built before 1700, perhaps by James Dickinson, son
of Thomas and Jennet Dickinson
Picture by Marv Adams

The Dickinson-Pillsburn house, as it is now known, believed to have been built about 1700, is a fine example of the two story, overhang type. A plaque on the front of the house indicates it was built in 1735. This is possible if another structure was originally built on the lot, as town records as early as 1704 indicate the Dickinson family occupied this lot. The front overhang is at the first story level and the west end overhang at the second story. This house has two rooms to a floor with central chimney built on a stone foundation twelve feet square. No leanto has ever been added. In one of the chambers is a very unusual fireplace, evidently a later addition, which has no timber or iron to support the bricks, but is built in the form of an arch held in place by a key brick. This house is located on Jewett Street in the Parish of Byfield within the limits of the present town of Georgetown. It was owned and occupied in 1704 by Samuel Dickinson and after several transfers, came to his descendant Paul Pillsbury.

The furnishings of the earliest houses were extremely simple. Furniture consisted of benches, forms (or long settees), and stools and tables, usually of home manufacture. The houses usually had one large room called the hall, or kitchen. Here the family work was done. They washed, ironed, cooked, made the butter, cheese, and candles. The big fireplace was the the center of activity. It furnished the means of warmth and cooking. In the fireplace were the fire dogs (andirons) and cobirons on which the great logs of wood were laid. The brass or copper warming pan stood near the chimney and the bellows hung beside it, while over the fireplace were the ever present firearms. Hardly an inventory of the seventeenth century fails to mention one or more guns and often a sword.

It is not difficult to construct a rough picture of what an early New England town street must have looked like. It was usually made up of wooden houses, each standing in its own orchard, arranged for the most part, in rows. In Rowley, there is no record of a market place. The only two public buildings were the meeting house and the school.

The town records for Rowley contain many interesting items. Because timber was prized for the construction of buildings and for fuel, the destruction of trees on common land became an early problem. The Rowley Records show the following action by the town in March 1701-2 when it was voted, "if any person or Persons either masters or parents sons or servants shall fall lop or girdle any trees greater or smaller upon the common called the sheep common on both sides the Mill River until it come to Jonathan Baileys uper field and at the other end of the Towne any where at Thomas Dickinsons land except it be alders or birches shall pay fifteen shillings for every tree...."

The tree question came up again in 1709, and a law was passed by the town "that if any person shall fall lop or cary away any tree or part of a tree from the day and date hearof they shall forfitt and pay for each tree above: 12 inches over 20s (twenty shillings) and for every lesser trees 10s (ten shillings) excepting old wood that is already down."

A large tract of land known as the West Ox Pasture was laid out between the Bradford Street and Batchelder Plain lots on the east, extending westward across Batchelder Brook to Wethersfield Street. It contained nearly one square mile of territory and was owned by Mr. Thomas Nelson, Mr. Ezekiel Rogers, Thomas Barker, George Abbott, Widow Brocklebank, Lieut. John Remington, Deacon Maximilian Jewett, Joseph Jewett, Thomas Dickinson, Mighill Hopkinson, Constance Crosby, Elder Humphrey Reyner, Captain Sebastian Brigham and Mrs. Margaret Shove.

It is likely that Thomas Dickinson, in addition to farming, was also a weaver. In his will dated March 8, 1661-62, he gives to his son, James, his looms and furniture belonging thereto.

Thomas Dickinson was buried January 29, 1662, in Rowley. His widow, Jennet, remarried. Her second husband was John Whipple of Ipswich. Widow Jennet Whipple was buried in Rowley on February 1, 1686.
    The will of Thomas Dickinson was proved in Inswich court April 17, 1662, by the witnesses. Essex Co. Probate Files, Docket 7,678.

"I Thomas Dickinson of The Towne of Rowley in The County of eses being weake of Body but of perfect vnderstanding And memmory doe make And ordaine This my last will and Testament In primis my will is That my welbeloued wife Jennett Dickinson shalbe my Solle excequtrise for To pay all my debts and to pay my childeren Those portions Tat I by will doe Giue vnto Them; And also to demand and Recouer all debts that are pr ,au be die vnto me by bills bonds or otherwise and To doe any Thinge belonging To such an Excequtorise. Item I will and Giue vnto This my welbeloued wife halfe of ¦my¦ Dwelling house halfe of my barne halfe of my orchard and halfe of my swampe below my orchard and all my land oboue the The barne about Twellue Acres be it more or lese And Three Acres of meadow one acre of it in betchelor meadow and Two Acres in the northeast feild as also one acre more of salt marsh in the marsh feild bounded by deacon Jewets marsh on the west and by marsh of John pickards on the north and also i doe Giue bnto hir Two Gates on the Towne common al this I doe Giue hir dureing hir natuall life Item I will And Giue vnto my son James dickinson The other halfe of my houseing barne orchard and swampe below the orchard and all other my lands meadowes and Commons that belonge bnto me with The Towne of Rowley (excepting my village land and Two Acres of meadow in The great meadow be it more or lese.) Item I doe Giue vnto my son James dickinson foure score Acres of land more or lese being my deuission of land in that land Commonly called merrimack land buting against merrimacke Riuer with the priueledges belonging bnto the said fourscore acres of land and likewise I doe Giue vnto my son James my houseing barne orchard and swampe and lands aboue the barne and meadow and commons That I haue giuen bnto my welbeloued wife for her naturall life to be his bnto his proper use and behoufe after his mothers decease. Item I doe further Giue vnto my son James my cart and plough and furneture belonging There To also I giue bnto him my loumes and furneture belonging There To
    Item out of The Rest of my estate That is in my village land and Two Acres of meadow in the Great meadow that was before

excepted and in my stocke moueables bills bonds or any other estat
that is or may be due vnto me out of This Remaneing part of my
estat I will and Giue vnto my foure daughters each of Them one
hundred pounds and my will is that fifty pounds That I haue giuen
vnto my daughter Sarah alredy shalbe acounted as part of that which
I doe now giue And if any of my childeren die before they attaine
to the age of Twenty one yeares or day of marriage Then There
portions at be devided equally among the rest and if my Son James
depart This life gaueing noe child Then the one halfe of those
lands I giue him to Returne to be equally devided among The Rest
of my daughters or Theire heires The other halfe I giue vnto his
wife if then liueing to be for hir use dureing hir nattural life
and then to returne after hir decease to be equally devided among
my other daughters or there childeren if ther be any then liueing
Item I will and Giue (the Three hundered and fifty poinds being
paid out of this estat that I here apoint for the payment of my
daughters portions) all the Remaineing part of that estat vnto my
welbeloued wife To be vnto hir owne proper use and To despose of
as she shall Thinke meete; And my will is that my wife shall haue
hir liberty to chuse which halfe of my dwelling house she will for
to liue in dureing hir life; And I appoint John pickard and Samuell
Brocklebanke To be ouerseers of This my last will and Testament
which I Confirme with my owne hand this eights of march one
Thoussand Six hundred and sixty one or sixty two
                              Thomas Dickanson
      Witness: Samuell Brocklebanke, John trumble"

ESSEX COUNTY,
MASSACHUSETTS

The map above shows the shape of Essex County, Massachusetts today. In the mid 1600's the northern boundry of the Bay Colony was the Merrimac River and the southern boundary did not extend below Lynn. In 1643, Essex County had only the eight towns shown. The approximate town boundaries at that time are indicated by the dotted lines.

As the population grew and religeous and economic differences began to separate the population, more towns were formed and the town boundaries were changed repeatedly.

THIRD GENERATION

THOMAS[3] ADAMS

Thomas[3] Adams, second son of Nathaniel[2] and Mercy (Dickinson) Adams was born at Ipswich, Massachusetts, on June 14, 1672. He married Bethia _____ in early 1694. Although not adequately proved, it is believed Bethia's maiden surname was Blanchard.

Thomas lived his entire life in Ipswich. He was likely to have been a farmer, at least part of the time. Many of the early settlers had other skills used to provide income during part of each year.

Thomas and Bethia had nine children, all born at Ipswich.

(1) **BETHIA[4]**: born October 21, 1694; died June 26, 1710.

(2) **SARAH[4]**: born April 29, 1697; married Josiah Bishop on February 7, 1717.

(3) **THOMAS[4]: born August 31, 1699; died in early 1765; married Deborah Knowlton on April 17, 1722. Thomas and Deborah had five sons.
   (1) **Thomas[5]**: born February 15, 1722/23.
   (2) **Ephraim[5]: born in 1724 at Ipswich, Massachusetts; died March 26, 1797, in New Ipswich, New Hampshire. Ephraim married, first, Lydia Kinsman, and second, Rebecca Locke.
   (3) **Ezekiel[5]**: born about 1725; married Judith Preston on June 27, 1749; died December 15, 1793, at Hamilton, Massachusetts.
   (4) **Benjamin[5]**: baptized August 4, 1728; married, first, his cousin, Priscilla Adams, on April 18, 1751, and second, Susannah Ralph, widow of David Everett, on February 19, 1795; died May 5, 1815. Benjamin was disabled by rheumatism contracted in the Campaign of 1776 (Revolutionary War), near White Plains, in consequence of having his blanket stolen from him while he slept. Priscilla Adams, first wife of Benjamin, died February 19, 1791, at New Ipswich, New Hampshire.
   (5) **Joseph[5]**: born November 1733 at Hamlet parish, Ipswich; died May 1734.

(4) **JOSEPH[4]**: born November 12, 1702, at Ipswich, Massachusetts; married, first, Priscilla Warner on January 10, 1727/28. Priscilla Adams died in Concord January 6, 1734. He married, second, Dorothy Merriam on November 4, 1736. Joseph died May 10, 1790, at Concord. Joseph and Priscilla Adams had three children.
   (1) **Priscilla[5]**: born January 3, 1728/29; married her

cousin, Benjamin Adams, in Concord on April 18, 1751; died in New Ipswich, New Hampshire, February 19, 1791.
(2) **Lydia**[5]: born October 16, 1730; died July 3, 1731.
(3) **Mary**[5]: born May 5, 1733, at Concord; died September 9, 1733.

Joseph and Dorothy Adams had six children.

(1) **Dorothy**[5]: born August 26, 1737, at Concord; died April 10, 1766.
(2) **Ruth**[5]: born January 14, 1739, at Concord; married Peter Fletcher of New Ipswich, New Hampshire, September 8, 1761; died April 28, 1816.
(3) **Mary**[5]: born March 14, 1742; married Isaac Appleton of New Ipswich, New Hampshire, April 24, 1760; died May 22, 1827.
(4) **Bethia**[5]: born June 3, 1744; died September 30, 1753.
(5) **Mercy**[5]: born January 14, 1747; married, first, Benjamin Pollard of Lincoln on April 21, 1768, and second, Jonas Whiting. She died in Norway, Maine, August 12, 1815.
(6) **Lydia**[5]: born August 22, 1750; married Joseph Chandler April 28, 1774; died December 10, 1829.

(5) **LYDIA**[4]: born December 16, 1704; married, first, Benjamin Woodbury on January 12, 1722/23, and second, Rice Knowlton, Jr. on December 12, 1727.

(6) **ELIZABETH**[4]: born June 22, 1707; married Peter Lamson on April 18, 1728.

(7) **BENJAMIN**[4]: born April 22, 1710; died September 15, 1785; married Persis Potter, who died September 10, 1783. He settled in Marlboro first, then in about 1738 removed to North Brookfield, Massachusetts. Benjamin and Persis had fifteen children:
    (1) **Persis**[5]: born November 13, 1732.
    (2) **Silas**[5]: born November 17, 1733; died young.
    (3) **Rebecca**[5]: born February 29, 1736; married Obadiah Bartlett, who was born on April 5, 1730, on May 9, 1753.
    (4) **Silas**[5]: born September 14, 1738.
    (5) **Lucy**[5]: born March 20, 1740.
    (6) **Persis**[5]: born April 16, 1742; married Silas Stevens on November 21, 1782.
    (7) **Mary**[5]: born March 3, 1744; married Emerson Woolcott on December 2, 1767.
    (8) **Sarah**[5]: born March 30, 1746; married Dr. Joseph Stow on May 22, 1765.
    (9) **Benjamin**[5]: born April 20, 1748, at Brookfield, Massachusetts; married Eunice Hale on December 16, 1773; died February 23, 1829, at Brookfield.

(10) **Ephraim**[5]: born May 23, 1750, at Brookfield, Massachusetts; married, first, Eunice Moulton on May 19, 1774, and second, Sybil Bemis on May 14, 1785; died January 3, 1822.

(11) **Joel**[5]: born April 19, 1752; married Joanna Hale on July 14, 1776.

(12) **Charles**[5]: born April 23, 1754, at Brookfield, Mass.

(13) **Lydia**[5]: born March 11, 1756, at Brookfield, Mass.

(14) **Darius**[5]: born June 27, 1758, at Brookfield, Mass.

(15) **Lemuel**[5]: born November 22, 1760; died young. (Name could be Samuel).

(8) **CHARLES**[4]: born June 29, 1712 (recorded old style, 29:4:1712); died September 17, 1786; married Mary Perkins, who died April 24, 1800, on October 30, 1733. He moved to North Brookfield, Massachusetts, before 1748 and bought what is known as the "Knowlton place"; had no children, and gave his property to a nephew, Charles A. Knowlton, whom he had raised.

(9) **BETHIAH**[4]: baptized 8:6:1714; probably died young.

Thomas Adams died October 24, 1729. He was buried at Ipswich, Massachusetts. Thomas' widow died there also, recorded as "The widow Adams", died January 12, 1742.

THE WILL OF THOMAS³ ADAMS
(Nathaniel², William¹)
****

In the Name of God Amen This 24th day of March Anno Domini 1724/5 I Thomas Adams senior of Ipswich in the County of Essex, in the Province of the Massachusets Bay in New-Eng. Husbandman, Being at this time sick and infirm in Body but of a sound and disposing mind, for which I bless God and Calling to mind my own mortality, I have thought fit to make and ordain this my Last Will and Testament. and first of all, I commend my immortal soul to God who gave it and Bequeath my body to the earth its originall, to be buried in a Decent manner nothing doubting, but at ye resurrection I shall receive it again a glorious body from ye almighty power of God. And respecting such worldly goods, as God in his unmerited bounty has bestowed on me my will is as followeth.

[   ] - To my Loving Wife Bethiah Adams I give the use of one third part of all my Lands, the use of one end in one of my houses as she shall choose, and a sufficient priviledge in the Barne for her stock. my wife shall have two cows, and six sheep out of my stock for her own, to be kept upon her thirds. And she shall have all my Moveables within doors, during her natural life to be disposed of at her Death among our children, at her pleasure. Her wood sufficient for her use shall be cutt off of her thirds and brought to ye door By my Executor after-named.

Nextly to my two Eldest sons Thomas and Joseph I give all my Lands, common rights, houseing, outhousing, and buildings, with all moveables without dores, to be Equally divided between them, Excepting that to Thomas my Eldest son, I give all my interest in Piggeon Hills and my interest in the new Barne. my said two Eldest sons, I Constitute the Executors of this my Last Will and Testament, and order them to Pay all my just debts, and the following legacies which I give to my other children.

Vis -

To my Daughter Sarah Bishop I give Five pounds in addition to what she has had already.

To my daughter Lydia Woodbury I also give five pounds, in addition to what she has had already.

To my son Benj^{a}. I give seventy pounds, to be paid him at the age of Twenty one.

To my son Charles I also give seventy pounds to be paid him at ye age of twenty one.

To my daughter Elizabeth I give Fifty pounds, to be paid her at ye age of Twenty one, or upon her marriage if she should marry before twenty one.

My two Executors above named shall pay all the above mentioned lLegacy in an Equall proportion

Signed, Sealed, and Published

In presence of us -

Samuel Wigglesworth   Thomas Adams

Hannah Safford (her mark)

James Whipple [   ]

FOURTH GENERATION

THOMAS[4] ADAMS

Thomas[4] Adams, oldest son of Thomas[3] and Bethia Adams, was born in Ipswich, Massachusetts, August 31, 1699. He lived in that part of Ipswich now known as Hamilton on lands left him by his father. He died in early 1765. His will was proved March 25, 1765, at Ipswich, Massachusetts.

As a young man, Thomas was known to be interested in the settlement of New Ipswich, New Hampshire. The History of New Ipswich by Charles Henry Chandler provides the following detail. Thomas received two eighty-acre lots under the Massachusetts grant, which he probably lost. He held five shares under the Masonian charter, giving him title to more than two square miles of land, upon 240 acres of which his sons Ephraim and Benjamin were the original settlers. His will, written in 1750, mentions his brother Joseph and refers to deeds of land in New Ipswich left to his sons Ephraim and Benjamin. Thomas never resided in New Ipswich. He lived his entire life in Ipswich, operating his farm.

The land grants which enabled Thomas Adams to acquire property in New Hampshire dated to the very early period of settlement in New England. The original royal patent of "Laconia", granted in 1622 to Sir Ferdinando Gorges and John Mason, embraced all the line of the Atlantic coast lying between the Merrimack and St. Lawrence rivers to the distance of many miles inland. Subsequently, Mason, who probably had several business transactions with Gorges, obtained a second patent containing a considerable tract of territory lying between the Merrimack and Piscataqua rivers, and which he called New Hampshire. Reference, Collier's Encyclopedia, copywrite 1964, volume 15, page 498.

John Mason expected to benefit greatly from the land and from mining precious metals in New Hampshire. He never realized his plans. The properties of John Mason became known as the Masonian charter, or Masonian Grant. As those properties passed to his heirs and were sold, they were acquired by individuals interested in expanding the settlements in New England. One of those persons was Thomas Adams.

On April 17, 1722, Thomas Adams married Deborah Knowlton. Research has shown there is some confusion as to which Deborah Knowlton married Thomas Adams. The History of New Ipswich by Chandler, published in 1914, identifies the wife of Thomas Adams to be Deborah Knowlton, born December 31, 1698, daughter of Thomas and Margery (Goodhue) Knowlton.

Ezekiel and Sarah (Leach) Knowlton had a daughter named Deborah who was born October 29, 1699. Published genealogies referenced in the bibliography of this work for both the Knowlton and Leach families indicate this is the Deborah who married Thomas Adams. The fact that Thomas and Deborah Adams named one of their sons Ezekiel, presumably after Deborah's father, and the credibility of the works on the Knowlton and Leach families, convince this writer that Thomas Adams did, in fact, marry the daughter of Ezekiel and Sarah.

Thomas and Deborah Adams had five sons. all born at Ipswich.

(1) **THOMAS**[5]: born February 15, 1722/23; a yeoman; married Elizabeth Brown, intentions published April 14, 1744; died between January 28 and April 6, 1790. He was survived by his wife. Thomas and Elizabeth Adams had eleven children, all born at Ipswich.

    (1) **Deborah**[6]: born May 1, 1745; died young.
    (2) **Elizabeth**[6]: born December 5, 1746; married Daniel Appleton of Buxton, intentions published June 29, 1776; died September 5, 1832.
    (3) **Hannah**[6]: born February 10, 1749.
    (4) **Abigail**[6]: born September 21, 1750; married Thomas Ross of Salem on November 26, 1771; died before 1790.
    (5) **Bethiah**[6]: born December 12, 1752; married Samuel Brown of Wenham on March 7, 1775.
    (6) **Lucy**[6]: born November 1, 1754; married William Brown of Ipswich on February 10, 1778.
    (7) **Sarah**[6]: born January 15, 1756; probably died young.
    (8) **Thomas**[6]: born September 2, 1757; married Anna Porter on April 19, 1783; died in Gilmanton, New Hampshire, May 6, 1844.
    (9) **Moses**[6]: born about 1759; was a cabinet maker; married Sarah Hubbard of Ipswich on August 14, 1784; had five children; died October 7, 1796.
    (10) **Lydia**[6]: living in 1790.
    (11) **Mary**[6]: married, first, Ephraim Smith on September 27, 1781, and second, William Price of Gilmanton, New Hampshire.

(2) EPHRAIM[5]: baptized October 18, 1724; died March 26, 1797; married, first, Lydia Kinsman on April 6, 1749, and second, Rebecca Locke on November 18, 1761. Ephraim and Lydia, who died at age 32 on November 5, 1760, had five children:
    (1) **Ephraim**[6]: born December 15, 1749; married, first, Elizabeth Stearns, and second, Bridget ____ ; died April 15, 1825. Ephraim was a soldier in the Revolution, having responded to the Concord alarm in 1775.
    (2) **Thomas**[6]: born September 12, 1751; died October 11, 1820; married Molly Farnsworth on December 18, 1777. She was born about 1756 and died June 24, 1842. Thomas served in the Revolution, and was probably the Thomas Adams named on the company roll of Captain Abijah Smith or of Captain Francis Towne, or of both.

(3) **Stephen**[6]: born November 6, 1753, said to have enlisted for the Revolution from Rindge in the company of Captain Philip Thomas in 1775. If true, he served at the battle of Bunker Hill. Positive identification is uncertain, as there were several soldiers with the same name.

(4) **Daniel**[6]: born August 24, 1755; married Sarah Clark; died about 1790.

(5) **Lydia**[6]: born July 16, 1757; died October 1800, married Nathan Wheeler. Nathan was born in Concord, Massachusetts, on January 9, 1744, and died May 7, 1834. Nathan and Lydia lived in Temple, New Hampshire. Children: Nathan, Lydia, and Josiah.

Ephraim and his second wife, Rebecca Locke, had seven children, all born at New Ipswich, New Hampshire.

(1) **John**[6]: born November 10, 1762; died December 9, 1763.

(2) **John**[6]: born February 29, 1764; died in the army in 1781.

(3) **Ebenezer**[6]: born October 2, 1765; married, first, Alice Frink on July 9, 1795, ans second, Beulah Minott on May 17, 1807; died August 15, 1841. Ebenezer Adams was a graduate of and later a full professor at Dartmouth College.

(4) **Rebecca**[6]: born July 27, 1767; married Abel Shedd on January 20, 1802.

(5) **James**[6]: born May 20, 1769; married Ruth Conant on November 3, 1795.

(6) **Betsy**[6]: born March 13, 1772; died April 14, 1816; married Dr. Luther Jewett of St. Johnsbury, Vermont, on February 7, 1797; had eight children.

(7) **Quincy[6]: born September 29, 1775; died in the winter of 1814/1815; married Dolly Elliot.

(3) **EZEKIEL**[5]: born about 1725; was a yeoman; lived in that part of Ipswich known as Hamilton; married Judith Preston of Beverly, intentions published February 9, 1748/49. She died in Hamilton August 28, 1793. He died there December 15, 1793. Ezekiel and Judith Adams had six children, all born in Hamlet parish, Ipswich.

(1) **Ezekiel**[6]: was a cordwainer; married, first, Sarah Whipple on January 14, 1773, second, Anna _____, before 1789, and third, Miss Lucy Whipple of Hamilton in January 1795. Ezekiel lost twin children at birth when his first wife, Sarah, also died.

(2) **Isaac**[6]: a mariner and yeoman; lived in Hamilton for a while.

(3) **Stephen**[6]: was a cooper; moved to Jaffrey, New Hampshire.

(4) **Nehemiah**[6]: baptized April 16, 1769.

(5) **Benjamin**[6]: baptized July 16, 1780.
(6) **Asa**[6]: baptized April 23, 1780.

(4) **BENJAMIN**[5]: baptized August 4, 1728; died May 5, 1815;
married, first, on April 18, 1751, Priscilla Adams, a cousin
and daughter of his father's brother, Joseph, and his wife,
Priscilla (Warner) Adams. Benjamin's wife, Priscilla, was
born January 3, 1728/29, and died February 19, 1791. Benjamin
married, second, Susannah, daughter of Stephen Ralph and the
widow of David Everett. Benjamin was the father of eleven
children.
    (1) **Joseph**[6]: born February 3, 1752; died March 30, 1752.
    (2) **Priscilla**[6]: born March 15, 1753; died February 17,
1777; married John Warner on October 12, 1772.
    (3) **Sarah**[6]: born February 1, 1755; died March 15, 1775.
    (4) **Benjamin**[6]: born February 7, 1756; died May 6, 1758.
    (5) **Mary**[6]: born March 1, 1758.
    (6) **Deborah**[6]: born June 5, 1760; died July 19, 1760.
    (7) **Hannah**[6]: born August 27, 1761.
    (8) **Benjamin**[6]: born September 9, 1763.
    (9) **Joseph**[6]: born December 13, 1765.
    (10) **Sarah**[6]: born August 11, 1768; died November 20,
1768.
    (11) **Eunice**[6]: born March 8, 1770; married Aaron Appleton
on November 17, 1799, and had six children.

Benjamin traveled to New Ipswich with his brother,
Ephraim, and settled on the same lot and the lot adjoining to
the west. The two brothers held their land in common for many
years until Benjamin moved his home to the western lot. He
was a valued citizen and served as town clerk and was a
selectman for nine years. He served upon at least two calls
for troops in the Revolutionary struggle. He was present for
the battle at White Plains. While encamped near White Plains,
his blanket was stolen from him while he was asleep. The
resulting exposure caused a life-long lameness and ultimately
a complete inability to walk.

(5) **JOSEPH**[5]: born November 1733; died May 1734.

As stated earlier, it is believed that Thomas Adams lived his
entire life at Ipswich, Massachusetts. He is believed buried in
the area of Ipswich, although details of his death and burial have
not been learned. Some information about the family is available
from his will, which follows.

```
*****************************************************
```
THE WILL OF THOMAS[4] ADAMS
(Thomas[3], Nathaniel[2], William[1])

```
*****************************************************
```

In the Name of God Amen
I Thomas Adams of Ipswich in the County of Essex yeoman Knowing
that it is apointed for all once to die And being of a sound mind
and memory do make and ordain this my last will and Testament That
is to say principally and first of all I give and Recommend my soul
into the Hands of God that gave it and my Body I Recommend to the
Earth to be Buried in Christian burial at the discretion of my
Executors. and as touching worldly Estate wherewith it hath
Pleased God to Bless me in this life I gave and dispose of the same
in the following manner -
[   ] To my loving wife Deborah I give ye use of one half the house
I now dwell in and a sufficient Priviledge in my Barnes for her
stock and two Cows and six sheep out of my stock to be kept by my
Executors After mentioned upon her thirds also I give her one
Eighth part of ye yearly produce of my Estate Excepting ye hay and
grass which she is to have only sufficient for her stock also I
give her fire wood sufficient for her use brought and Cut at her
door by my Executors in Equal halfs the during my widdow and in
Case they or Either of S[d] Executors do refuse or neglect ye above
said duty to their mother she may upon making aplicaton to ye judge
of probate have her thirds set off at any time she remaining my
widow.
also I give her all my moveables within doors to her one disposed
Except those hereafter mentioned
Item To my oldest son Thomas I give the homested that I bought of
Bro Joseph Adams with all ye Buildings thereon also the
southeasterly part of [   ] madow land Bounded at a white oak tree
in ye walk by a small stone thence running on a straight line to
a stake standing near the head of the Brook in S[d] madow thence as
ye Brook runs to John Bowles his land thence on ye Bowleses land
and his own land to ye tree first mentioned. also half our old
lott that I bought of Paletiah Kinsman in the thickwooods Eight so
Caled
also twelve acres of that Lott of Land I gought of John Patch and
Nehemiah Dodge at the End of said Lott adjoining to ye way that
Leeds to Isaac Cummings also one half a tract of Land Caled
Bedlocks also ye one half of my marsh and thickbank in ye Hundreds
so Caled also my Desk my Sword my Cane and one third part of my
sider Casks
I order him my son Thomas to pay out unto my son Benjamin his Heirs
or order one Hundred Pounds in lawfull silver money -
to my son Ephraim I give one Right throughout in all the divisions
in New Ipswich as by a deed that I gave him may appear -
I give him one Hundred Pounds in lawfull silver money out of that
part of my Estate that I have and shall give to my son Ezekiel

-34-
```
```

including what his Brother Ezekiel hath already ingaged to Pay unto
him ye said Ephraim to his Heirs or order
                              I give
To my son Ezekiel the House I now Dwell in with the Homested and
ye other buildings thereone with the other Lands which I have
expressed in a Deed that I have given to him my half that tract of
Land Caled bed Locks and half ye marsh and Thackbank in ye Hundred
so Caled and one quarter and half a Quarter of an old Common Right
in ye thickwoods Eight so Called viz Quarles his Right so Caled and
the Northerly part of vensons maddon Land Bounded Southesterly and
Southwesterly on his Bro Thomas his Line and Northerly and
Northeasterly on Land that was Common: also Eight acres out of that
Lott which I Bought of John Patch and Nehemiah Dodge adjoining
thereto also my Looms and one third part of my sider Casks and
I order him my S^d son Ezekiel to pay to my son Ephraim his Heirs or
order one Hundred Pounds Lawfull Silver money Excluding what he
Hath already ingaged to pay to him ye S^d Ephraim
Item To my son Benjamin I give one Right through in all the
Divisions in a Township Caled New Ipswich as I have expressed in
a deed that I gave him of ye same
also I give to him ye S^d Benjamin one Hundred Pound Lawfull Silver
money out of that part of my Estate I gave to my son Thomas he
Refusing or neglecting to pay ye same according to my order
moreover all my money that I have or that is Due to me or Bond Noat
or any other wayes I give to my wife and our four sons to be Equaly
Divided
all my just Debts and Funernall Charges Being first paid all the
Rest of my Estate both Real and personal I give to my four sons to
be Equaly Divided
I Constute and ordain my son Thomas and son Ezekiel to be Executors
to this my Last Will and Testement and I do hereby utterly Disallow
Revoke and [   ] all and Every other Testement and will Executors
By me in any ways Before made and named Ratiefing and Confirming
this and No other to be my Last will and testement In wittenis
where of I have hereunt left my hand and seal this nineteenth Day
of March Anno Domini One thousand seven Hundred and Fifty.

Signed Sealed published pronounced and Declaird
by ye S^d Thomas Adams as his last will and
Testement in ye Presence of ye subscribers
Samuel Wigglesworth
Jthn Thompson   Thomas Adams
Martha Wigglesworth

        ****

KNOWLTON FAMILY

Deborah Knowlton, daughter of Ezekiel and Sarah (Leach) Knowlton, married Thomas Adams on April 17, 1722. She was born October 29, 1699, probably in Manchester, Massachusetts. Deborah was the great-great-grandaughter of Captain William Knowlton who sailed from London for Nova Scotia in 1632. The bulk of the family history which follows has been extracted from <u>The History and Genealogy of the Knowltons of England and America</u> by the Reverend Charles Henry Wright Stocking, D.D., published by the Knickerbocker Press, 1897.

The known Knowlton lineage of Deborah Knowlton is shown here.

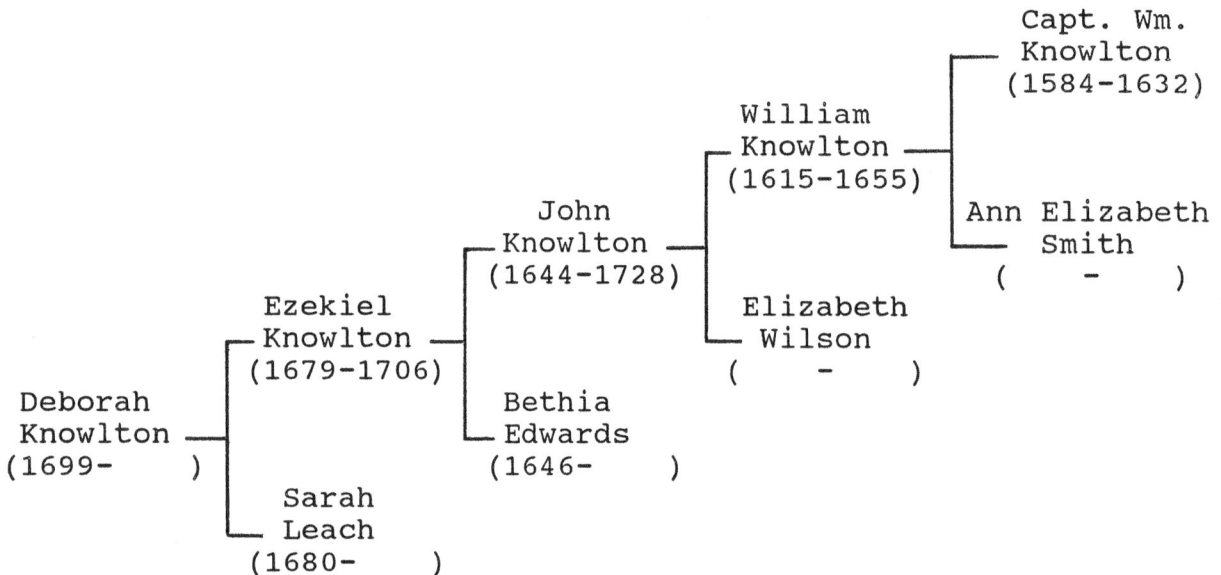

```
                                                                    Capt. Wm.
                                                                  ┌ Knowlton
                                                                  │ (1584-1632)
                                                     William      │
                                                   ┌ Knowlton ────┤
                                                   │ (1615-1655)  │
                                        John       │              │ Ann Elizabeth
                                     ┌ Knowlton ────┤              └ Smith
                                     │ (1644-1728)  │                (    -    )
                          Ezekiel    │              │ Elizabeth
                        ┌ Knowlton ──┤              └ Wilson
                        │ (1679-1706)│                (    -    )
            Deborah     │            │ Bethia
            Knowlton ───┤            └ Edwards
            (1699-   )  │              (1646-    )
                        │ Sarah
                        └ Leach
                          (1680-    )
```

Captain William Knowlton was born in 1584 in England. With his wife, Ann Elizabeth (Smith), and some of their children, he sailed from the port of London for Nova Scotia in 1632. In England a record was kept of those emigrants who took the oath of loyalty to the English Crown when they left. As no record of Knowlton appears in the Customs Department at London, it has been inferred that William was independent in political action and probably a religious non-conformist.

Every resident in each English parish was enrolled in its records. Captain Knowlton was probably so enrolled at Chiswich. Unfortunately, the old parish church was siezed by Cromwell in 1645 and used as a garrison. The records were destroyed. For this reason, much of the proof of the early English lineage of this

Knowlton family is lost.   The family name dates to the time of William the Conqueror.

Captain Knowlton was at least part owner of the ship in which he sailed for America.   He died on the voyage, probably not far from Nova Scotia.   In 1839, a land surveyor in Nova Scotia found an ancient headstone there bearing the inscription, " William Knowlton, 1632."

It is believed his ship was sold at Anneapolis, the first settlement in Nova Scotia, and the location of their landing in 1632.   His widow and children continued to Massachusetts, probably Hingham.   The widow is believed to have remarried in Hingham.

The children of Captain William and Ann Elizabeth Knowlton include:
   (1) **John**: born 1610.
(2) **William: born 1615; died 1655; married Elizabeth Wilson.
   (3) **Thomas**: born 1620.
   (4) **Samuel**: born 1621.

William Knowlton, son of Captain William Knowlton, eventually settled in Ipswich, Massachusetts, where he was a cordwainer.   A cordwainer is a shoemaker.   He was once fined for having a pack of cards in his house.

Further details of the life of William Knowlton are not clear, as there was more than one William Knowlton living in Ipswich and it is not possible to distinguish between the activities of the two from the records kept at the time.

William and Elizabeth Knowlton had seven children.
   (1) **Thomas**: born 1640.
   (2) **Nathaniel**: born 1641; married Deborah Grant, May 3, 1662.
   (3) **William**: born 1642; married Susannah _____.
(4) **John: born 1644; married Bethia Edwards.   Reference, Boston Transcript.
   (5) **Benjamin**: born 1646; married Hannah Mirick on November 30, 1676.
   (6) **Samuel**: born 1647; married Elizabeth Witt in 1669.
   (7) **Mary**: born 1649; married Samuel Abbe on October 12, 1672; lived in Wenham, Massachusetts.

William Knowlton died in 1655.   Administration of the estate of William Knowlton, who died intestate, was granted July 25, 1655, to his brother, Thomas Knowlton, to whom was committed the care of the widow and children.   The following is from the Essex Co. Probate Files, Docket 16,099.

"Inventory taken July 17, 1655, by Theophilus Wilson and Thomas Knowlton: house and ground, medow and Upland, 20li.; 3

pewter disshes and tin candlestick, 10s; brass kettle, 12s.; little bras pot with holes, 1s. 6d.; little brass kettle old, 2s.; 2 paire of pott hooks, 1s 8d.; pr. of tongs, 1s. 6d.; broken brass scillet, 1s. 6d.; broken brass ladle, 6d.; 4 Woodden trayes, 2s. 6d.; straining dish, a tunnle, 2 wooden platers and a old traye, 1s. 8d.; lumber, 5s., friing pan, 18d., 6s. 6d.; 2 boxes and a old chest, 5s.; 2 old narrow axes, 1s.; A sive, 12d., tin tunnle, 9 trenchers, 1s. 9d.; A kow, 4li. 5s.; 2 yerlings, vantage, 3li. 11s., 8lie.; 3 Calves, 2li. 10s.; 4 shoats, 2li. 10s.; 2 siekles, 1s.; A broad how, 4s.; gun and sword, 14s.; fflock bed and boulster, fflock bed tick and blanket, 1li.; total 37li. 8s. 1d. Depts that are owing to others for hilling of the ground, 34s., 1li. 14s.; debts besids, 7li.; mor owing, 12s.; mor owing to others 12s.

Received in Ipswich court, 25: 7: 1655."

A copy of this taken out of the records of the Ipswich court March 11, 1655, received into court March 31, 1691.

"Debts oweing from the estate of William Knowlton: To my selfe Tho. Knowlton wch I lent him, 7li.; payd to men for hilling his corne, 1li. 16s.; payd to Jer. Belcher, 3s.; John Browne, 16s. 9d.; Mr. Wilm Norton, 5s.; Henry Muddle, 15s.; payd to by cloths for the children 1li. 16s. 6d.; payd for makeing them & a wastcot for her, 14s. 2d.; to the widdow Varney, 11s.; for a peece of marsh, 12s.; for bringing the goods to the Towne, 10s.; to Wilm Coggswell 7s., Goodman ffowler, 6s., 13s.; for 4 hatts, 1li. 1s. 8d.; for shirts for the boyes, 10s.; for Scooling for the boyes, 14s. 6d.; to Goodman Kinsman, 11s. 10d., to Isaack Coussins, 20d., 13s. 6d.; for the Coffin & Grave, 6s. 6d., to goodman Lomas, 6s. 8d.; to John Emerson, 2s.; 6 paire of shoes for the boyes & a paire for the girle, 14s. 6d.; for a paire of Indenters administration and Inventory & coppes, 3s.; oweing in my booke before his death for corne & shoes, 2li.; The widdow hath of the houshold stufe, 3li. 9s. 1d.; A petecoat, wastcoat, hatt & a paire of shoes, 2li. 8s. 10d.; a pound of Cotton woole, 1s. 8d.; total 27li. 14s. 4d."

Thomas Knowlton received of the estate of his brother William Knowlton, deceased, 37li. 8s. 1d. An account of what he has paid out of the said estate: "to Robert Kinsman, 11s. 10d.; John Browne, 16s. 9d.; Isaac Cuzens, 2s. 5d.; his Coffin, 5s.; making Cloathes, 14s. 2d.; shoes, 18s. 6d.; Skins for the Boyes, 8s.; to Edward Lumax, 6s. 8d.; Mr. John Emerson, 2s. 8d.; Good. Lord, 2s. 3d.; more paid in June 7li.; for ye burial of him to mr. Wilson, 1s. 6d.; cotten wool and ye Rate then due, 2s. 1d.; for Bringing my Brother to Town when Buried, 12s.; for hilling of his Corne, 1li. 16s.; bringing their Goods to Towne, 10s.; paid to mr. Cogswell, 1s.; Goodwofe Fuller, 6s.; Skins for the boyes, 9s. 6d.; four hatts, 1li. 1s. 8d.; one Hatt, 13s. 6d.; A Coat, 1li.; in Shifts, 10s.; to Henry Muddle, 15s.; A coat, 16s.; more in Shoes, 5s. 4d.; to Goodwife Varny, 11s.; Robert Cross, 1s. 8d.; A Coat for William

Knowlton, 13s. 6d.; two yards of Cloath, 14s. 11d.; to Richard Jacob, 6s.; my Sister of me in Houshold Goods and a Cow, 8li. 7s. 11d.; total 31li. 12s. 10d. And two boyes I kept from their age of five years till they were Eight years old and Cloathed and keept them to Scool, 36li. And I keept a Girle from her age of one year and halfe old till shee Maried.

Received by the court Sept. 24, 1678.

Deacon Thomas Knowlton testified to the truth of a copy of the above account and also that he hath disbursed much more than what is written.

June 19, 1690, before Mr. Samll. Appleton Assist.

Received in Ipswich Court Mar. 31, 1691."

"The request of Thomas Knowlton, sr. of Ipswich, dated Mar. 31, 1691, to the Ipswich court shewing that many years since, he was appointed administrator of the estate of his brother William Knowlton, who died in 1655, leaving a widown and seven children, the youngest about one and one half years old, and he was forced to take care especially of the youngest of them. The estate amounted to about 37li. 8s. 1d. and was insufficient to pay the debts with and bring up the children; he gave in to the court in 1678, two accounts of disbursements, one ofr 31li. and one for 36li., and as by the accounts it appeared he had paid 50li. more than was inventoried he thought he had been cleared and that his disposal of the estate was for the benefit of the family, especially when they received it an by his sister's importunity consented to the sale of the land, which was valued at about 20li., but now having done that for the widow and children, will this court take such cognizance of the cause as to examine whether the entry of the cleaing of said estate be sufficient, if not will they see just cause to do it yet."

"Ipswich court, Jan. 2, 1715, granted administration (D.B.N.) on the estate of William Knowlton, Ipswich, to his grandson Capt. Jno. Knowlton of Ipswich, he giving bond of 200li., Rice Knowlten and Issac Giddings, sureties. Witness: Samuel Daland, Danl. Rogers."

"Mary Mitchell formerly Mary Knowlton, daughter to William Knowlton of Ipswich, deceased, desires that 'my Cusen John Knowlton' of Ipswich, late of Manchester, may have administration of any estate that may be thought to be her father's. Dated Winddum, Nov. 10, 1715."

"Thomas Knowlton of Norwich, New London Co., desires that 'my Cusen John Knowlton' of Ipswich, late of Manchester, may have administration of any estate that may have his father's, William Knowlton. Dated, Norwich, Nov. 12, 1715."

"William Knowlton desires that 'my Cusen John Knowlton' of Ipswich may have administration of any estate that may have been his father's William Knowlton. Dated Wenham, Dec. 5, 1715."

It has been taken for granted the dress of the Puritans was very plain and simple, that they lived in an age of homespun and had little of the finery. A glance at the inventories in wills, especially of the well-to-do, sometimes disproves this. It must be remembered that many who came to New England were of the better class and were used to living and dressing well in England. As early as 1634, "the General Court, takeing into consideration the great, supflous, & unnecessary expences occaconed by reason of some newe & imodest fashions, as also the ordinary wearing of silver, golde, & silke laces, girdles, hatbands, *7c. hat therefore ordered that noe pson either man or woman, shall hereafter make or buy appel, either wollen, silke, or lynned, with any lace on it, silver, golde, silke, or thread, vnder penalty of forfecture of such cloathes &c. Massachusetts Bay Colony Records, 1, 136.

It sometimes happened that a man was reprimanded by the Court because his wife or daughter had indulged in the wearing of finery beyond what the law allowed. A number of Ipswich men were called to explain why their wives or daughters were allowed to wear so much finery. Among them was one Thomas Knowlton, who formerly lived in Rowley. This Thomas Knowlton is the prominent Deacon who was also a shoemaker.

John Knowlton, son of William and Elizabeth (Wilson) Knowlton, was born in 1644 in Ipswich, Massachusetts. He was a captain of the local militia at Ipswich. He was made a freeman in Ipswich in 1669 and took the oath in Manchester in 1680. Status as a freeman indicated the man was free of debt and of good standing in his church. John Knowlton was a carpenter by trade, but he was also a very enterprising man. He dealt largely in real estate. He died in 1728. His will was probated August 24, 1728.

John Knowlton was first married to Bethia Edwards, daughter of Rice and Joan (or Joanna) Edwards. Bethia lived in Wenham, Massachusetts. She married John Knowlton about the time he became a freeman in 1669. By most accounts John and Bethia had a large family. Some of their children were:
  (1) **John**: born 1670; married Abigail Bachelor (or Batchelder) on December 20, 1697.
  (2) **Robert**: born 1672; married and had five children.
 (3) **Ezekiel: born 1679; married Sarah Leach on January 29, 1698.

Bethia Knowlton died sometime after 1707. John then married Susanna Hutton of Wenham. There were no children born to this marriage, although Susanna may have brought children from a previous marriage to the family.

Rice Edwards, father of Bethia (Edwards) Knowlton, was born in England about 1615. After traveling to New England, he settled in Watertown, Massachusetts. He married, first Elnor (perhaps

Eleanor), and second, Joan (or Joanna) in Salem in 1643. In 1635 Rice Edwards moved to Boston, and in 1647 to Wenham.

Rice Edwards' children, all born to his second wife were:
(1) **John**: born 1644.
(2) **Bethia: born 1646; died after 1707; married John Knowlton.
(3) **Mary**: born about 1648.
(4) **Elizabeth**: born about 1650.
(5) **Thomas**: born 1652.
(6) **Sarah**: born 1654.
(7) Daughter whose name is not known; married William Cleaves.
(8) **Benjamin**: born 1662.

On April 18, 1681, an agreement signed between Rice and son Benjamin provided that Benjamin would receive most of the family estate in return for providing for Rice. A dispute arose over this arrangement after the death of Rice and was settled with other family members receiving furniture. The agreement dividing the furniture was signed by the family members on April 15, 1683.

Ezekiel Knowlton, father of Deborah, and son of John Knowlton is believed to have been born at Ipswich, Massachusetts, in 1679. His father relocated the family from Ipswich to Manchester in 1679, so there is some conjecture that Ezekiel could have been born at Manchester.

Ezekiel Knowlton was a weaver and made his home at Manchester. Ezekiel's wife, Sarah, was the daughter of Robert and Sarah Leach of Manchester, Massachusetts. Her parents lived their entire lives in Manchester.

Ezekiel and Sarah Knowlton are known to have had at least four children.
(1) **Deborah: born October 29, 1699; married Thomas Adams on April 17, 1722.
(2) **Robert**: born July 17, 1701; married Lydia Bishop on December 24, 1724.
(3) **Ezekiel**: born February 7, 1703; married Emma Foster on December 23, 1724.
(4) **Sarah**: born October 24, 1704; married John Woodbury on February 2, 1722.

Ezekiel is believed to have died in 1706. His wife was appointed administratrix of his estate on November 4, 1706. There is one report that Ezekiel drowned in an accident at Sable Isle in 1719. It is unlikely that this is the case in view of the manner in which the estate was handled.

Deborah Knowlton, daughter of Ezekiel and Sarah (Leach) Knowlton, married Thomas Adams. Her biography is contained in the preceding chapter dealing with her husband.

LEACH FAMILY

Sarah Leach married Ezekiel Knowlton. She is the mother of Deborah Knowlton, who married Thomas Adams and the daughter of Robert Leach and his wife, Sarah. Although nothing has been learned of her mother's ancestry, Sarah Leach's father's lineage has been determined and is presented here.

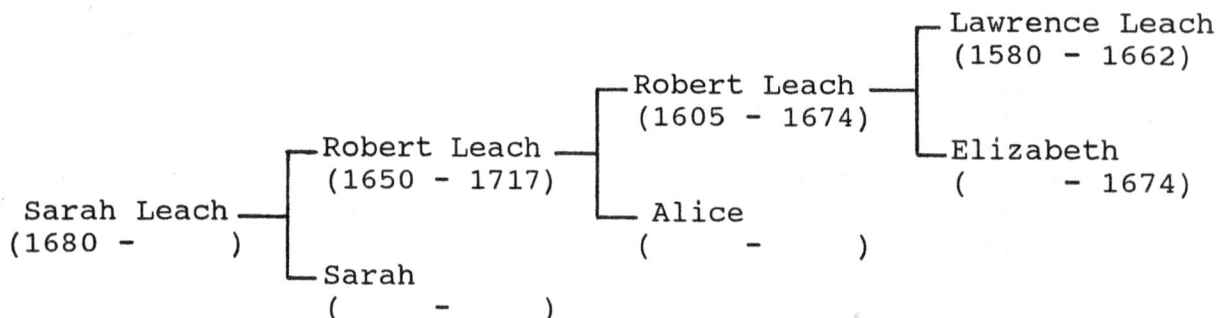

```
                                                       ┌─Lawrence Leach
                                                       │  (1580 - 1662)
                                      ┌─Robert Leach ──┤
                                      │  (1605 - 1674) │
                   ┌─Robert Leach ────┤                └─Elizabeth
                   │  (1650 - 1717)   │                   (     - 1674)
Sarah Leach ───────┤                  └─ Alice
(1680 -    )       │                     (    -    )
                   └─Sarah
                      (    -    )
```

Sarah Leach's great-grandfather, Lawrence Leach, was highly regarded in England and was sent by the Massachusetts Bay Company to assist in governing the Massachusetts Bay Colony. The details of his life are presented by F. Phelps Leach in his book, Lawrence Leach of Salem, Massachusetts, and Some of His Descendants, published in 1924.

Lawrence Leach is said to be descended from John DeLeche, surgeon to King Edward III of England. This connection is based largely on the family coat of arms which is consistent thru the ages.

Lawrence Leach was sent to Salem by the Massachusetts Bay Company in 1629. He traveled from England with his wife, Elizabeth, and some of his children. He was introduced to Governor John Endicott of the Massachusetts bay Colony by letter dated April 17, 1629, from Governor Craddock of Gravesend, England. The lengthy letter dealt extensively with the affairs of the colony. Lawrence Leach was one of the seven men originally chosen to manage the public affairs of Salem, Massachusetts. He held office in Salem for many years.

He was sworn a freeman at Salem on May 18, 1630. He was one of the jurymen in Boston which in 1630 served on the trial of the first capital case ever heard in Massachusetts. He was one of the founders of the church at Salem. He engaged in farming and milling. His mills were so important that a road was laid to them in 1657. He also had an iron foundry, which was the first in the colonies.

-42-

Lawrence Leach and his wife, Elizabeth, are believed to have had the following children:

(1) Robert: born in England, 1605; married, first, Mary (or Miriam) and second, Alice; died in 1674.
(2) **Clement:** born in England and remained there.
(3) **John:**
(4) **Margaret:** born in 1616; came to New England on the ship "Susan and Ellen" in 1635.
(5) **Ambrose:** born in 1616.
(6) **Richard:** born in England in 1618.
(7) **Edmund:**
(8) **Rachel:**
(9) **James:**
(10) **Giles:** born at Salem, Massachusetts, in 1632.

Upon his death, Lawrence Leach left all his possessions to his wife, Elizabeth. No history of Elizabeth's family is known, as her maiden surname has not been determined.

Robert Leach, the oldest son of Lawrence and Elizabeth Leach, was born in England in 1605. He traveled with his parents to Salem in 1629. Robert Leach was first married to Mary (or Miriam). She was admitted to the church September 9, 1639, and died February 11, 1648. Following her death, Robert married Alice. From the dates of birth of the children of Robert Leach, we know that Alice was the mother of the Robert Leach, son of this Robert Leach, who is next in the line of descendency traced here. It is also believed that Alice was married once before she married Robert Leach, so the children listed here could include Robert's children born to Mary and to Alice as well as children born to Alice from her first marriage. The children are:
(1) **Mary:**
(2) **Elizabeth:** married John Fosket.
(3) **Sarah:**
(4) **Bethiah:**
(5) **Abigail:** married John Day on December 10, 1682, at Manchester. He was born April 28, 1657, and was living in 1715. He was a soldier in King Philip's War and received a grant of land at Kettle Cove for his services.
(6) Robert: born in 1650 at Manchester; married, first, Sarah, and second, Hannah; died in 1717.
(7) **Samuel:** born in 1655 at Manchester.

Robert Leach may have owned land in several areas, including Salem, Manchester, and Charlestown. It is clear that he was from an influential family and received many grants of land for his services. In Salem, he received a grant on land in 1637 and took the freeman oath in 1644. He was one of the founders of Manchester and settled there in 1636. At Manchester, he was Town Clerk until 1648 and was a Selectman from 1658 to 1661.

Records pertaining to Robert Leach are confusing, as some indicate he died in 1688. There is also a record of him having served as a Selectman in Salem in 1680. It must be concluded these records are in error as more reliable records indicate he died in 1674 and that his widow remarried in 1676. These records indicate that widow Alice Leach married Robert Elwell in 1676. They had no children. Nothing more is known of Alice Leach, as her maiden surname has not been determined.

Robert Leach, son of the senior Robert Leach just discussed, was born in Manchester in 1650. It is clear from the date of death of his father's first wife and the rest of the biographical data presented he is the son of Robert and Alice Leach. Robert married, first, Sarah in 1678, and second, Hannah in 1684.

Robert and Sarah Leach had two children.
(1) **Sarah: born June 11, 1680; married Ezekiel Knowlton on January 29, 1698.
(2) **Robert**: born 1682-3.

Sarah, wife of Robert Leach, died about 1683. Nothing is known of her lineage, as her maiden surname has not been determined.

Robert married Hannah in 1684 and had eight more children.
(1) **Hannah**: born 1685; married her cousin, Samuel, who was born in 1682.
(2) **John**: born 1687-8.
(3) **Mary**: born 1690-1.
(4) **Elizabeth**: born 1692-3; died October 4, 1713.
(5) **Joseph**: born 1694.
(6) **Ann**: born May 23, 1696; married Joseph Pitman on December 16, 1715.
(7) **Paul**: born 1698.
(8) **Charles**: born October 7, 1702.

Robert was a soldier in King Philip's War. He was a Selectman at Manchester in twelve different years between 1687 and 1705. During the term of his office as a Selectman in 1700, a deed for the town of Manchester was obtained from the Indians. The deed was acknowledged at Salem on December 18, 1700. Robert lived his entire life in Manchester and died there in 1717.

Sarah Leach, daughter of Robert and Sarah Leach, was born June 11, 1680, at Manchester. She married Ezekiel Knowlton who was born at Ipswich, but who had moved to Manchester with his parents in the year of his birth.

The known biography of Sarah and Ezekiel Knowlton is contained in the Knowlton Family section of this work. Deborah Knowlton, daughter of Ezekiel and Sarah (Leach) Knowlton, married Thomas Adams.

FIFTH GENERATION

EPHRAIM[5] ADAMS

Ephraim[5] Adams, second son of Thomas[4] and Deborah (Knowlton) Adams, was born in Ipswich, Massachusetts, in 1724. He was baptized on October 18, 1724. Ephraim must have spent his early years going to school and working on his father's farm at Ipswich.

Most of the details of the life of Ephraim Adams which follow are from The History of New Ipswich, New Hampshire, by Charles Henry Chandler and A Genealogical and Historical Record of the Descendants of William Locke, of Woburn, by John Goodwin Locke, published by James Munroe and Company, 1853.

Ephraim Adams was a soldier against the French in 1646. After his return from service, he married Lydia Kinsman (born about 1728; died November 5, 1760) on April 6, 1749, and moved to New Ipswich, New Hampshire. It is likely that Ephraim moved to New Ipswich about the same time as his brother Benjamin, as they built houses at about the same time and are known to have lived on the same farm for many years. The 240 acres they farmed in New Ipswich was part of a larger grant of land given their father under the Masonian charter. Ephraim and Benjamin were the original settlers on this land, identified as N.D., 21.

New Ipswich was located along a road built between 1735 and 1737 to connect other towns. At a meeting of the Proprietors of Upper Ashuelot (now the town of Keene), held at Concord, Massachusetts of the last Wednesday of May 1735, a committee was appointed to "join with such as the lower town proprietors shall appoint, to search and find out whether the ground will admit of

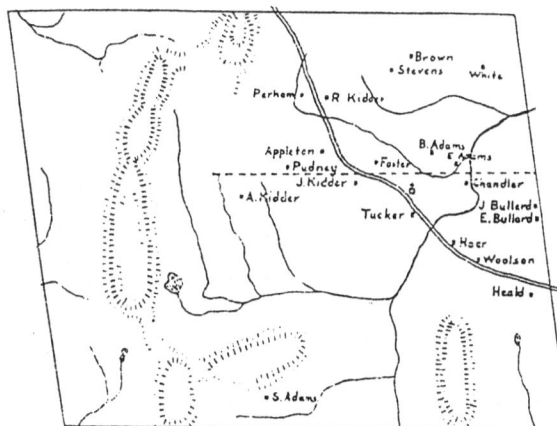

LOCATIONS OF THE FIRST SETTLERS OF
NEW IPSWICH, NEW HAMPSHIRE

a convenient road from the two townships on Ashuelot river, down to the town of Townsend." On June 30, 1737, a meeting was held at the meeting house frame, and "Jeremiah Hall was recompensed for his services in searching for, and laying out, a road to Townsend."

The road built to Townsend, thru now what is New Ipswich, is shown on the map, the first known map of this area, as a simple dotted line. This "old country road," the first token of civilization established within the bounds of what would become New Ipswich, had a great influence in locating the sturdy pioneers in the wilderness, as is indicated by the positions of the homes of twenty early settlers placed on the map. Note the locations of the homes of B. Adams and E. Adams, next to one another just above the roadway.

The children born to Ephraim and Lydia Adams were:

(1) EPHRAIM[6]: born December 15, 1749; died April 15, 1825; married, first, Elizabeth Stearns (born November 11, 1751, died March 29, 1810) and second, Bridget _____ (born about 1747, died October 25, 1813). His children, all born to his first wife, were:

    (1) **Ephraim[7]**: born October 15, 1773.
    (2) **Issac[7]**: born July 13, 1775.
    (3) **Lydia[7]**: born June 7, 1777; married William Perkins of Leominster, Massachusetts, and lived at Enosburg, Vermont; had thirteen children.
    (4) **Elizabeth[7]**: born December 13, 1778; died February 22, 1868; married, first, Joseph Spear on June 21, 1801, second, Mr. Cross of New Hampshire, and third, Joseph Joslyn of Jaffrey.
    (5) **John[7]**: born February 10, 1781.
    (6) **Rebekah[7]**: born November 1782; married Aaron Knight on February 3, 1803.
    (7) **Sarah[7]**: born July 30, 1784; died March 19, 1814; married Nicholas Richards of Enosburg, Vermont.
    (8) **Susanna[7]**: born November 4, 1785; died November 6, 1819; married Thomas Stearns of Leominster, Massachusetts.
    (9) **Lucinda[7]**: born January 26, 1788; died in 1848; married Johas Stearns of Leominster, Massachusetts.
    (10) **Melinda[7]**: born February 8, 1790; died in 1868; married Asa Knight on February 6, 1807.
    (11) **Timothy Kinsman[7]**: born September 30, 1791.
    (12) **Benjamin Stearns[7]**: born August 6, 1794; married and moved to Tennessee.
    (13) **Cynthia[7]**: born September 5, 1796; died in 1883; married Hiram Fassett and lived in Enosburg, Vermont.

(2) THOMAS[6]: born September 12, 1751; died October 11, 1820; married Molly Farnsworth (born about 1756, died June 24, 1842) on December 18, 1777. He served in the Revolution, and was probably the one bearing the name Thomas Adams on the company roll of Captain Abijah Smith or of Captain Francis Towne, or of both.

(3) **STEPHEN**[6]: born November 6, 1753. He is said to have enlisted from Rindge in the company of Captain Philip Thomas in 1775. Positive identification is almost impossible due to the large number of different soldiers having the same name.

(4) **DANIEL**[6]: born August 24, 1755; died about 1790; married Sarah Clark (born in Townsend, Massachusetts, on November 21, 1754). Sarah's mother was Sarah Locke who was sister to her husband's stepmother. In about 1778, Daniel moved to a part of Fitzwilliam which is now Troy. The children of Daniel and Sarah were:

   (1) **Stephen**[7]: born October 29, 1779; married December 1, 1803; lived at Hinesburg, Vermont; had eight children.
   (2) **Daniel**[7]: born March 22, 1781; married Mercy Olney on December 3, 1806; lived at Zingwick, Quebec; had seven children.
   (3) **William**[7]: born March 10, 1783; died October 15, 1851; married, first, Susan Raymond, second, Betsey Tarbell, and third, Phebe Hatch.
   (4) **Thomas**[7]: born March 9, 1785; Died September 12, 1841; married Sarah Sawtelle of Jaffrey in June 1805; lived in Jaffrey; had ten children.
   (5) **Sarah**[7]: born January 25, 1787; married John Frost on March 11, 1805; lived at Jaffrey; had nine children.
   (6) **Lydia**[7]: born July 13, 1789; lived at Nashua.
   (7) **Samuel**[7]: born April 30, 1791; moved to Canada and was last known to be a soldier in the British army in 1812.

(5) **LYDIA**[6]: born July 16, 1757; died in October 1800; married Nathan Wheeler (born in Concord Massachusetts on January 9, 1744, and died May 7, 1834); lived in Temple, New Hampshire.

Ephraim's first house in New Ipswich, New Hampshire, built about 1749 or 1750, was still standing in 1914 when Chandler's history of New Ipswich was published. The house was surrounded by "flankers" for protection from the indians. (Flankers are structures provided as protection of other structures or positions.) There is no record of the house ever having been attacked. In 1757, the town voted not "to repair Mr. Adam's flankers in order for defence."

Ephraim was a leading citizen and had great influence in public matters, due not only to his sound sense, but also to the clear and quaint methods in which his views were presented. Although he was elected to the position of selectman only once, he was relied upon frequently in times of special stress. He represented the town in the Provincial Congress and for four years in the State Legislature, 1782 - 1785. He was chairman of the Committee of Inspection, and of the Committee for Correspondence and Safety when it was first formed. He served later on the latter committee at a time when its duties were very difficult and its power was almost dictatorial, just following the Revolution. Skillful management was almost as essential as earnest purpose, and his record bears the mark of a conscientious, patriotic, and well-balanced man. Ephraim was one of two deacons elected at the organization of the church in New Ipswich.

Ephraim served in the army during the Revolution. The records of his service are somewhat confusing because his oldest son, Ephraim, also served. The two men may have actually served under the same command in some cases. It is impossible, in some cases, to tell which Ephraim Adams is referenced in the documents of the day.

From the information found, the following periods appear to correctly identify the service of the elder Ephraim Adams:

+ July 18, 1777, thru the autumn of that year in the Northern army on Lake Champlain under Captain Joseph Parker.

+ Starting in September 1778 for a period of about three months in the company of Captain Abijah Smith to reinforce the army in New York. There seems to be no doubt that he served in Captain Smith's company at the battle of White Plains.

Although dates are confusing, it appears that Ephraim Adams was among a company of men from New Ipswich, New Hampshire, who marched to Saratoga, New York, and served during the time of the battle of Stillwater and the surrender of Burgoyne.

Copies of muster records for Ephraim Adams' service in the Revolution can be found at the end of this chapter.

Following the death of his first wife, Ephraim married Rebecca Locke, daughter of James and Elizabeth (Burnap) Locke. Ephraim and Rebecca were married at New Ipswich on November 18, 1761. Ephraim and Rebecca had seven children.

(1) JOHN[6]: born November 10, 1762; died December 9, 1763.

(2) JOHN[6]: born February 29, 1764; died 1781 in the army, where he was probably the one who enlisted in February of that year "for three years or the war".

(3) EBENEZER[6]: born October 2, 1765; died August 15, 1841; married, first, Alice Frink on July 9, 1795, and second, Beulah Minott on May 17, 1807. Ebenezer prepared for college

at New Ipswich and graduated from Dartmouth College in 1791. He was principal of the academy at Leicester, Massachusetts, for fourteen years; of an academy at Portland, Maine for two years; and instructor at Phillips Academy, Exeter, for two years. In 1809, he was appointed professor of Latin, Greek, and Hebrew at Dartmouth College, but a year later was transferred to the chair of Mathematics and Natural Philosophy where he remained for the remaining 31 years of his life. The following children were born to Ebenezer Adams. The first five to his first wife and the last two to his second wife.

> (1) **Alice Amelia**[7]: born June 2, 1796; died at Portland, Maine, on February 11, 1820; married Reverend Thomas Jewett Murdock on June 16, 1819.
> (2) **Adeline Augusta**[7]: born January 17, 1798; married June 28, 1819.
> (3) **John Frink**[7]: born November 3, 1799; married Elizabeth Lovell Walker on July 2, 1835; graduated from Dartmouth College in 1817; was a lawyer at Moblile, Alabama; had three children.
> (4) **Charles Augustus**[7]: born October 2, 1801; died in South Carolina March 9, 1824.
> (5) **Harriet Russell**[7]: born September 14, 1804; died July 30, 1830; married on November 14, 1816, the Hon. John Aiken who was a lawyer in Manchester, Vermont, and a graduate of Dartmouth College in 1819.
> (6) **Eliza Minott**[7]: born February 9, 1810; married on August 23, 1833, Ira Young, who graduated from Dartmouth College in 1821, and who succeeded his wife's father at Dartmouth upon his becoming professor emeritus.
> (7) **Ebenezer**[7]: born August 6, 1813; died July 23, 1837; graduated from Dartmouth College in 1831.

(4) REBECCA[6]: born July 27, 1767; married Abel Shedd on January 20, 1802.

(5) JAMES[6]: born May 20, 1769; died September 19, 1803; married Ruth Conant on November 3, 1795; lived in Grafton, Vermont; had nine children. Ruth Conant was born May 2, 1772, and died March 14, 1807.

(6) BETSY[6]: born March 13, 1772; died April 14, 1816; married Dr. Luther Jewett of St. Johnsbury, Vermont; had eight children.

**(7) QUINCY[6]: born September 29, 1775; married Dolly Elliot, daughter of Rev. William and Dorothy (Merrill) Eliot, on April 8, 1800, at Mason, New Hampshire; died in the winter of 1814/15. He lived on his father's farm at New Ipswich following his father's death. In about 1805 he exchanged farms with Francis Cragin of Temple and moved to that town.

He received fatal injuries in an accident when he fell beneath his sled and was crushed. The children of Quincy and Dolly Adams are:

(1) **John Quincy[7]: born December 19, 1800, at New Ipswich, New Hampshire; married Lovina Walker on March 16, 1828, at Boston, Massachusetts; died November 12, 1873, at Keene, Ohio.

(2) **Maria**[7]: born November 14, 1802, at New Ipswich, New Hampshire; married Sam Colby on November 13, 1831, at Mason, New Hampshire.

(3) **Augusta**[7]: born July 25, 1805, at Temple, New Hampshire; married James Cowee on April 12, 1827; died February 22, 1877, in Ohio.

Ephraim Adams' will is dated December 27, 1796. He died March 26, 1797. A copy of the original handwritten will is available in the archives of the Family History Library at Salt Lake City, Utah. A transcription of that will is presented here.

Will
Adams Ephme

In the name of God Amen. The Twenty seventh day of December Anno Domini one thousand seven hundred and ninety six. I Ephraim Adams of New Ipswich in the County of Hillsboro and state of New Hampshire calling to mind the mortality of my body and knowing that it is appointed for all men once to die, do make and ordain this my last will and testament that [   ] principally and first of all I give and recommend my soul into the hands of God who gave it and my body I recommend to the earth to be buried in a decent christian burial at the discretion of my executor nothing doubting but at the general ressurection I shall receive the same by the mighty powers of God and [   ] that that worldly estate wherewith it hath pleased God to blefs me in this life I gie, demise, and dispose of the same in the following manner

[   ], My Will is that all my Just debts be paid by my executor hereafter named.

Item,   I give and bequeath unto Rebecca my dearly beloved Wife, her heirs and afsigns one third part of my personal estate: also the free use and improvement of one third part of my real estate during her natural life.

Item,   I give and bequeath unto my eldest son Ephraim Adams [   ] his heirs and afsigns seventeen pounds two shillings & four pence, which sum together with what he has already received is his full share of my Estate.

Item,   I give and bequeath unto my son Thomas Adams his heirs and afsigns thirty five pounds three shillings and four pence as his full share of my estate with what he has already received.

Item,   I give and bequeath unto my son Stephen Adams his heirs and afsigns eighty three pounds as his full share of my estate and as a full discharge of the demands he may have against my estate which bequest is upon this condition that he calls upon my executor first within two years after my decease.

Item, I give and bequeath unto the children of my late son Daniel Adams twenty pounds two shillings & four pence to be equally divided amongst them who shall be living at my decease.

Item, I give and bequeath unto my daughter Lydia Wheeler her heirs and afsigns eleven pounds three shillings and six pence which sum together with what she has heretofore received is considered as her portion of my estate.

Item, I give and bequeath unto my son Ebenezer Adams his heirs and afsigns thirteen pounds two shillings & seven pence as his full portion of my estate together with what he has already received.

Item, Item I give and bequeath unto my daughter Rebecca Adams her heirs and afsigns fifty nine pounds eight shillings & three pence being her share of my estate.

Item, I give and bequeath unto my daughter Betsy Adams her heirs and afsigns fifty nine pounds eight shillings & three pence being her full share of my estate.

Item, I give and bequeath unto my son James Adams his heirs and afsigns twenty one pounds nine shillings and five pence as his share of my estate in addition to what he has received.

Item, I give and bequeath unto my son Quincy Adams his heirs and afsigns all the rest and residue of my Estate both real and personal not in this Will disposed of otherwise wherever the same is situate, he the said Quincy paying the debts and legacies herein mentioned in the following manner, viz, all sums of Money mentioned as legacies to be considered at the rate of six shillings and eight pence per [   ] and the legacies to become payable within one year after my decease excepting then pounds on each legacy which is to become payable at my wifes decease. Stephen Adams' legacy however is not subject to this last exception but the whole to be considered as due in one year after my decease.

My Will further is that so long as either of my daughters remain single or unmarried my executor provide them with suitable & convenient home room.

And I do hereby appoint & constitute my son Quincy Adams aforesaid sole executor of this my last Will & Testament and I do enjoin it upon him to give his mother her choice either to take her thirds as herein mentioned or to fulfill to her the conditions of a bond he has signed respecting her support and I do hereby revoke and disannul all former Wills, bequest & executors heretofore named & bequested in any manner whatsoever declaring this and no other to be my last will & Testament.

Signed, Sealed, published pronnoced & delivered by the said Ephraim Adams as his Last Will & Testament the day above written in presence of w   Ephraim Hartwell
                        Solomon Brooks   Ephraim Adams   seal
                        Timo [   ]

THE TOMBSTONE OF EPHRAIM ADAMS

"Here lies interred the remains of Dea'n Ephraim Adams who departed this life 26 March 1797
    In early life he exhibited the Christian Was chosen first deacon of the church in this place in which office as well as in every other public and private station he was well reported of for faith and good works
    The favor of a Christian name shall leave behind a lasting fame"

Left card

a Wyman's Regiment. | **N. H.**

Ephraim Adams

Appears with the rank of *Pt* on a

Muster and Pay Roll*

of Captain Joseph Parker's Co. raised out of Col. Enoch Hale's Reg't. Joined the Northern Army at Ticonderoga. Mustered and paid July 18, 1776, by Enoch Hale, Muster and Pay Master,

(Revolutionary War,

State of New Hampshire

dated *Hillsborough ss July*   , 17,76.

Advance pay to officers, 2 mo.; ⎫ £9 - 18 -
to soldiers, 1 mo. and bounty ⎭

Travel, 1d per mile   -£ - 4 -

Amount   £ 10 - 2 -

Remarks: ....

*Certified copy of an original roll in the possession of the State of New Hampshire.

Brodie

(545)   Copyist.

Right card

a | | **N. H.**

Ephraim Adams

Appears as shown below on an

Account*

of the men that went into the Continental Army—

(Revolutionary War.)

Account dated

Not dated . 17 .

Ephraim Adams five months
engaged July 1776 12. 0

The five months men here
included are militia

*From copy, printed by the State of New Hampshire, not verified in the R. & P. Office by comparison with the original record, that record not having been received October 12, 1895, among the others loaned to the office by the State.—R. & P., 431,372.

Number of record:

452 *H. Austin*

MUSTER RECORDS FOR EPHRAIM ADAMS, REPRODUCED
IN NEW HAMPSHIRE FROM ORIGINAL RECORDS OF
SERVICE IN THE REVOLUTIONARY WAR

Ephraim Adams

Appears with the rank of .... *Private* on a

Pay Roll *

of Captain Edmund Briant's Company in Col.
Daniel Moore's Regiment of New Hampshire
Volunteers, marched from New Ipswich and
join'd the Continental Army at Saratoga, 1777,

(Revolutionary War,)

dated .... *Feby 6th* ...., 177*8*.

Entry .... *Sep 28* ...., 177*7*.

discharge .... *Octo 25* ...., 17 .

Time in Service *28*

Rate per month ....

Amount Wages .... *4. 4.*

Travel from Ipswich to Ben- } *130. 1. 12. 6*
nington @ 3d per mile,

Travel from Saratoga home } *160. 1. 6. 8*
at 2d per mile,

Whole amount *7. 3. 2*

Remarks:

* From copy (verified in the R. & P. Office in Nov., 1895,) of an
original record borrowed from the State of New Hampshire.—
R. & P. 431,372.

(545i)   *Procter*   *Copyist.*

Ephraim Adams

Appears as shown below on a

List *

under the following heading:

.... *Jaffrey Account* ....

(Revolutionary War.)

List dated ....

.... *not dated* ...., 17 .

Ephraim Adams
13 Days at Cambridge $ 1. 8.

* From copy (verified in the R. & P. Office, War Dept., in Nov.,
1895,) of an original record borrowed from the State of New
Hampshire.— R. & P. 431,372.

Number of record:

101

(545m)   *Jr Jacobson*   *Copyist.*

MUSTER RECORDS FOR EPHRAIM ADAMS, REPRODUCED
IN NEW HAMPSHIRE FROM ORIGINAL RECORDS OF
SERVICE IN THE REVOLUTIONARY WAR

LOCKE FAMILY

Rebecca Locke was born in Hopkinton, Massachusetts, on May 13, 1735. She was the daughter of James and Elizabeth (Burnap) Locke. Rebecca married Ephraim Adams of Ipswich on November 18, 1761. Rebecca was the great-granddaughter of William Locke, who emigrated from England. Most of what is known of the Locke family comes from <u>A Genealogical and Historical Record of The Descendants of William Locke, of Woburn</u>, by John Goodwin Locke, published by James Munroe and Company, 1853.

The Locke lineage and that of the related Cutter and Clarke families, traced to those who first came to New England, is shown here.

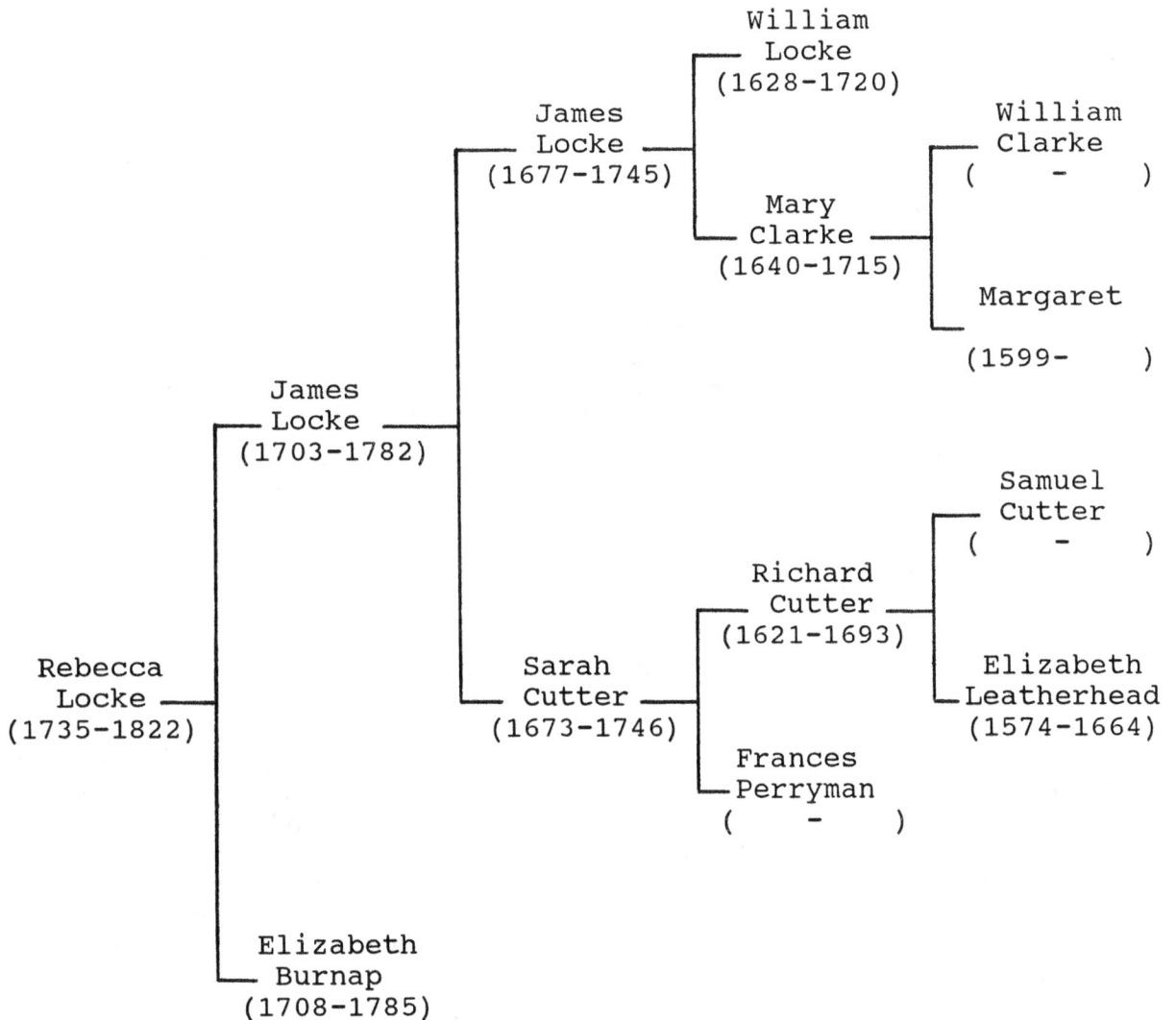

```
                                            William
                                          ┌ Locke
                                          │ (1628-1720)
                               James      │                    William
                             ┌ Locke ─────┤                  ┌ Clarke
                             │ (1677-1745)│                   │ (    -    )
                             │            │ Mary             │
                             │            └ Clarke ──────────┤
                             │              (1640-1715)       │
                 James       │                               │ Margaret
               ┌ Locke ──────┤                               └
               │ (1703-1782) │                                 (1599-    )
               │             │
               │             │                                 Samuel
               │             │                               ┌ Cutter
               │             │                               │ (    -    )
               │             │                  Richard      │
               │             │                ┌ Cutter ──────┤
               │             │                │ (1621-1693)  │ Elizabeth
 Rebecca       │             │ Sarah          │              └ Leatherhead
 Locke ────────┤             └ Cutter ────────┤                (1574-1664)
 (1735-1822)   │               (1673-1746)    │
               │                              │ Frances
               │                              └ Perryman
               │                                (    -    )
               │
               │ Elizabeth
               └ Burnap
                 (1708-1785)
```

William Locke was born at Stepney Parish, London, England. He emigrated to New England in the company of an uncle, Nicholas Davies, leaving England aboard the Planter March 22, 1634, at the age of six.

Although little is known of his life, William was a farmer and probably also worked as a carpenter. From the book Elisha S. and Lavina (Locke) Andrus... Their Ancestors and Descendants, published by John V. Beck, 1985, we learn an interesting item. Apparently William did not believe that church membership was essential to life in his New England community of Woburn, then known as Charlestown Village. He and some friends were charged with claiming a right to vote to elect a Governor. He was charged and was fined. As a result of this experience, he changed his views and became a member of the church. For many years after that he was a deacon and became one of the pillars of the church.

THE HOUSE OF WILLIAM LOCKE AT
WOBURN, MASSACHUSETTS

William Locke married Mary Clarke in Woburn, Massachusetts, on December 27, 1655. She was born in Watertown, Massachusetts, on December 20, 1640. Her parents, William and Margaret Clarke came to New England in the spring of 1635 aboard the ship Plain Joan. They settled in Watertown where William Clarke was granted several parcels of land, the largest of which was 58 acres. In 1650, he purchased 60 acres of land at Woburn and within a few years moved there to live.

William and Mary Locke had nine children, eight of whom lived to adulthood. All of the children were born in Woburn.

    (1) **William**: born December 27, 1657; died January 9, 1658.
    (2) **William**: born January 18, 1659.
    (3) **John**: born August 1, 1661.
    (4) **Joseph**: born March 8, 1664.
    (5) **Mary**: born October 16, 1666.
    (6) **Samuel**: born October 14, 1669.
    (7) **Ebenezer**: born January 8, 1674.
(8) James: born November 14, 1677; died December 11, 1745; married Sarah Cutter on December 5, 1700.
    (9) **Elizabeth**: born January 4, 1681.

Mary Locke died July 18, 1715, at Woburn, Massachusetts. William Locke died at Woburn on June 16, 1720. His tombstone records his age as "91 years, 6 months".

In his will, William Locke wrote "with refference to my son James Locke I lett him go to work for himself to gett something to begin the world with, and also gave him about thirty pounds in money, to him his full portion already, and now I give him ten shillings more as a token of my love".

James purchased his first farm September 9, 1699, from a man named James Converse. It was 46 acres at Woburn of an area known as Pine Mountain. It was described as "bounded, South East by ye Woodland of Henry Gardner and Josiah Johnson, North East by ye Woodland of Josiah Johnson, North West by ye Woodland of John Carter, and South West partly by Cambridge line and partly by Woodland of John Carter". Also "twenty acres of swamp bottom, so called, with the liberty to take it up for himself, where the top is his own, according to an order of the Town of Woburn".

In 1715, James Locke "purchased from Josiah Johnson, ten acres of Woodland, bounded South Westerly on Cambridge and Lexington lines, North Westerly on said James Locke, North Easterly on land in possession of Widow Garner (Gardner ?) and South Easterly on Charlestown line". The following is from the Woburn Town Records. May 17, 1700. "Then layed out to James Locke of Woburn 23 acres and a half where the top is his already, at a place called Pine Mountain, on the South side thereof, near Cambridge line; bounded by the Woodland of Josiah Johnson East; South by ye Woodland that was Matthew Johnson's and Sam. Blodgett's, and the said James Locke's Woodland elsewhere twenty acres thereof upon Samuel Converse's account and three acres and a half given him by the proprietors of this town of Woburn, at their meeting April 22, 1700". These tracts of land constituted the beginning of his homestead, and here he built his first house.

James Locke married Sarah Cutter on December 5, 1700. She was born August 31, 1673, the daughter of Richard and Frances Cutter of Cambridge, Massachusetts.

Sarah's father, Richard Cutter, was the son of Samuel Cutter and Elizabeth Leatherhead. Richard was born in England and traveled from Newcastle-upon-Tyne to New England about 1640. He would have been about 20 years old and is assumed to have been unmarried. He was a cooper. He was admitted as freeman June 2, 1641. All freemen were required to be "orthodox members of the church, 20 years old and worth L200". Richard was a member of the Ancient and Honorable Artillery Company of Boston.

Richard Cutter first married Elizabeth Williams. He settled in Middlesex County, Massachusetts. Elizabeth died March 5, 1661/62 at about 42 years of age. She is buried in the cemetery at Old Cambridge. On February 14, 1662/63, according to Middlesex records, Richard married widow Frances (Perryman) Amsden. Sarah was the second child born to Richard and Frances Cutter.

James Locke, who was married to Sarah Cutter, was elected to numerous positions of honor in his town. He was chosen Surveyor of Highways March 3, 1717/18; Constable March 2, 1718/19; and hayward on three occasions. A hayward is the person responsible for fences and hedges around a common.

Sarah (Cutter) Locke died sometime after 1746. James Locke died intestate on December 11, 1745. Sarah is known to have survived her husband, as her name is mentioned in the court orders distributing her husbands assets after his death.

James and Sarah (Cutter) Locke had eight children.
(1) **Hannah**: born July 11, 1701; married Thomas Pierce on November 5, 1722.
(2) **James: born June 17, 1703; died September 1, 1782; married Elizabeth Burnap on January 11, 1727.
(3) **Ruhannah**: born April 23, 1705; married, first, Benjamin Whittenmore on June 15, 1726, and second, John Bond.
(4) **Sarah**: born July 5, 1707; married William Jones on December 25, 1733.
(5) **Phebe**: born August 15, 1709; married, first Daniel Brewer on September 9, 1732/33, and second, Isaac Hartwell on July 14, 1776.
(6) **Rebeckah**: born November 11, 1711; married William Munroe on March 6, 1735.
(7) **Mary**: born October 12, 1713; married John Wright on January 4, 1738.
(8) **Jonathan**: born January 17, 1717; married Phebe Pierce on February 1, 1746.

James Locke, son of James and Sarah (Cutter) Locke, was born June 17, 1703, at Woburn, Massachusetts. He married Elizabeth Burnap, who was born May 1, 1708, at Reading, Massachusetts, on January 11, 1727, at Hopkinton.

James Locke was a farmer, and first settled in Hopkinton about 1725. He was appointed Administrator on his father's estate in Woburn in June 1745. On the division of the estate, his share was 146 pounds, 6 shillings, 8 pence. He remained at Hopkinton, where all ten of his children were born, until about 1749. At that time, he removed to Ashby, then known as Townsend, where he purchased a farm - the first surveyed in that part of Townsend. The survey is dated April 1736 and was recorded in the Proprietors' books December 4, 1736. The farm was situated in the North-Easterly part of Ashby, on what, for many years, was the principal road from Townsend through New Ipswich, New Hampshire, to Keene, New Hampshire. This road was laid out January 15, 1750, and is described as "Beginning at Pearl Hill Brook, near the Bridge, near John Conant's fence; thence Northerly to John Steven's; thence towards the bridge across Willard's stream; thence up to James Locke's; thence to the Brook running out of Locke's meadow to the Beaver Dam, and across said Dam, so on to the Westerly side of Pine Hill, near Ebenezer Taylor's House, to the Province Line". At the same time, the town voted to pay James Locke 10 pounds for building a bridge across the stream that runs out of his meadow, and to maintain the bridge for ten years.

James and Elizabeth Locke had ten children.

(1) **Elizabeth**: born April 19, 1728; was admitted to the church in Hopkinton in 1742; resided some years at Southborough, afterwards with her parents at Ashby; was a distinguished school teacher for forty years. She died unmarried. She was uncommonly large, weighing 250 pounds, and was found dead in her bed on June 26, 1799, at age 71.
(2) **James**: christened November 23, 1729; married Hannah Farnsworth, December 17, 1753.
(3) **Sarah**: born June 24, 1732; married William Clark, Jr. on January 17, 1753.
(4) **John**: born December 16, 1733; married Beulah Newton.
(5) **Rebecca: born May 13, 1735; died 1822; married Ephraim Adams on November 18, 1761.
(6) **Jonathan**: born December 7, 1737.
(7) **David**: born February 22, 1740.
(8) **Ebenezer**: born May 22, 1742.
(9) **Martha**:
(10) **William**: born April 12, 1748.

In 1767, Ashby incorporated and was no longer part of Townsend. Mr. Locke became one of the most influential men in the town. For many years he was the moderator of the town meetings.

When the church was organized in 1776, he was first on the list of members. In 1773, James Locke sold all of his real estate to his son Jonathan, who lived with and took care of his parents. Following his death on September 1, 1782, his widow moved to New Ipswich, New Hampshire, to live with her daughter Rebecca, who had married Ephraim Adams. Upon her death on November 25, 1785, she was buried at New Ipswich with the following inscription on her tombstone:

"Sleep virtuous dust within your peaceful urn,
There rest in hope, till thy blest Lord's return."

The inscription on James Locke's tombstone at Ashby is:

"Death is the lot, the tomb the place,
For all the sons of Adam's race."

BURNAP FAMILY

Elizabeth Burnap married James Locke and was the mother of Rebecca Locke. Rebecca Locke married Ephraim Adams, one of the principals of this genealogical study. The New England ancestry of Elizabeth Burnap is shown here.

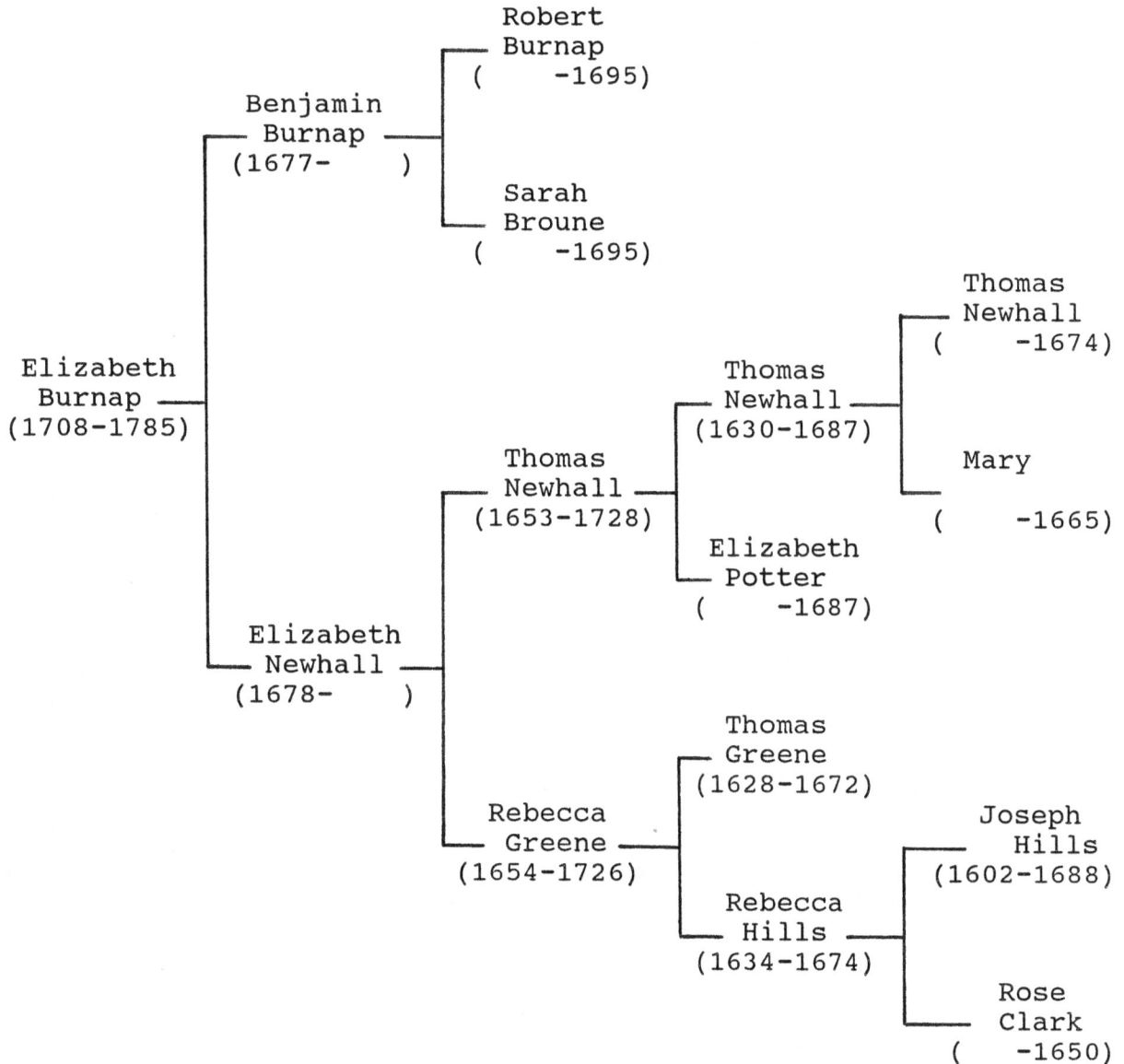

```
                                       Robert
                                     ─ Burnap
                                     (     -1695)
                     Benjamin
                   ─ Burnap ────
                   (1677-   )
                                       Sarah
                                     ─ Broune
                                     (     -1695)

                                                            Thomas
                                                          ─ Newhall
                                                          (     -1674)
                                         Thomas
                                       ─ Newhall ────
Elizabeth                              (1630-1687)
Burnap ──                                                  Mary
(1708-1785)           Thomas
                    ─ Newhall ────                         (     -1665)
                    (1653-1728)
                                         Elizabeth
                                       ─ Potter
                                       (     -1687)
     Elizabeth
   ─ Newhall ────
   (1678-   )
                                         Thomas
                                       ─ Greene
                                       (1628-1672)
                     Rebecca                                Joseph
                   ─ Greene ────                         ─ Hills
                   (1654-1726)                           (1602-1688)
                                         Rebecca
                                       ─ Hills ────
                                       (1634-1674)
                                                           Rose
                                                         ─ Clark
                                                         (     -1650)
```

Elizabeth Burnap's grandfather, Robert Burnap, was born and lived in Reading, Massachusetts. He was the son of Robert and Ann Burnap. The younger Robert Burnap served as a selectman in Reading for nineteen years. He first married Ann (surname not known) and had at least four children. Ann Burnap died in 1661. Second, he married Sarah Broune. Nothing is known of the ancestry of Sarah Broune as her family has not been located. Robert and Sarah Burnap had at least seven children. The birth information provided here comes from <u>Vital Records of Reading, Massachusetts, to the Year 1850</u>, compiled by Thomas W. Baldwin, A.B., S.B., Member of the New England Historic Genealogical Society, published in Boston, 1912. In this record, Robert Burnap's first name is consistently spelled "Robbart".

Children born to Robert and Ann Burnap:

(1) **Sarah**: born November 6, 1653.
(2) **John**: born May 16, 1655.
(3) **Robert**: born "last of Feb., 1657"; died 1674.
(4) **Mary**: born June 17, 1661.

Children born to Robert and Sarah Burnap:

(1) **Joseph**: born March 24, 1663; married Tabitha _____ in 1690.
(2) **Elizabeth**: born February 21, 1664; married Jonathan Eaton in 1683.
(3) **Lydia**: born April 8, 1667.
(4) **Isaack**: born April 29, 1671.
(5) **Samuel**: born September 15, 1675; died 1676.
(6) **Benjamin: born June 8, 1677; married Elizabeth Newhall January 18, 1700.
(7) **Dorcas**: born August 22, 1679; married William Sawyer in 1700.

Benjamin Burnap, father of Elizabeth Burnap, married Elizabeth Newhall January 18, 1700. Elizabeth Newhall was the daughter of Thomas and Rebecca (Greene) Newhall.

Not much is known of Benjamin's life. He apparently lived in the town of Reading, Massachusetts, for much of his life, as the births of his children place him there over a long period of time. From the Vital Records of Reading find the following records of children born to Benjamin and Elizabeth Burnap:

(1) **Rebecca**: born April 2, 1701.
(2) **Benjamin**: born November 14, 1702.
(3) **David**: born March 24, 1704.
(4) **David**: born March 13, 1705.
(5) **Elizabeth: born May 1, 1708; married James Locke January 11, 1727; died November 25, 1785.
(6) **Lydia**: born February 21, 1709/10.
(7) **Jonathon**: born January 19, 1711.
(8) **Sarah**: born August 31, 1713.

(9) **Hannah:** born October 26, 1715.
(10) **Mary:** born February 25, 1719/20.
(11) **Easter:** born April 9, 1723.

One can only wonder about the two births recorded for sons named David. A birth date recorded as March 13, 1704/05 according to the Julian Calendar would translate to March 24, 1705, in the Gregorian Calendar. It is very possible that a first son died shortly after birth and that the next child was then also named David. No records were found to explain this.

Elizabeth Burnap married James Locke and her biography is included in the chapter dealing with the Locke Family.

The history of the Newhall family which follows was developed from The Record of My Ancestry, by Charles L. Newhall, published at Southbridge, 1899; and the History of Lynn, Essex County, Massachusetts, by Alonzo Lewis and James R. Newhall.

Elizabeth Burnap's mother, Elizabeth Newhall, was descended from a prominent family which came to New England early in the development of the new colony. As stated earlier, she was the daughter of Thomas and Rebecca Newhall. She was the great granddaughter of Thomas and Mary Newhall who came from England to New England in 1630. They arrived in Salem, Massachusetts, and settled at Lynn shortly after arriving. Thomas was a farmer and acquired 30 acres of land which was virtually in the center of town. There is no record of Thomas ever becoming a freeman, though it is most likely that he was. His family was one of fifty in Lynn in 1630. There were only five families at Lynn in 1629.

Thomas and Mary Newhall had at least four children.

(1) **Susanna:** born about 1624 in England.
(2) **John:** born in England.
(3) **Thomas: born in 1630; married Elizabeth Potter December 29, 1652; was buried April 1, 1687, aged 57.
(4) **Mary:** born about 1637.

Thomas Newhall, born in 1630, grandfather of our subject, Elizabeth Newhall, was the first white child born in Lynn, Massachusetts. He married Elizabeth Potter December 29, 1652. She was the daughter of Nicholas Potter, a bricklayer who settled in Lynn is 1651 and moved to Salem about 1660.

In the March term of 1663, Thomas was tried by the Quarterly Court for striking the wife of a neighbor, William Longley. He had apparently hit her with a pole over some property line dispute after she tried to hit him with an axe. The results of the trial are not recorded.

In 1679, there was a great celebration for the fiftieth anniversary of the settlement of Lynn. Here one finds some measure of the respectability of Thomas Newhall, as he was seated among the chief dignitaries of the town at the end of the table. Here also, we find reference to the fact that he owned the mill that produced the best cider in the whole region. Thomas Newhall also owned the orchards that provided the stock for his cider mill.

Thomas and Elizabeth (Potter) Newhall had ten children.

(1) **Thomas: born November 18, 1653; married Rebecca Greene of Malden in 1674; died July 3, 1728.
  (2) **John:** born February 14, 1656.
  (3) **Joseph:** born September 22, 1658; married Susanna Farrar in 1678; settled in Lynnfield; had eleven children; died in a snow storm.
  (4) **Nathaniel:** born March 17, 1660.
  (5) **Elizabeth:** born March 21, 1662; lived only three years.
  (6) **Elisha:** born November 3, 1665.
  (7) **Elizabeth:** born October 22, 1667.
  (8) **Mary:** born February 18, 1669.
  (9) **Samuel:** born January 19, 1672.
(10) **Rebecca:** born July 17, 1675.

One of the early tragedies of Lynn was the drowning of daughter Elizabeth. She was found dead in an uncovered pit dug by a neighbor and filled with water as a place to keep live fish. There was an inquest, but no finding of wrongdoing is recorded.

Elizabeth (Potter) Newhall was buried at Lynn on February 22, 1687. Thomas Newhall was buried on April 1, 1687.

Thomas Newhall, father of our subject Elizabeth, was born in Lynn, Massachusetts. He married Rebecca Greene in November 1674 and moved to Malden. Rebecca Greene was the daughter of Thomas and Rebecca (Hills) Greene.

A deed of gift dated November 9, 1674, is recorded in Middlesex Deeds giving land to Thomas Newhall, Jr., of Lynn, and his wife Rebecca. The gift is given by Joseph Hills, Rebecca's maternal grandfather. On March 16, 1681, Thomas bought, for 530 pounds, the sixty acre farm of Joseph and Ann Hills located in Malden.

Thomas Newhall was a weaver. He was a soldier in King Philip's War. He was a Lieutenant in the local militia and was a selectman in Malden for four one-year terms.

Thomas and Rebecca (Greene) Newhall had nine children, all born in Malden.

(1) **Rebecca**: born 1676; died October 7, 1694.
(2) **Elizabeth: born 1678; married Benjamin Burnap of Reading on January 18, 1700.
(3) **Thomas**: married Mary _____.
(4) **Hannah**: married Joseph Lamson on February 13, 1708/09.
(5) **Daniel**: born 1685; married Sarah Fosdick of Charlestown.
(6) **Lydia**: born April 17, 1687; married Samuel Wade (born December 31, 1683) of Medford on October 17, 1706.
(7) **Samuel**: born April 26, 1689; married Sarah Sargeant (born in Malden on October 30, 1695) on December 3, 1713.
(8) **Martha**: married Nathaniel Wilson on January 5, 1709.
(9) **Elisha**: married Rebecca Gay of Stoneham in 1721.

SIXTH GENERATION

QUINCY[6] ADAMS

Quincy[6] Adams was born in New Ipswich, New Hampshire, on September 29, 1775, where his father, Ephraim[5], and his uncle Benjamin[5] Adams had established a very successful farm on land given them by their father, Thomas[4].

A transcribed birth record for Quincy Adams from the archives of New Hampshire is provided at the end of this chapter. Although of poor quality, it serves an important purpose in proving the lineage of this Adams family.

Quincy lived on the family farm for a short time following the death of his father in 1797, then exchanged farms with Francis Cragin of Temple, New Hampshire, and moved to that town. Several records have been located which place the exchange of property in 1804 or 1805. In the 1800 census Quincy is reported as living in Hillsborough County, New Hampshire. In the 1810 census he is found living in Temple Township, Hillsborough County, New Hampshire.

Temple is one of the oldest and prettiest villages in Hillsborough County. It is a town of rustic charm set in rolling hills and woods. The township sits in a glacier carved area and has a variety of landscape features, from high hills to broad valleys and flats where orchards and crops are tended.

The town was originally settled by individuals who had exercised claims to the land thru the Masonian Grant, the grants of the Colony of Massachusetts, and various court grants to individuals who had faithfully served the English Crown. Many of the grants overlapped and courts continued to rule on the actual boundaries between Massachusetts and New Hampshire and the extent of the various grants from at least 1736 until after 1787. The situation was made very complicated by the fact that some of the lands included in the grants were sold by the individuals who believed they held proper grants in the first place.

Ephraim and Benjamin Adams, sons of Thomas Adams, settled at New Ipswich, New Hampshire, in about 1749 or 1750 on land obtained by their father under the Masonian charter (or Masonian Grant). They continued to prosper on the property and were apparently never adversely affected by the problems of land ownership which were settled in the courts.

When Quincy Adams inherited his father's land in 1797, the ownership was not contested. The farm in Temple for which Quincy exchanged his New Ipswich property was also not in contested ownership. Francis Cragin was a descendant of an original settler in Temple.

Quincy Adams married Dolly Elliot (sometimes spelled Eliot), on April 8, 1800. Dolly is the daughter of William and Dorothy (Merrill) Eliot. The marriage was performed by Dolly's father, a baptist minister. She was born March 3, 1779, at Mason Township, Hillsborough County, New Hampshire.

Quincy and Dolly Adams are believed to have had three children. The birth records of the first two children are well documented. The third child, Augusta, is attributed to Quincy and Dolly Adams as a result of circumstantial, but convincing, information provided by family members. This position is supported by the 1810 Federal Census which shows that Quincy and wife Dolly lived at Temple, Hillsborough County, New Hampshire, with three children, one boy and two girls, all under the age of ten.

**(1) JOHN QUINCY[7]: born December 19, 1800, at New Ipswich, New Hampshire; married Lovina Walker on March 16, 1828, at Boston, Massachusetts; died November 12, 1873, at Keene, Ohio.

(2) MARIA[7]: born November 14, 1802, at New Ipswich, New Hampshire; married Samuel Colby of Mason, New Hampshire, on November 13, 1831; intentions published October 23, 1831, at Charlestown, Massachusetts; died in 1883. Samuel Colby was born May 9, 1798, at Salisbury, New Hampshire. He died in May 1878. Samuel and Maria Colby lived in Springfield, New Hampshire, on a farm owned by his father. They had six children, all born at Springfield, New Hampshire.
  (1) **Christopher Columbus Colby**: born September 24, 1832; married, first, Leora L. Wood, and second, Josephine C. Christopher had one son.
    (1) **Norman H. Colby**: born February 4, 1863, at Manchester, New Hampshire; married Katherine D. McKillop, daughter of John and Mary Ann (Hill) McKillop, on July 16, 1891; died July 3, 1909, at Manchester, New Hampshire.
  (2) **Helen Augusta Colby**: born November 21, 1834; died August 30, 1835.
  (3) **John Demetruis Colby**: born June 21, 1836; married Elizabeth M. Hamm, daughter of Peter and Anna (Bartlette) Hamm, on January 13, 1856. John D. Colby enlisted in the Union Army to serve in the Civil War on August 20, 1862. He mustered in on August 29, 1862, with the 11th New Hampshire Volunteers, and was granted a disability discharge on March 13, 1863. John and Elizabeth (Hamm) Colby had six children.
    (1) **Charles Cliffton Colby**: born October 20, 1856, at Duck Lake, Michigan.
    (2) **Frank M. Colby**: born May 17, 1858, at Canandaigua, New York.
    (3) **Clara L. Colby**: born August 18, 1861, at Rochester, New York.

(4) **Harry W. Colby**: born March 2, 1864, at Manchester, New Hampshire.

(5) **Herbert E. Colby**: born January 8, 1869, Chicago, Illinois.

(6) **Carrie H. Colby**: born October 29, 1870.

(4) **Charles Madison Colby**: born August 19, 1838; married Lucy A. Collins, daughter of Joseph and Alice C. (Greeley) Collins, on August 17, 1857.

(5) **Henry Adams Colby**: born February 1, 1841; died at Washington D.C. of wounds received in the Civil War.

(6) **Leora M. Colby**: born April 29, 1844; married John H. Johnson on November 13, 1867, at Springfield, New Hampshire.

(3) AUGUSTA[7]: born July 25, 1805; married James Cowee on April 12, 1827, Intentions Published April 2, 1827, at Mason, New Hampshire; died February 22, 1877. The published intentions indicate that Augusta Adams was from Rindge, New Hampshire. James Cowee was born December 28, 1802, at Gardner, Worcester, Massachusetts, and died Neovember 22, 1891, at Randolph, Ohio. James Cowee was the son of James and Susannah (Baldwin) Cowee. Augusta and James Cowee had six children.

(1) **James Edwin Cowee**: born February 15, 1828, at Mason, New Hampshire; married Persis K. Gardner on November 22, 1855; died February 24, 1858.

(2) **John Quincy Cowee**: born April 13, 1830 at Durham, New York; married Emerenza C. Drinkwater on November 9, 1855; died September 18, 1921, at Burlingame, Kansas.

(3) **Emily Maria Cowee**: born April 23, 1835, Durham, New York; married M. A. Barnes on March 16, 1859; died January 30, 1892. Emily and M. A. Barnes had three children.

  (1) **Edwin M. Barnes**: born in 1860; died in 1937.

  (2) **Clara Barnes**: born in 1868.

  (3) **Olive A. Barnes**:

(4) **Merrill Elliott Cowee**: born November 7, 1839 at Durham, New York; married Keziah Kizzie Hook on August 30, 1866, at Keene, Ohio; died March 21, 1872, at Washara, Kansas. Merrill and Keziah Cowee had three children.

  (1) **Edwin Stanton Cowee**: born November 11, 1867, at Burlingame, Kansas; married Ada Myrtle Akers on December 23, 1896; died June 13, 1928.

  (2) **Dorothy A. Cowee**: born in 1869; married Frederick Ginter; died in 1951.

  (3) **Frank Alvin Cowee**: born in 1871; married Etta Belle O'Neal; died in 1954.

(5) **Lucy Louina Cowee**: born August 16, 1842, at Marathon, New York; married Joseph Cooper on January 6, 1866; died on August 23, 1913. Lucy and Joseph Cooper had two children.

(1) **Gleason Charles Cooper:** born in 1866.

(2) **Mary Augusta Cooper:** born in 1872; married George W. Raines.

(6) **Dorothy Elizabeth Cowee:** born August 31, 1848, at Catskill, New York; married James Walker Hamilton on October 16, 1878, Randolph, Ohio; died August 21, 1913, at St. Helena, Napa County, California. Dorothy, always known as "Ibbie", and James Hamilton had three children.

    (1) **unnamed boy (twin):** born in 1879; died young.

    (2) **unnamed girl (twin):** born in 1879; died young.

    (3) **Hugh Kenneth Hamilton:** born November 14, 1880, at East Liberty, Logan County, Ohio; married Gladys Melrose Manweiler on July 14, 1915; died September 28, 1965, at Santa Cruz, California. Hugh and Gladys Hamilton had two children.

        (1) **Quincy Kline Hamilton:** born February 19, 1920, at Modesto, California; married, first, Carmen Iocle Birge on September 1, 1944, and second, Mable Mae (Clover) Sherrod on July 24, 1964.

        (2) **Particia Dorothy Hamilton:** born December 30, 1926, at San Jose, California; married Robert Rodney Winterberg on October 20, 1946, at Visalia, California. Patricia and Robert Winterberg have three children, all born at Stockton, California.

            (1) **Deborah Lynn Winterberg:** born July 18, 1955; married Alan Roscelli on September 24, 1977.

            (2) **Jody Michele Winterberg:** born January 26, 1961; married Jeffrey Charles Council on May 28, 1983. Jody and Jeffrey Council have two children, both born at Stockton, California.

                (1) **Wendy Michele Council:** born August 1, 1985.

                (2) **Matthew Thomas Council:** born January 30, 1988.

            (3) **Lynette Diane Winterberg:** born March 31, 1965; married Bill Henry Dillard on September 18, 1987. Lynette and Bill Dillard have three children, all born at Stockton, California.

                (1) **Crystal Lyne Dillard:** born March 1, 1987.

                (2) **April Nicole Dillard:** born November 7, 1988.

                (3) **Melisa Marie Dillard:** born May 15, 1990.

Quincy Adams was killed in an accident during the winter of 1814/15. He fell through his horse drawn sled and was crushed. He left no will. By court action on March 27, 1817, Dolly Adams was granted full power to administer the estate. A copy of the administrative order is provided.

It is believed that Dolly Adams moved to Mason, New Hampshire, to live near or with her father following the death of her husband. At Mason, on November 5, 1822, she married John Robins (Robbins) whose first wife had died the previous year. Dolly's father performed the marriage.

Dolly's father's will, made November 6, 1828, mentions his children, including Dolly Robins. A transcription of the will is included in the chapter of this work dealing with the Eliot family.

Dolly Robins died at Mason, New Hampshire, in June 1831, at age 52 years.

This birth record was copied from original records at New Ipswich, New Hampshire, on August 19, 1900

It reports that a white, male named Quinsy Adams was born the 12th child of Ephraim Adams and wife Rebeckah on Sept. 29th, 1775, at New Ipswich.

Quincy is reported to be the 12th child born to Ephraim Adams. He was the 12th child born to his father and the 7th child born to Ephraim Adams' second wife, Rebecca (Locke) Adams.

ADMINISTRATION.

Adams Dolly

HILLSBOROUGH, ss. AT a Probate Court, holden at *Amherst* in and for said County, on the *27th* day of *March* Anno Domini, 18*77*

Before *John Harris* Esquire,

JUDGE of the Probate of Wills, &c. for said County.

RESPECTFULLY shews *Dolly Adams* of *Temple* in said County, *widow* That *Quincy Adams* late of *Temple* in said County, *laborer* has lately deceased intestate, having, while he lived, and at the time of h*is* death, estate in said County, and that the said deceased died, leaving

your petitioner his widow

WHEREFORE the said *Dolly* prays that Administration, on the estate of said deceased, may be granted to *her* . This application was preferred at this Court, and, upon examination, it appears that the facts therein alleged are true. It is, therefore, decreed, by the said Judge, that the prayer of said petition be allowed, and that Administration on the estate of said deceased be granted to the said *Dolly Adams* *s*he giving bonds, as the law directs.

Attest, *Ch. H. Atherton* REG'R.

~~~~~~

STATE OF NEW-HAMPSHIRE.

HILLSBOROUGH, ss. *John Harris* ESQUIRE,

JUDGE of the Probate of Wills, and for granting Letters of Administration on the estates of persons deceased, having estate in the County aforesaid:

To *Dolly Adams*

(L. S.) of *Temple* in said County, *widow* GREETING.

WHEREAS *Quincy Adams*

late of *Temple* in said County, *laborer* deceased, having, while *he* lived, and at the time of *his* death, estate in the County aforesaid, lately died intestate, whereby the power of committing Administration of all and singular the estate of the said deceased, and also the hearing, examining and allowing the account of such Administration, doth appertain unto me.

TRUSTING therefore in your care and fidelity, I DO, by these presents, commit unto you full power to Administer all and singular, the estate of the said deceased : to ask, gather, levy, recover and receive all and whatsoever credits of the said deceased, which to *him* while *he* lived, and at the time of *his* death did appertain ; to pay all debts, in which the said deceased stood bound, so far as the value of the estate of said deceased can extend ; and well and faithfully to dispose of the same estate, according to law. You are to make a true and perfect Inventory of all and singular the estate of the said deceased ; and to exhibit the same into the Registry of the Court of Probate, for the County aforesaid, within three months next ensuing ; and to render a plain and true account of your said Administration upon oath, within one year next following.——AND I DO hereby ordain, constitute and appoint you Administrat*rix* on all and singular the estate aforesaid.

In Testimony whereof, I have hereunto set my hand, and the seal of the Court of Probate, Dated at *Amherst* in said County, the *27th* day of *March* Anno Domini, 18*77*

John Harris

A true Copy of Record,

Attest, *Ch. H. Atherton* REG'R.

ELIOT FAMILY

Dolly Eliot (name also spelled Elliot), daughter of William and Dorothy (Merrill) Eliot, married Quincy Adams on April 8, 1800, at Mason, New Hampshire. William Eliot was a baptist minister and performed the marriage of his daughter to Quincy Adams. Quincy Adams is the son of Ephraim and Rebecca (Locke) Adams. The ancestry of William Eliot is shown here. The history of the Eliot family in New England and America follows.

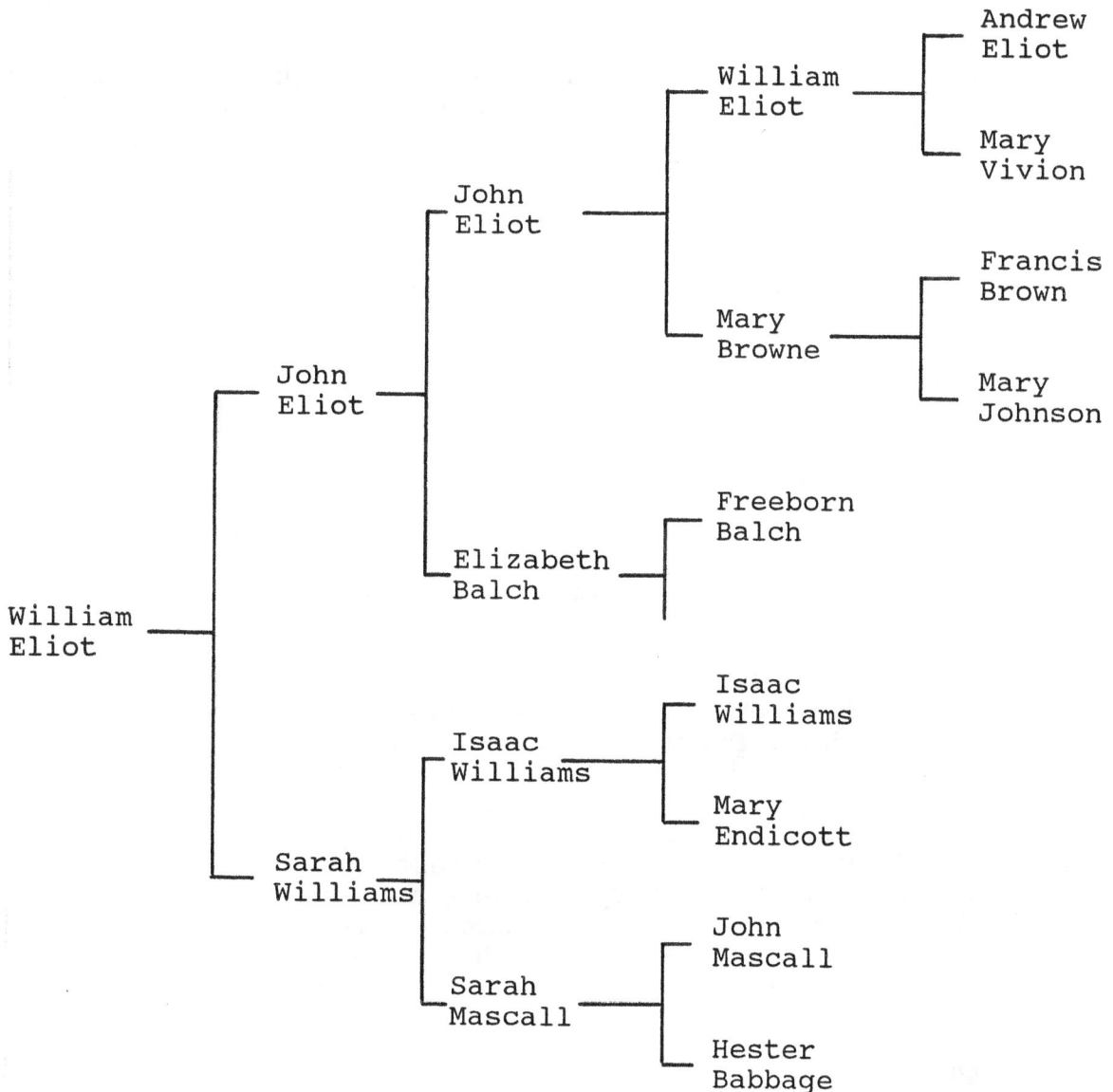

```
                                                         ┌─ Andrew
                                             ┌─ William ─┤   Eliot
                                             │   Eliot   │
                                ┌─ John ──────┤           └─ Mary
                                │   Eliot    │               Vivion
                                │            │           ┌─ Francis
                                │            │           │   Brown
                                │            └─ Mary ─────┤
                                │                Browne  │
                 ┌─ John ────────┤                        └─ Mary
                 │   Eliot      │                            Johnson
                 │              │
                 │              └─ Elizabeth ──── Freeborn
                 │                  Balch          Balch
                 │
  William ───────┤
  Eliot          │                                ┌─ Isaac
                 │                                │   Williams
                 │              ┌─ Isaac ──────────┤
                 │              │   Williams      │
                 │              │                 └─ Mary
                 │              │                     Endicott
                 └─ Sarah ───────┤
                     Williams   │                 ┌─ John
                                │                 │   Mascall
                                └─ Sarah ──────────┤
                                    Mascall       │
                                                  └─ Hester
                                                      Babbage
```

-73-

ANDREW ELIOT: born in East Coker, England, in 1627. His baptism is recorded there on April 24, 1627. Andrew Eliot is the son of William and Emma Eliot, who did not emigrate to North America. Andrew Eliot married, first, Grace Woodier on April 23, 1649, at East Coker, England, and second, Mary Vivion in 1654, also at East Coker. Andrew Eliot died March 1, 1703/04, at Beverly, Massachusetts. He is buried at the Beverly Graveyard.

Andrew's first wife, Grace (Woodier) Eliot died February 8, 1652. Andrew and Grace Eliot had one son.

(1) ANDREW: born January 30, 1650, at East Coker, Somersetshire, England; married Mercy Shattuck in 1680 at Beverly, Massachusetts; died September 21, 1688, when he was lost at sea off Cape Sable.

Andrew and second wife, Mary, emigrated to New England sometime before 1670. He was a man of property, education, and ability. He was a member of the established Church of England. Andrew and Mary (Vivion) Eliot had three children, all born at East Coker, England.

**(1) WILLIAM: born 1654/55; married Mary Browne, daughter of Francis and Mary (Johnson) Brown; on July 10, 1681, at Beverly, Massachusetts, died February 19, 1721/22, at Beverly.

(2) EMMA: born about 1655.

(3) MARY: born January 11, 1662.

Andrew Eliot became a member of the church at Beverly in 1670. He was frequently employed in public service and served in a number of courts. He was one of the jurors at the Salem Witch Trials. He, with the other jurors, afterwards made a public recantation and greatly reproached himself for the part he had taken.

Andrew Eliot's will was drawn February 26, 1703/04, and proved April 3, 1704. The will is still on file in Salem. His wife, Mary, made a will dated December 8, 1718. It was proved August 1, 1720, giving reason for the assumption she died in July 1720.

The link establishing this Andrew Eliot to be the father of William Eliot is weak. The information establishing the link is found in the LDS Family History Library and in the book, Eliot Family, by Walter Graeme Eliot, published in 1887.
Upon emigrating to New England, he settled first in Salem, Massachusetts, and then in Beverly. For a time he worked as a tailor.

WILLIAM ELIOT emigrated to New England with his parents sometime before 1670. On July 10, 1681, at Beverly, Massachusetts, he married Mary (Browne) Parker, widow of Nathan Parker. Mary and Nathan Parker had one daughter, Mary. Mary Browne was the daughter of Francis and Mary (Johnson) Brown of Newbury, Massachusetts. She was born April 15, 1657, at Newbury.

William and Mary Eliot had eight children.

(1) **Andrew:** died young.
(2) **Andrew:**
(3) **Judith:** born March 24, 1685; married Thomas Cocks.
(4) **William:** born September 14, 1685, at Beverly, Massachusetts; married Anna Porter on October 21, 1708, at Beverly.
(5) **Mary:** baptized February 5, 1691; married William Tuck.
(6) **John: born May 16, 1693, at Beverly, Massachusetts; married, first, Elizabeth Balch on April 20, 1715, at Beverly, and second, Hannah Waldron, on April 20, 1720; died in April 1751, at Beverly.
(7) **Emma:** baptized may 16, 1697.
(8) **Elizabeth:** baptized October 8, 1699.

William Eliot's will is on file in Salem, Massachusetts. It was made January 19, 1721/22, and was proved on February 19, 1721/22.

JOHN ELIOT, son of William and Mary (Browne) Eliot, sometimes spelled his name "Eliott". He lived in Beverly, Massachusetts, and perhaps for some time in Newbury. John and Elizabeth (Balch) Eliot had two children, both born at Beverly.

(1) **Skipper:** born January 1, 1715/16; married Joanna.
(2) **John: born March 10, 1717/18; married Sarah Williams on March 25, 1742, at Beverly, Massachusetts; died at Sutton, Massachusetts, on June 25, 1781.

Following the death of his first wife, Elizabeth, John married Hannah Waldron of Wenham, Massachusetts. John and Hannah (Waldron) Eliot had seven children.

(1) **Nathaniel:** christened July 2, 1721.
(2) **Francis:** born July 26, 1723; died November 2, 1745, at Cape Breton, Massachusetts.
(3) **Elizabeth:** born June 26, 1725; married John Canada.
(4) **Abigail:** born Feburary 11, 1726/27; died young.
(5) **Abigail:** born June 15, 1729; married, first, C. Larcom, and second, Israel Dodge.
(6) **William:** born June 22, 1731; married Elizabeth Woodberry on February 12, 1754; lost at sea on March 5, 1755.
(7) **Hannah:** born January 1, 1736; married Peter Woodberry.

John Eliot made his will April 6, 1751. It was proved May 6, 1751, thus the guess that he died in April 1751. He left land known as Hardy's land to his two sons from his first marriage, Skipper and John. He left land on Beaver Pond, near Beverly, to his sons Nathaniel and William. William, the residuary legatee, got the homestead and its lands, a pasture known as Woodberry's pasture, and all the personal estate. John Eliot's second wife, Hannah, survived him and she is named in the will to be the Executor, along with their son William.

JOHN ELIOT, son of John and Elizabeth (Balch) Eliot, moved from Beverly to Bradford, Massachusetts, where he farmed and raised his family. He lived for a while in Nottingham West, now Hudson, New Hampshire. Later he moved to Mason Township, New Hampshire, where he had purchased land in 1766, while still living at Hudson.

John's wife, Sarah Williams, was born May 25, 1723, at Salem, Massachusetts. She was the daughter of Isaac and Sarah (Mascall) Williams. She died about 1791 at Bradford, Massachusetts.

John and Sarah (Williams) Eliot had five children.

(1) William: born December 9, 1748, at Bradford, Massachusetts; married, first, Dorothy Merrill, in 1772, at Hudson, New Hampshire, and second, Rebecca Hildreth, in March 1787; died June 4, 1830, at Mason Township, Hillsborough County, New Hampshire.
(2) **Abigail:** born in 1750, at Bradford, Massachusetts; married, first, Abiather Winn, second, William Burns, and third, Justus Daken.
(3) **Sarah:** born in 1753, at Bradford, Massachusetts, married John Tarbell.
(4) **Andrew:** born September 11, 1755 (or 1756), at Bradford, Massachusetts; married Hannah Dakin on January 29, 1782.
(5) **David:** born at Mason Township, New Hampshire; married, first, Hannah Adams (daughter of Benjamin Adams, who is the brother of Ephraim Adams, who is the father of Quincy Adams), and second, Lucy Emory.

Sarah Williams' ancestry includes John Endicott, credited by many historians to have been the first Governor of Massachusetts. Her connection to the Endicott lineage is given here.

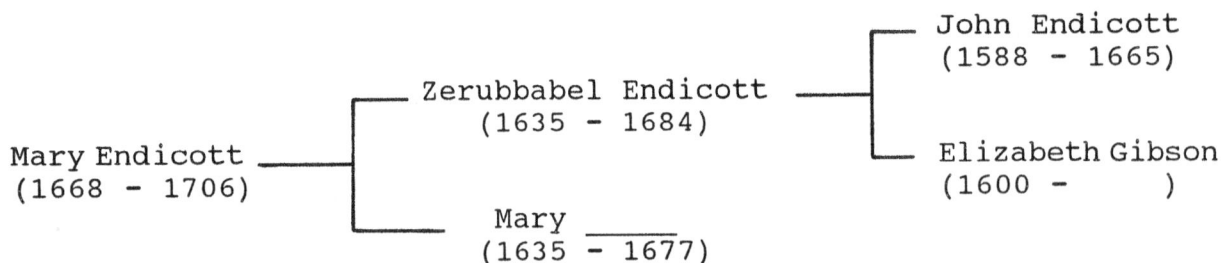

```
                                                        ┌─ John Endicott
                                                        │  (1588 - 1665)
                           ┌─ Zerubbabel Endicott ──────┤
                           │  (1635 - 1684)             │
Mary Endicott ────────────┤                             └─ Elizabeth Gibson
(1668 - 1706)             │                                (1600 -      )
                           │
                           └─ Mary _____
                              (1635 - 1677)
```

Mary Endicott, the grand-daughter of Governor John Endicott, married Isaac Williams, a grandfather of Sarah Williams, as shown on the lineage chart on page 73.

John Endicott came to New England in the ship *Abigail*, from Weymouth, England. He arrived at Salem, Massachusetts, in September 1628. He was one of the six original purchasers of the Massachusetts Bay from the Plymouth Council on March 19, 1627. He was the first of the purchasers to travel to the new colonies.

Matthew Craddock was the first Governor of the Massachusetts Company, but he remained in England. As such, John Endicott is credited by many historians as being the "real" first governor of Massachusetts, having taken office officially on September 7, 1630.

WILLIAM ELIOT, in 1766, at age 18, moved with his parents, John and Sarah (Williams) Eliot, to Mason Township, Hillsborough County, New Hampshire. The land purchased by his father in the northwest part of Mason was still unbroken wilderness.

William Eliot married Dorothy Merrill, daughter of the Rev. Nathaniel and Elizabeth (Sargent) Merrill, in 1772 at Hudson, New Hampshire. Dorothy Merrill was born February 11, 1748/49, at Hudson, New Hampshire. William and Dorothy had six children, four sons and two daughters.

> (1) **Molly:** born August 2, 1773, at Mason Township, New Hampshire; died May 22, 1866.
> (2) **Elizabeth (Betty):** born March 3, 1775, at Mason Township, New Hampshire; died March 17, 1850.
> (3) **William:** born February 3, 1777.
> (4) **Israel:** born April 10, 1781.
> ******(5) **Dolly:** born March 3, 1779, at Mason Township, New Hampshire; married, first, Quincy Adams on April 8, 1800, at Mason, and second, John Robins (Robbins) on November 5, 1822, at Mason; died June 5, 1831, at Mason.
> (6) **Sarah:** born May 29, 1783, at Mason Township, New Hampshire; died about 1850.

Dorothy (Merrill) Eliot died June 14, 1785, at Mason, Township, New Hampshire. William Eliot married Rebecca Hildreth, daughter of Mr. Oliver Hildreth of Townsend, on March 20, 1787. William and Rebecca (Hildreth) Eliot had twelve children, eight sons and four daughters, all born at Mason.

> (1) **Seth:** born May 8, 1792.
> (2) **Joseph:** born April 12, 1789; married Susan Worden of Westminster, New Hampshire; died at Monmouth, Illinois.
> (3) **Israel:** born January 1, 1788; drowned sometime after graduating from Middlebury College; buried at Mason.

(4) **David**: born September 24, 1790.
(5) **Rebecca**: born July 9, 1794; died January 12, 1823.
(6) **Samuel**: born March 22, 1796; died September 7, 1860, aged 64, at Boston, Massachusetts; buried at Boston.
(7) **Susan**: born March 4, 1798; married Mr. Lane; died at South Framlingham, Massachusetts.
(8) **Jesse**: born December 24, 1799; married, first, Phoebe Yeomans on June 27, 1827, and second, Mary C. Willis on May 16, 1842; died March 24, 1880, aged 81, at Batavia, New York.
(9) **Elcy**: born October 15, 1803; died April 13, 1834.
(10) **Mel**: born May 5, 1805.
(11) **David**: born May 18, 1809.
(12) **Julia**: born January 12, 1811; died August 27, 1844.

During the entire period of the Revolutionary War, William Eliot served on many of the important committees for town business. He became a member of Mr. Farrar's church in New Ipswich, New Hampshire, in 1772. He was one of the original members of the Congregational Church in Mason on October 13, 1772, when that church was formed. His wife, Dorothy, joined in 1776.

With the introduction of the Baptist movement following the Revolutionary War, William Eliot embraced that faith and servied it as a minister for the rest of his life. He was ordained in 1788 and served as a minister for 41 years.

Rev. William Eliot died June 4, 1830, at Mason Township, Hillsborough County, New Hampshire. His will was made at Mason on November 6, 1828. A transcription of the will is provided on the next page.

Rev. William Eliot performed the marriage services for both of the marriages of his daughter, Dolly. The remaining biography for Dolly Elliot is contained in the Adams chapter for her first husband, Quincy.

THE WILL OF WILLIAM ELIOT

****

The following transcription of the will of William Eliot is made from a copy of the original which is filed at the Hillsborough County, New Hampshire, Court of Probate. Illegible words have been replaced with brackets.

****

Be it remembered that I William Eliot of Mason in the County of Hillsborough and State of New Hampshire [   ] considering the uncertainty of this [   ] life and being of sound mind and memory (blessed be God for [   ] [   ],) do make and establish this my last Will and Testament, in manner and form following, that is to say - Item 1. I give myself to God, my Creator, to be at his disposal, both in life and death.

2. I give and bequeth to my sons William Eliot, Joseph Eliot, Seth Eliot, and Jesse Eliot, twenty dollars cash to be paid by my Executor at my decease [   ] all my money and notes if any left to be equally divided to each of my sons above named. Also my wearing apperal. 3rd I give to my Daughters Polly Johnson, Betty Wilson, Dolly Robbens and Sally Hutchinson and Suzey Lane twelve dollars each to be paid by my Executor at my decease.

4th I give to my two daughters Elcy Eliot and Julia Ann Eliot all my Household furniture (excepting one bed and bedding I give to Elis) equally to be divided. but I give my loom [   ] and Spinning Wheels to Julia Ann. Also I give to Julia Ann fifty dollars to be paid her at the age of eighteen by my Executor. Likewise I give to Elcy thirty dollars to be paid at my decease. together with their deceased mothers clothing. to be equally divided between them.

5th I give to my daughters Love joys Heirs fourty dollars each to be paid at my decease by My Executor. and Julia Ann to have a home with my Executor and for him to take care of her while out of health and lives single. Also I give to Elcy and Julia Ann all my moveables about house   clock, [   ] and so on.

6th I give and bequeath to my son Samuel Eliot all the residue and remainder of my estate after paying my just debts. excepting six sheep which are hereby given to Elcy and Julia Ann. also he is to give me a decent burial. And I do hereby constitute and appoint him the said Samuel the sole Executor of this my last Will and testament hereby revoking all former wills by me made.

In witness whereof I have hereinto set my hand and seal, november 6th in the year of our Lord one thousand eight hundred and twenty eight.

                                        William Eliot

Signed and sealed by the above
William Eliot in presence of us.
Abram Robens
Eben Adams
Andrew Elliot

****

SEVENTH GENERATION

JOHN QUINCY[7] ADAMS

John Quincy[7] Adams, only son of Quincy[6] and Dolly (Elliot) Adams, was born in New Ipswich, New Hampshire, on December 19, 1800.

When John Quincy was only four or five years old, his family moved to Temple, a town just a short distance north of New Ipswich. For reasons unknown, and a few years after the death of his father, Quincy Adams exchanged his father's farm, which he had inherited, for one in Temple owned by Francis Cragin, and moved to that town.

Quincy Adams died in a farm accident in the winter of 1814/15 leaving his wife, Dolly, and three children, including John Quincy Adams who was 14 years old at the time.

What happened to John Quincy Adams between the time of the death of his father and his marriage in Boston is not known. It is likely that John Quincy's mother moved to Mason, New Hampshire, to be near her father. Dolly (Elliot) Adams married John Robins at Mason on November 6, 1822. John Quincy more than likely went, or was sent, to Boston for education or for business opportunity, or both.

At Boston, John Quincy Adams engaged in the mercantile business and married Lovina Walker on March 16, 1828. Lovina Walker was born at Waterboro, Maine, on November 22, 1807. She is the daughter of Edward and Susanna (Scribner) Walker.

Although Edward Walker was born in Maine and returned to Maine late in life, he served in a Massachusetts company during the Revolutionary War. It is likely that John Quincy Adams met his wife during the time the Walker family spent in Massachusetts following the war.

In Boston, John Quincy Adams prospered in the mercantile business. In 1831 he moved west. He settled in Keene Township, Coshocton County, Ohio, where he spent the rest of his life farming. John Quincy Adams died on November 12, 1873. His estate passed to his wife, though she declined to serve as executor and those duties were fulfilled by her second son, Edward.

Lovina Adams continued to live on the farm and did so until she died on January 7, 1891.

John Quincy and Lovina Adams had seven children.

**(1) JOHN QUINCY[8]: born March 9, 1830, at Boston, Massachusetts; died October 13, 1893, at Keene, Ohio; married Sarah Jane Wilson on January 22, 1856, at Greensburg, Indiana.

(2) EDWARD WALKER[8]: born January 24, 1832; married Olivia M. Gleason; died in 1913. Olivia Gleason was born in 1840 and died in 1923. Edward and Olivia Adams had five children.

    (1) Lorna Lovina[9]: born in 1868; married Samuel Black Linhart; died in 1941. Samuel Linhart was born in 1865 and died in 1936. Lorna and Samuel Linhart had three children.

        (1) **Dorothy Elizabeth Linhart**: born in 1900.
        (2) **Lois Olivia Linhart**: born in 1903.
        (3) **Edward Adams Linhart**: born in 1906.

    (2) John Quincy[9]: born in 1870; married Grace M. Norris; died in 1956. Grace Norris was born in 1883. John Quincy and Grace Adams had four children.

        (1) **Edna Olivia**[10]: a twin born in 1918.
        (2) **Erma E.**[10]: a twin born in 1918.
        (3) **John Quincy**[10]: born in 1921.
        (4) **Janice Maxine**[10]: born in 1922; died in 1987.

    (3) Dorothy Ann[9]: born in 1872; married Joseph Dwight Wetz; died in 1960. Joseph Wetz died in 1937.

    (4) Edward Gleason[9]: born in 1875; married, first, Sophie Moore, and second, Mary Lutz; died in 1965. Sophie Moore was born in 1877 and died in 1929. Edward and Sophie Adams had two children.

        (1) **Ruth Moore**[10]: born in 1906; died in 1968.
        (2) **Helen L.**[10]: born in 1920; married Claude M. Pearson, Jr.

    (5) Clifford Raymond[9]: born in 1879; married Nellie R. McGinnis; died in 1946. Nellie McGinnis was born in 1879 and died in 1969. Clifford and Nellie Adams had six children.

        (1) **Elizabeth Woodruf**[10]: born in 1908; married Guy Deneve Williams. Guy Williams was born in 1908.
        (2) **Edward William**[10]: born in 1910; married, first, Dorothy Brown, and second, Merla Davenport. Dorothy Brown was born in 1916.
        (3) **Dorothy Ann**[10]: born in 1912; married Wilbur Maurice Annable. Wilbur Annable was born in 1904.
        (4) **Robert McGinnis**[10]: born in 1914; married Mary Alice Henderson. Mary Henderson was born in 1914.
        (5) **Margaret Gleason**[10]: born in 1916; married Paul Eugene Henderson. Paul Henderson was born in 1904 and died in 1978.
        (6) **Jean Eleanor**[10]: born in 1920; married Jacob Robbins.

(3) SARAH M.[8]: born December 19, 1833; married Sam T. Spangler on July 31, 1853. Sarah and Sam Spangler had three children.

    (1) **Ella L. Spangler**: born March 14, 1854, in Keene, Ohio.
    (2) **Emma A. Spangler**: born October 21, 1855, in Keene, Ohio.

(3) **George Franklin Spangler**: born March 2, 1858, in Buffalo Grove, Iowa.

(4) JAMES C.[8]: born February 2, 1836; died 1887; married Mary A. _____. James and Mary Adams had one son.
  (1) **Milo Melvin[9]**: born in 1859 in Keene, Ohio.

(5) AUGUSTA MEHITABLE[8]: born November 22, 1839; married William Dawson on October 2, 1861, in Keene, Ohio. Augusta and William Dawson had ten children, all born in Coshocton County, Ohio.
  (1) **John Quincy Dawson**: born August 10, 1862.
  (2) **Merrill E. Dawson**: born January 31, 1864.
  (3) **Effie Lovina Dawson**: born January 29, 1866.
  (4) **Ora Belle Dawson**: born March 12, 1868.
  (5) **Abba M. Dawson**:
  (6) **Kate L. Dawson**:
  (7) **William M. Dawson**:
  (8) **Perly E. Dawson**: born in 1874; died young.
  (9) **James H. Dawson**: born in 1875; died in 1876.
  (10) **Clyde W. Dawson**: born in 1877; died in 1903.

(6) BETTY (BETSY) LINNA[8]: born November 22, 1841; married William Shank, M.D.; died in 1923. William Shank was born in 1846 and died in 1900.

(7) DOROTHY A.[8]: born August 14, 1843; married Edwin Collar Gleason; died in 1908. Edwin Gleason was born in 1845 and died in 1935. Dorothy and Edwin Gleason had two children.
  (1) **John M. Gleason**: born in 1872; married Rosalind Hock; died in 1955.
  (2) **Maud Adella Gleason**: born in 1876; married Hugh Boyd Finlay; died in 1957. Maud and Hugh Finlay had two children.
      (1) **Grace Adella Finlay**: born in 1908; married Clarence Frederick Miller.
      (2) **Dorothy Belle Finlay**: born in 1911; married William Gleason Taylor.

TOMBSTONE OF JOHN QUINCY ADAMS AT
KEENE TOWNSHIP, COSHOCTON COUNTY, OHIO

This birth record was copied from original records in New Ipswich, New Hampshire, in 1900.

Although in very poor condition, it is included because it provides a significant link in establishing the lineage of the Adams family.

This birth record reports a male child named John Quincy Adams was born the first child to Quincy Adams and wife Dolly on December 19, 1800, at New Ipswich.

EIGHTH GENERATION

JOHN QUINCY[8] ADAMS

John Quincy[8] Adams was born in Boston, Massachusetts, on March 9, 1830. He was the eldest son of John Quincy[7] and Lovina (Walker) Adams. His father, John Quincy[7], was born in New Ipswich, New Hampshire, and had moved to Boston as a young man to pursue education and business opportunity.

In 1831, with young John Quincy only one year old, his parents moved to Ohio. They settled in Coshocton County in an area which would become known as Keene Township. Here the elder John Quincy would live out his life while engaged in farming.

Young John Quincy was trained in farming. As he grew to manhood he was provided the best education available and adopted the avocation of teacher. On December 5, 1848, John Quincy was awarded his first teaching certificate and began teaching at a girl's seminary in Coshocton County, Ohio.

In July 1852, John Quincy Adams moved to Indiana to pursue teaching as a career. He settled in Decatur County, and taught in the area of Greensburg. Family information indicates that John Quincy eventually became the principal of a high school in Greensburg, Indiana. If this is true, it would have been at a private high school, as the high school district in Greensburg was not formed until 1869, well after John Quincy moved on to Kansas. While residing in the city of Greensburg, John Quincy met his future wife, Sarah Jane Wilson.

On January 22, 1856, John Quincy Adams married Sarah Jane Wilson, one of his students. Sarah Jane was born June 24, 1838, the daughter of John Dickson and Sarah (Foster) Wilson. She was a native of Decatur County.

In July 1859, together with their first two children, John Quincy and Sarah Jane Adams moved to Linn County, Kansas. They first settled near friends who had preceded them to Kansas in an area now known as Blue Mound, a name given the area by Mr. Adams. The name derived from a description of the area. There was a gentle mound to the north of the homestead that took on a beautiful azure blue color when the day was hazy or misty. In 1861, John Quincy Adams purchased 160 acres of farmland just north of Blue Mound. At about this time, John Quincy Adams was made postmaster and he established the post office at his home. He named the post office Blue Mound and it did not take long for the community to take on the same name.

To feed his family, John Quincy hunted on the prairie for small game. He hunted turkey and rabbits and whatever else was available. He used the turkey feathers he collected for making brooms.

John Quincy and Sarah Jane Adams had ten children. The 1860 census reports John Quincy and Sarah Adams living in Mound City Township, Linn County, Kansas with two children, Sarah age 1 and John age 3. The author believes this to be an error. The census incorrectly gives Ida Belle's name as Sarah. There is no record to substantiate that John Quincy and Sarah Jane Adams ever had a daughter named Sarah.

WILLIAM AND IDA BELLE (ADAMS) CHITWOOD

Ida Belle Adams was the oldest daughter born to
John Quincy and Sarah Jane Adams. She was born
in Indiana and came to Kansas with her parents
as an infant.

The children and descendants of John Quincy and Sarah Jane (Wilson) Adams are as follows:

(1) JOHN QUINCY[9], Jr.: born February 24, 1857, at Greensburg, Indiana; married, first, Mary Brooks, and second, May ____; made his home in Los Angeles, California. John and Mary Adams had four children.

(1) **John Quincy**[10]: died in infancy.
(2) **Mable**[10]: married Percy Vernon Hammon on April 22, 1908; had two children.
    (1) **Eleanor Hammon**:
    (2) **Marjorie Hammon**:
(3) **Ethel**[10]: married Norman Young; had two children.
    (1) **Norman Young, Jr.**:
    (2) **Ione Young**:
(4) **Bernal**[10]: committed suicide.

(2) IDA BELLE[9]: born May 31, 1859, at Spring Hill, Indiana; married William Harrison Chitwood on January 17, 1886; died June 3, 1952, in Topeka, Kansas. For at least part of their married lives, Ida and William Chitwood made their home in Stanley, Kansas. William Chitwood was born in Linn County, Kansas, on August 19, 1859. He died April 1, 1939, in Topeka, Kansas. Ida and William had:
(1) **Edna Chitwood**: born December 7, 1886; married Milton Paul Gartrell (born February 24, 1876, at Chicago, Illinois) on July 27, 1912. Milton Gartrell died August 21, 1959, at Topeka, Kansas. Edna and Milton Gartrell had one daughter.
    (1) **Janice Gartrell**: born May 26, 1920, in Johnson County, Kansas.
(2) **Avis Chitwood**: born December 29, 1893, near Mound City, Kansas; never married; died January 25, 1994, at Topeka, Kansas, at age 100; buried at the Mount Hope Cemetery. Avis Chitwood was an accomplished artist and a family historian.

(3) MARO MELVIN[9]: born July 27, 1862 at Blue Mound, Kansas; died January 29, 1944; married Rachel Mary Stanley (born January 8, 1862) on February 25, 1886; made his home in Kincaid, Kansas. Rachel Adams died July 12, 1925. Maro was married a second time, but had no children from that marriage. Maro Melvin and Rachel Adams had six children.
(1) **Guy Harrison**[10]: born August 1, 1888; died August 8, 1913; married Edna Chamberlain (born January 6, 1889) on August 1, 1907. Edna Adams died October 9, 1921. Guy and Edna Adams had three children.
    (1) **Robert**[11]: died at birth
    (2) **Merril Melvin**[11]: born April 4, 1909; married Willamena Bogan (born December 1, 1913) on February 16, 1932; died December 27, 1992, at Allen County Hospital in Iola, Kansas. Merril was a farmer in the area of Kincaid, Kansas. He specialized in dairy cattle and poultry operations. He lived his entire life within 1-1/2 miles of his birthplace. Merril and Willamena "Billie" Adams had six children.

(1) **Edna Charlene**[12]: born March 12, 1933; married Paul Carter Hosley (born July 24, 1930) on February 22, 1953. Edna (Adams) and Paul Hosley had two children.

    (1) **David Ray Hosley**: born October 18, 1956; married Rita Jo Timm. David and Rita Hosley have two children.

        (1) **Crystal Dawn Hosley**: born March 23, 1981.

        (2) **Ashley Marie Hosley**: born August 3, 1985.

    (2) **Kevin Paul Hosley**: born September 18, 1960.

(2) **Wayne Leland**[12]: born April 10, 1938; married Judith Ann Bahr (born November 6, 1942) on July 25, 1962. Wayne and Judith Adams have two children.

    (1) **Lisa Merril**[13]: born February 22, 1963.

    (2) **Lance Bradford**[13]: born September 14, 1964.

(3) **Marvin Merril**[12]: born June 2, 1940; married Rosa Oliva Marin (born April 9, 1940) on October 26, 1963. Marvin and Rosa Adams have three children.

    (1) **Hilda Yvette**[13]: born April 14, 1964.

    (2) **Matthew Marvin**[13]: born October 25, 1971.

    (3) **Erica Renee**[13]: born February 13, 1974.

(4) **Sharilyn Kay**[12]: born August 7, 1949; married William Ross Lamb (born May 24, 1945) on January 21, 1969. Sharilyn (Adams) and William Lamb have four children.

    (1) **Barry James Lamb**: born January 5, 1970.

    (2) **Merril Ross Lamb**: born March 2, 1974.

    (3) **Kyla Dianne Lamb**: born May 3, 1977.

    (4) **Kendra Annette Lamb**: born May 22, 1979.

(5) **Lanette Marlene**[12]: born February 21, 1951; married Micheal Lour. Lanette (Adams) and Micheal Lour have one child.

    (1) **Tina Marlene Lour**: born November 17, 1979.

(6) **Calvin Ray**[12]: born May 8, 1952; is a single parent with three children.

    (1) **Robbie Ray**[13]: born August 16, 1971.

    (2) **John Quincy**[13]: born September 8, 1974.

    (3) **Renda Liana**[13]: born May 7, 1980.

(3) **Lucienne**[11]: born May 6, 1913; married Walter P. Bucholz (born January 12, 1912) on August 12, 1939. Lucienne and Walter Bucholz have one son.

(1) **Lyle Dean Bucholz**: born October 28, 1941; married Joyce Cunningham (born July 1, 1940) in 1968. Lyle and Joyce Bucholz have one daughter.

    (1) **Kimberly Sue Bucholz**: born October 3, 1969.

(2) **George Clair**[10]: born September 24, 1892; died June 9, 1965; married Anna Marie Smith (born September 23, 1890) on May 21, 1914. George and Anna Marie Adams had two children.

    (1) **Margery Clair**[11]: born August 7, 1915; married Howard Raymond Donald (born September 8, 1915) on June 21, 1937. Following their marriage, Howard and Margery lived in the Texas panhandle while Howard worked at a carbon black plant. After only a couple of years, they returned to Kansas where they spent their working years farming. Margery (Adams) and Howard Donald have four children.

        (1) **Karen Lee Donald**: born July 15, 1940; married Ed Hack (born July 12, 1937) on August 26, 1959. Karen and Ed Hack have three children.

            (1) **Steven Ward Hack**: born November 27, 1960; married Katherine Joan Kiper (born December 18, 1959) on March 11, 1983. Steven and Katherine Hack have two children.

                (1) **Kelsey Anne Marie Hack**: born December 29, 1987.

                (2) **Garrett Wesley Hack**: born September 12, 1990.

            (2) **Andrea Lynn Hack**: born August 27, 1963; married Mark Alan Herndon (born September 1, 1960) on November 26, 1987.

            (3) **David Alan Hack**: born December 14, 1965.

        (2) **Dwight Clair Donald**: born July 26, 1942; married Judith Ann Zink (born October 11, 1941) on April 16, 1966. Dwight and Judith have three children.

            (1) **Dana Lynn Donald**: born May 26, 1969.

            (2) **Amy Marie Donald**: born March 21, 1977.

            (3) **Laura Diane Donald**: born March 21, 1979.

        (3) **Dee Ann Donald**: born March 10, 1946; married Stephen Joe Parsons (born June 26, 1949) on February 19, 1972. Dee Ann and Stephen have two children.

            (1) **Justin Michael Parsons**: born May 26, 1975.

            (2) **Jennifer Diane Parsons**: born March 5, 1984.

(4) **Dale Alan Donald**: born March 9, 1949; married Sherry Leake (born April 14, 1953) on February 19, 1977. Dale and Sherry have two children.

      (1) **Ashley Marie Donald**; born January 27, 1978.

      (2) **William Blake Alan Donald**: born January 10, 1982.

(2) **Stanley Weaver**[11]: born April 16, 1921; married Doris Eileen Ayers (born December 4, 1931) on May 6, 1951. Stanley was a farmer most of his life. He retired to Reed's Spring, Missouri. Stanley and Doris Adams have three children.

      (1) **Stanley Weaver**[12]: born February 12, 1953. Stanley Adams is the father of two children.

            (1) **Veronica Christy**[13]: born February 23, 1985.

            (2) **Owen Clair**[13]: born October 29, 1986.

      (2) **Gwendolyn**[12]: born January 29, 1955, married a Mr. Hubble. Gwendolyn (Adams) Hubble is the mother of two children.

            (1) **David Allen Hubble**: born August 7, 1980.

            (2) **Christina Michelle Hubble**: born January 23, 1982.

      (3) **Melvin Bruce**[12]: born April 30, 1957. Melvin Adams is the father of three children.

            (1) **Apolonia Eilene**[13]: born July 12, 1985.

            (2) **Francisco Stanley**[13]: born May 12, 1987.

            (3) **Nathaniel Ian**[13]: born March 22, 1989.

(3) **John Quincy**[10]: born October 3, 1894; died July 10, 1974; married Ada May Rogers (born April 27, 1897) on February 25, 1917. Ada Adams died December 2, 1993, and was buried at Lone Elm Cemetery, Lone Elm, Kansas. John Quincy and Ada Adams had five children.

      (1) **John Quincy**[11],**Jr.**: born February 15, 1918; married Mae Myrtle Ross (born April 23, 1917) on November 22, 1940; live at Kincaid, Kansas. John Quincy Adams (or JQ, as he prefers to be called) was a farmer and stockman most of his life until his retirement in 1982. In 1965, JQ became a director and helped to organize American Investors Life Insurance Company of Topeka, Kansas. He still serves on that board. Mae Adams has a masters degree and a degree in education from Pittsburg State University, Pittsburg, Kansas. She taught and served as a school principal for a total of 38 years before retiring. John Quincy and Mae Adams have an adopted son.

            (1) **Randal Joe Adams**: born January 13, 1950; married, first, Kathleen K. Robinson (born

April 29, 1951) on August 23, 1969, and second Gerrie Duvall (born September 4, 1950) on June 5, 1983. Randal and Gerrie live in Tulsa, Oklahoma, where Randal works as a C.P.A. and a Certified Financial Planner (C.F.P.). He holds a law degree from Kansas University, Lawrence, Kansas. Randal and his first wife, Kathleen, had one son.

   (1) **John Michael Adams**: born August 4, 1970.

(2) **Enola**[11]: born May 6, 1920; married Jess Leland Coleman (born November 5, 1916) on September 24, 1942.

(3) **Pauline**[11]: born November 24, 1922; died January 12, 1989, after working 37 years for TWA in Kansas City.

(4) **Helen**[11]: born September 29, 1927; married Norman Francis Lally (born May 22, 1923) on December 2, 1946. Helen (Adams) and Norman Lally have four children.

   (1) **Norman Francis Lally, Jr.**: born December 10, 1949; married Gretchen Louis Mattson (born October 4, 1951) on August 18, 1973. Norman and Gretchen Lally have two children.

      (1) **Scott Mattson Lally**: born March 18, 1982.
      (2) **Kate Elizabeth Lally**: born July 3, 1986.

   (2) **Victoria Lynn Lally**: born June 12, 1954; married Ted Robert Aggeler (born December 24, 1953) on August 20, 1977. Victoria and Ted Aggeler have three children.

      (1) **Rachel Leigh Aggeler**: born February 17, 1982.
      (2) **Clayton James Aggeler**: born November 9, 1983.
      (3) **Luke Allen Aggeler**: born November 18, 1986.

   (3) **Gregory Mark Lally**: born February 21, 1961; married Tracy Helen Steele (born July 2, 1962) on May 29, 1981. Gregory and Tracy have three children.

      (1) **Lacey Marie Lally**: born June 8, 1982.
      (2) **Toby Micheal Lally**: born June 16, 1984.
      (3) **Dustin Matthew Lally**: born October 10, 1985.

   (4) **David John Lally**: born July 20, 1964.

(5) **Arliss Lyle**[11]: born April 5, 1934; married Bonnie Rae Goodall (born October 1, 1935) on June 7, 1953. Arliss and Bonnie Adams have four children.

(1) **Kendall Leland**[12]: born March 16, 1955; married, first, Alice Norman on February 8, 1975, and second, Regina Marie Culver (born September 9, 1962) on August 16, 1990. Kendall and Alice Adams had three children.

    (1) **Stacy Marie**[13]: born October 19, 1975.
    (2) **John Quincy**[13], III: born May 15, 1977.
    (3) **Clinton Leland**[13]: born May 16, 1978.

(2) **Lyle Jeffery**[12]: born August 4, 1956.

(3) **Renda Lynn**[12]: born February 1, 1960; married Michael Wayne Hammond (born June 29, 1958) on January 22, 1977. Renda (Adams) and Mike Hammond have two children.

    (1) **Chad Dewayne Hammond**: born May 23, 1977.
    (2) **Jared Michael Hammond**: born February 22, 1979.

(4) **Cindy Sue**[12]: born July 12, 1961; married Dennis J. Rhodes (born October 10, 1959) on December 1, 1979. Cindy (Adams) and Dennis Rhodes have three children.

    (1) **Kayla Rae Rhodes**: born November 15, 1980.
    (2) **Derek Leon Rhodes**: born July 21, 1983.
    (3) **Jaci Leigh Rhodes**: born December 28, 1988.

(4) **Russel Stanley**[10]: born January 6, 1900; died December 2, 1969; married Gladys Alice Stapleton (born October 17, 1899) on February 22, 1922. Russel and Gladys lived and farmed near Kincaid, Kansas, until 1949, when they relocated to a farm near La Harpe, Kansas. Following Russel's death in 1969, Gladys moved to Wamego where she died November 27, 1973. Russel and Gladys Adams had two children.

(1) **Russell Stanley**[11], **Jr.**: born March 7, 1926; married Ruby Louise Franklin (born May 12, 1931) on December 20, 1958. Russell and Ruby Adams adopted two daughters.

    (1) **Patrician Ann Adams**: born April 4, 1963.
    (2) **Cathleen Sue Adams**: born September 25, 1965; married Mark Christian Huseby (born December 25, 1965) on August 24, 1990.

(2) **Lois Clara**[11]: born April 22, 1935; married Gary Eugene Bartley (born October 19, 1933) on June 19, 1960. Lois (Adams) and Gary Bartley had two children.

    (1) **Stanley Eugene Bartley**: born August 7, 1963; married Stephanie Gayle Bechtel (born September 21, 1968) on August 31, 1991.
    (2) **Jon Jay Bartley**: born April 24, 1966.

(5) **Roscoe Melvin**[10]: born October 3, 1901; married Lenna Naomi Brooks (born January 12, 1909) on February 18, 1926; died July 20, 1965. Roscoe and Lenna had three children, only one of whom lived to adulthood.

(1) **Ruth Irene**[11]: born February 23, 1933, married Delbert Wayne Herrmann (born October 13, 1933) on December 27, 1953. Ruth (Adams) and Delbert Herrmann have two children.

(1) **Cathy Elaine Herrmann**: born August 30, 1957; married Wayne Robert Duderstadt (born October 2, 1957) on March 17, 1979. Cathy and Wayne Duderstadt have two children.

(1) **Eric Wayne Duderstadt**: born July 13, 1985.
(2) **Stacey Elaine Duderstadt**: born January 29, 1989.

(2) **Nancy Arlene Herrmann**: born February 6, 1961; married David Anthony Spieker (born September 21, 1957) on August 8, 1981. Nancy and David Spieker have two children.

(1) **Dustin Wayne Spieker**: born July 18, 1986.
(2) **Evan Anthony Spieker**: born May 25, 1989.

(2) **Milvin Paul**[11]: born July 24, 1938; died August 2, 1938.
(3) **Eva Louise**[11]: born December 1, 1940; died December 5, 1940.

(6) **Zella J.**[10]: born October 10, 1905; died July 11, 1988; married William Paul Brooks (born January 20, 1904) on January 1, 1925. William Brooks died April 11, 1976. Zella (Adams) and William Brooks had three children.

(1) **Williard Ira Brooks**: born January 22, 1928; married Joyce Manigonia (born June 26, 1926) on December 26, 1949. Williard and Joyce Brooks had six children.

(1) **Janice Elaine Brooks**: born March 21, 1951.
(2) **Carter Willard Brooks**: born February 21, 1953; died June 20, 1953.
(3) **Brenda Joyce Brooks**: born August 29, 1954.
(4) **Sheryln Sue Brooks**: born November 18, 1956.
(5) **Robert Willard Brooks**: born August 16, 1959.
(6) **Lynnette Yvonne Brooks**: born September 15, 1967.

(2) **Freda Maxine Brooks**: born June 29, 1931; married Stanley Ernest Dreher, Jr. (born April 27, 1926) on September 9, 1952. Freda and Stanley Dreher had two children.

(1) **Steven Paul Dreher**: born March 27, 1954; married Janet Lynn Scott (born June 1, 1957)

on October 21, 1978. Steven and Janet Dreher have two children.

> (1) **Jason Paul Dreher**: born January 21, 1981.
> (2) **Kristen Nicole Dreher**: born October 9, 1984.

(2) **Teresa Lynne Dreher**: born August 17, 1957; married Paul Eugene Hays (born September 19, 1950) on October 11, 1980. Teresa and Paul Hays have two children.

> (1) **Kasey Lynell Hays**: born March 26, 1982.
> (2) **Stephanie Jo Hays**: born December 26, 1984.

(3) **Wilber Willis Brooks**: born November 24, 1933; married twice, second time to Irene _____ (born August 12, 1928) on August 8, 1963. Two sons from a previous marriage were adopted into this marriage.

> (1) **Ward Paul Brooks**: born June 6, 1961.
> (2) **Timothy Willis Brooks**: born October 11, 1962.

Wilber and Irene Brooks had two daughters.

> (1) **Shelia Maxine Brooks**: born December 29, 1964.
> (2) **Sharon Melissa Brooks**: born April 4, 1969.

(4) **EDWARD J.**[9]: born October 25, 1864, at Blue Mound, Kansas; married, first, Hattie Burkhead, and second, Della Colyer; made his home near Wesley Chapel, Kansas; died in 1926. Edward and Hattie had no children. Edward and Della Adams had four children.

> (1) **Jay**[10]:
> (2) **Leta**[10]: married T.J. Rawie. Leta (Adams) and T.J. Rawie had two children.
>> (1) A baby boy who died in infancy.
>> (2) **Mary Elizabeth Rawie**:
> (3) **Lloyd**[10]:
> (4) **Estel**[10]:

In addition, Edward and Della raised Addie, Della's daughter and Edward's step-daughter.

During a trip to Mound City, Kansas, in August 1991, the author met a Mr. John Barnes who identified himself as a shirt-tail relative to the Adams family, as he was descended from the Burkhead family. He told a story, substantially confirmed by other family sources, that the marriage between Edward Adams and Hattie Burkhead lasted only one day. It seems that Hattie's father was afraid she would become an old maid. To avoid this, he arranged the marriage and saw that it happened. After only one night, Edward delivered his bride of one day back to her parents, presumably at her insistence. She resumed use of her maiden name and never remarried.

(5) IRA GUY[9]: born August 3, 1867, near Mansfield, Kansas; married, first, Ella Mae Ellington on December 24, 1889, and second, Mina Hunter; made his home near Wesley Chapel, Kansas, where he farmed. Ella Mae is the daughter of Isaac Millard and Sarah (Evans) Ellington. Ella Mae Adams died May 10, 1912. Guy, as he preferred to be called, was remarried in late 1912 to Mina Hunter. There were no children to this second marriage. Guy died December 10, 1934, at Fort Scott, Kansas. He is buried at the Wesley Chapel Cemetery with his first wife, Ella Mae.

IRA GUY ADAMS

This picture, taken about 1895, shows Ira Guy Adams and his first wife, Ella Mae (Ellington) Adams with their first son, Ralph Vernon Adams. Ella mae died in 1912 and Ira Guy remarried.

Guy and Ella Mae Adams had two children.

(1) **Ralph Vernon**[10]: born September 27, 1890; married Ethel Louise McGrew on January 2, 1912, at Mound City, Kansas; died May 15, 1968, at Garnett, Kansas. Ethel McGrew was born January 14, 1890, near Blue Mound, Kansas. She died April 16, 1970, at Fort Scott, Kansas. Ethel was the daughter of Emmet Logan and Emma Jane (Johnson) McGrew. Ralph Vernon and Ethel Adams had three children.

(1) **Ella Mae**[11]: born March 30, 1913, near Centerville, Kansas; married Ralph Lester Rigdon on March 4, 1931, at Greeley, Kansas. Ralph Rigdon was born May 5, 1902, near Greeley, Kansas. He was the son of William Everet and Eunice Louise (Martin) Rigdon. Ralph Lester Rigdon died April 6, 1982, at Kansas City, Kansas. Ella Mae (Adams) and Ralph Rigdon had four children.

(1) **Edna Mae Rigdon**: born February 8, 1935; married Morris Orland Allen on November 25, 1955, in Mound City, Kansas. Edna Mae and Morris Allen have four children.

(1) **Helen Louise Allen**: born September 14, 1956; married Charles Mattox; has three children.

(2) **Susan Ann Allen**: born March 22, 1959; married Siavash N. Meshkat (full given name is Seyyed Siavash Navadeh Meshkat Divan), a native of Lungarood, Guilan County, Iran; has two children.

(3) **Mark Lester Allen**: born December 19, 1960; married Debra Sue Thornton. Mark and Debra Allen have one son.

(1) **Mathew Aaron Allen**: born November 7, 1990, at Overland Park, Kansas.

(4) **David McKinley Allen**: born June 30, 1965; married Linda Kay Taylor. David and Linda Allen have one son.

(1) **Eric Morris Allen**: born March 22, 1991.

(2) **Verl LeRoy Rigdon**: born December 20, 1939, near Centerville, Kansas; married Laurel Ann Walder on March 3, 1959, at Oswatomie, Kansas. Verl and Laurel Rigdon had one son.

(1) **Keith Eugene Rigdon**: born December 20, 1959.

Verl and Laurel were divorced. Verl then married Judith Ann Melton. Verl and Judith have three children.

(1) **Sheiliy Sue Rigdon**: born March 29, 1967.

(2) **Scott Edward Rigdon**: born October 11, 1970.

(3) **Angela Marie Rigdon**: born April 11, 1973.

(3) **Harry Lewis Rigdon**: born January 17, 1945, near Centerville, Kansas; married Cynthia Ann Mahaffie on April 7, 1972. Cynthia was born September 26, 1946, in Olathe, Kansas. Harry and Cynthia Rigdon have two children.

    (1) **Jacob Lee Rigdon**: born February 18, 1973, in Olathe, Kansas.

    (2) **JoAnn Renne Rigdon**: born March 1, 1975, in Olathe Kansas.

(4) **Ethel Louis Rigdon**: born October 30, 1948, near Centerville, Kansas; married Donald Lee Cummings on June 8, 1968, in Emporia, Kansas. Ethel and Donald Cummings had one daughter.

    (1) **Vickie Charlene Cummings**: born January 10, 1970, in Emporia, Kansas.

Ethel and Donald were divorced. Ethel married, second, Junior Jones, but was later divorced and now lives, unmarried, under her maiden name.

(2) **Jennie Irene**[11]: born April 8, 1921, near Centerville, Kansas; married Earl J. McGee on September 7, 1939, at Mound City, Kansas; died June 13, 1987, at Springfield, Missouri. Earl McGee was the son of Carl and Rettie McGee. He was born August 28, 1915, near Centerville, Kansas. He died September 6, 1988, at Fort Scott, Kansas. Both Jennie and Earl McGee are buried at Wesley Chapel. Jennie Irene (Adams) and Earl McGee had eight children.

    (1) **Rettie Jean McGee**: born November 6, 1940, near Centerville, Kansas; married Kenneth Lee Weeks on October 23, 1964. Kenneth Weeks had four children from a previous marriage. They are Kenneth Wayne, Jerry Lee, Amy Louise, and Rose Ann Bess Weeks. Rettie and Kenneth Weeks have one daughter.

        (1) **Rettie Jaylene Weeks**:

    (2) **Vernon Earl McGrew McGee**: born October 7, 1945, near Centerville, Kansas; married, first, Della Mae Rickers. Vernon and Della McGee had two children.

        (1) **Charoletta May McGee**: born in 1972.

        (2) **Richard Earl McGee**: born June 19, 1973.

Vernon was married a second time, and later divorced.

    (3) **Brenda Kay McGee**: born August 8, 1950, in Fort Scott, Kansas; married, first, Fred Gerald Kinard on September 7, 1969, at Mound City,

Kansas; and second to Rick Graves. Brenda and Fred Kinard had two children.

> (1) **Rachel Natasha Kinard**: born October 28, 1972.
>
> (2) **Karen Monica Kinard**: born May 27, 1976.

(4) **Candy Sue McGee**: born March 23, 1953, at Fort Scott, Kansas; married Marvin David Bergeman; has two children, both born at Fort Scott.

> (1) **Aaron Eugene Bergeman**: born July 2, 1974.
>
> (2) **Cara Dionne Marie Bergeman**: born September 29, 1976.

(5) **Wayne Arlo McGee**: born August 28, 1955, in Fort Scott, Kansas; married Brenda Lee Bonner on August 16, 1980; has two children.

> (1) **Stephanie Amber McGee**: born August 1982.
>
> (2) **Andrea Janelle McGee**: born in 1984.

(6) **Larry Lewis McGee**: born October 8, 1958, in Fort Scott, Kansas; married Vicky Marie Lovett on May 27, 1984. Larry and Vicky have two children.

> (1) **Lauren Elizabeth McGee**: born January 29, 1990.
>
> (2) **Anna Victoria McGee**: born August 31, 1993.

(7) **Jane Rolleen McGee**: born February 7, 1961, in Fort Scott, Kansas; married Perry Townsend on July 15, 1989; has one child.

> (1) **Adam Michael Townsend**: born September 27, 1990.

(8) **Gary Dean McGee**: born August 13, 1963, in Fort Scott, Kansas; married Ellen Louise Ayers on June 9, 1990; has one son.

> (1) **Andrew Ray McGee**: born February 9, 1991.

(3) **Bernal McGrew**[11]: born August 8, 1924, near Centerville, Kansas; married, first, Donna Harper (later divorced), and second, Lola Bell Rook. Bernal is the father of one daughter.

> (1) **Diana**[12]: born January 15, 1949, in Fort Scott, Kansas. Diana Adams is not married.

(2) **Lester Don**[10]: married, first, Louise _____, second, Velma _____, and was believed to have been married a third time but the name of the wife is not known. Lester Adams was the father of one daughter.

> (1) **Donna**[11]:

(6) **DAISY**[9]: born October 30, 1869, near Mansfield, Kansas; married Albert B. Ashbaugh; made her home in Los Angeles, California; had one daughter.

    (1) **Hazel Ashbaugh**: married William Thompson; had three children.

        (1) **Betty Thompson**:
        (2) **Herbert Thompson**: married Rhoda _____.
        (3) **William Thompson**:

(7) **BRUCE B.**[9]: born November 2, 1873; married, first, Daisy Hinkle, and second, Leta _____; made his home in Hastings, Oklahoma. Bruce and Daisy Adams had one son.

    (1) **Bruce**[10],**Jr.**:
Bruce Adams and his second wife, Leta, had two children.
    (1) **Paul**[10]:
    (2) **Marjorie**[10]:

THE ADAMS FAMILY

This enlargement of a small portion of a picture of the Adams home near Mound City, Kansas, includes eight of the ten children of John Quincy[8] and Sarah Jane Adams. From left to right: Daisy, Ira Guy, John Q., Sarah Jane (mother of the eight shown), Ida Belle, Maro Melvin, Don Leon, Robert Clyde, and Myrtle.

(8) DON LEON^9: born December 19, 1876, near Mansfield, Kansas; died April 7, 1939; married Grace Petras Woodward on September 15, 1906; made his home in Santa Ana, California. Lee, as he was known most of his life, and Grace Adams had two children.

    (1) **Dorothy^{10}**: married _____ Brown; had no children.

    (2) **Don Leon^{10}, Jr.**: married Ella _____; had two children.

        (1) **Douglas^{11}**:

        (2) **Cynthia^{11}**:

(9) MYRTLE MAY^9: born August 10, 1881, near Mound City, Kansas; married Walter McRae (born September 1, 1874) on February 20, 1901; made their home near Mound City, Kansas. Walter McRae was a farmer and a stockman. Myrtle helped on the farm and served many neighbors as a midwife. Myrtle (Adams) and Walter McRae had five children.

    (1) **Velma Helen McRae**: born December 7, 1901; died January 7, 1902.

    (2) **Carl A. McRae**: born December 25, 1902; married Glenna Driskill (born July 18, 1902) on May 19, 1926; died October 1, 1963. Glenna died August 21, 1989. Carl and Glenna McRae had four children.

        (1) **Wanda Marie McRae**: born April 27, 1928; married Norman Kirk on July 22, 1952. Wanda and Norman were divorced in 1958. They had no children.

        (2) **Roy Eldon McRae**: born July 22, 1929; married Ferne Lucille Hobson (born April 23, 1929) on June 6, 1948. Roy and Ferne McRae have one son.

            (1) **Larry Eldon McRae**: married Georgia Dawn Grant (born November 4, 1951) on July 8, 1972. Larry and Georgia McRae have an adopted son.

                (1) **Timothy Grant McRae**: born May 15, 1990.

        (3) **Leo D. McRae**: born May 14, 1932; married Margaret Hatch (born January 30, 1932) on February 25, 1951. Leo and Margaret McRae have two children.

            (1) **Vicky Ellen McRae**: born June 27, 1953; married Joe David Flemming (born December 27, 1947) on November 27, 1971. Vicky and Joe Flemming have two children.

                (1) **Eric David Flemming**: born February 11, 1973.

                (2) **John Kevin Flemming**: born January 20, 1977.

            (2) **Ricky Leo McRae**: born October 11, 1957; married, first, Donna Burnitt on January 21, 1976, and second, Norman Sue (Cook) Berger. Ricky McRae has no children.

        (4) **Hilma Louise McRae**: born April 8, 1934; married Franklin Benton Brassfield (born July 6, 1935) on December 14, 1954. Hilma and Franklin Brassfield have two children.

(1) **Lois Elaine Brassfield**: born August 3, 1957; married William Shannon Black on July 18, 1974. Lois and William Black had eight children.

    (1) **Shannon Jason Black**: born May 14, 1976.

    (2) **Tiara Karen Black**: born March 20, 1978; died June 27, 1978.

    (3) **Cassandra Aaron Black**: born August 8, 1980.

    (4) **Ariel Kristin Black**: born July 11, 1983.

    (5) **Andria Breann Black**: born February 12, 1985.

    (6) **Kimberly Rachel Black**: born July 5, 1986.

    (7) **Devin Bradley Black**: born October 8, 1987.

    (8) **David Nathan Black**: born May 10, 1989.

(2) **Louise Mae Brassfield**: born February 7, 1961; married Scott Jenks in August 1977. Louise and Scott were divorced May 22, 1979. They had no children.

(3) **Ruby D. McRae**: born January 7, 1905; married Homer Nelson McDowell (born July 8, 1906) on February 19, 1930. Ruby and Homer McDowell had one son.

    (1) **Harold Lee McDowell**: born December 22, 1930; married first, Rosalyn Heck, and second, Barbara Emens (born April 7, 1939) on June 26, 1959. Harold and Barbara McDowell have two adopted children.

        (1) **Cathie Lynne McDowell**: born July 19, 1964; married Frank Infrancas on September 24, 1988. Cathie and Frank Infrancas have one daughter.

            (1) **Annie Michell Infrancas**: born July 14, 1989.

        (2) **Peggie Ann McDowell**: born March 30, 1968; married Quincy Martin Long (born February 19, 1966) on August 19, 1989.

(4) **Walter Earl McRae**: born June 1, 1911; married Elma Paddock (born May 29, 1912) on February 26, 1939; died July 19, 1988. Walter and Elma McRae had four children.

    (1) **Anna Louise McRae**: born March 31, 1941; married Ivor K. Davis in November 1967. Anna is now divorced. Anna and Ivor Davis had one child.

        (1) **Ivor K. Davis, II**: born March 12, 1968.

    (2) **Alice Elaine McRae**: born November 3, 1944; married Steven McClain (born August 24, 1947) on October 8, 1966. Alice and Steven McClain have two children.

        (1) **Tammie Sue McClain**: born March 23, 1967; married Marvin Lloyd Starkey on May 17, 1986. Tammie and Marvin Starkey have two children.

(1) **Jean Elaine Starkey**: born May 3, 1987.
(2) **Christopher James Starkey**: born May 30, 1989.
(2) **Steven Todd McClain**: born February 26, 1972.
(3) **Althea Marie McRae**: born September 4, 1946; married Kenneth Wallace (born June 27, 1947) on June 29, 1968. Althea and Kenneth Wallace have two children.
(1) **Michael Shannon Wallace**: born June 8, 1971.
(2) **Brian Lee Wallace**: born December 1, 1974.
(4) **Avis Mae McRae**: born August 4, 1951; married Richard Greenstreet (born March 16, 1945) on January 21, 1978. Richard brought a daughter, Sonya, into this marriage.
(5) **Mable May McRae**: born March 12, 1919; married Leo Brownback (born June 21, 1914) on May 2, 1943. After graduating from high school in 1937, Mable found work in Mound City at the Farm Security Office. She also worked in a restaurant for awhile before marrying Leo Brownback. After marrying Leo, who was a farmer and stockman, Mable had plenty to do at the home place and did not work away from the farm again. Mable and Leo Brownback have three children.
(1) **Loyd Allen Brownback**: born January 28, 1946; married Linda Sue Roberts (born May 21, 1948) on January 22, 1967. Loyd has worked for General Motors in Kansas City for many years. He also owns a farm and works it, just to stay busy. Loyd and Linda Brownback have two children.
(1) **Michelle Lyn Brownback**: born January 31, 1970.
(2) **John Allen Brownback**: born December 26, 1972.
(2) **Herbert Leo Brownback**: born October 22, 1949; married Mary Lou McNabb (born May 15, 1952) on January 29, 1972. Herbert has worked for Kansas City Power and Light for a number of years. He farms and raises some cattle on the side. Herbert and Mary Brownback have two children.
(1) **Chad Michael Brownback**: born January 30, 1976.
(2) **Christopher Leo Brownback**: born December 23, 1980.
(3) **Lois May Brownback**: born March 27, 1954; married Dale R. Wright (born July 8, 1950) on May 17, 1975. For a time Lois worked at the Linn County Courthouse in Mound City, only about seven miles from the Adams place. Lois and Dale Wright have two children.
(1) **Jason Dale Wright**: born December 1, 1980.
(2) **Melissa Ann Wright**: born July 26, 1983.

**(10) ROBERT CLYDE[9]: born March 16, 1885, near Mound City, Kansas; died October 17, 1955; married, first, Hattie Mapes on September 16, 1909, and second, Bertha Gladys Clark on September 19, 1919; made his home on the family farm near Mound City, Kansas. Robert Clyde and Hattie Adams had three daughters.

    (1) **Juanita Lenore[10]**: born September 5, 1910; married Earnest W. Rigdon on December 25, 1933. Juanita and Earnest had no children. Earnest Rigdon is the brother of Ralph Lester Rigdon who married Ella Mae Adams, daughter of Ralph Vernon Adams and grand-daughter of Ira Guy Adams. Ira Guy Adams is the brother of Robert Clyde Adams described in this chapter.

    (2) **Madeline[10]: born October 22, 1913; married Charles Edward Whitehead on July 26, 1936; had three daughters.

    (3) **Myrtle Helen[10]**: born November 19, 1915; married Clyde L. Bearly on March 4, 1939; had two children.

Robert Clyde and his second wife, Bertha Gladys (Clark) Adams had five children.

    (1) **Robert Clark[10]**: died young.

    (2) **Howard Marvin[10]**: born February 18, 1922; married Claire Luethe; had two children.

    (3) **Barbara Jane[10]**: born December 15, 1924, married Robert Dargatz on March 10, 1951. Barbara and Bob have no children.

    (4) **Mary Louise[10]**: born May 26, 1929; married James Stanley Buck on June 22, 1947.

    (5) **David Edward[10]**: born November 5, 1932; married Darlene (Ross) Munsen.

The locations where the children of John Quincy and Sarah Jane Adams lived were taken from the writ of partition ordering distribution of their father's estate following his death.

John Quincy Adams starting acquiring land in Paris Township, northwest of Mound City, Kansas, sometime after 1860. The earliest deed the author could locate for property in this area was dated in 1867. It is identified as the north east 1/4 of section 27 in Township 21, Range 23. Local tax records indicate he paid taxes on this same parcel which was purchased in 1867 in 1865. No explanation for this discrepancy has been found. It is believed that Mr. Adams moved to this location in 1866. The Adams house, built before 1870, still stands on this parcel in Paris township.

John Quincy continued to acquire land in the area until 1891, only two years before his death. By that time he had acquired a total of 1034 acres, not including the 160 acres at Blue Mound, which was sold by then.

John Quincy Adams farmed his lands and raised cattle. He was a breeder of short-horn cattle and the fine quality of his stock was well known in the area.

JOHN QUINCY AND SARAH JANE (WILSON) ADAMS
This picture of John Quincy Adams was taken in Pleasanton, Kansas, probably just a year or two before his death

John Quincy Adams died unexpectedly at his home on October 13, 1893. The cause of death was heart failure. He left no will.

A civil action concerning the disposition of the estate resulted in a writ of partition under which half of the estate was awarded to Sarah Jane Adams, the surviving spouse, and half was divided among the ten children. Sarah Jane retained the house and the property it occupied. The court also ordered that all personal property, including the furniture and the farm implements, be disposed of so that each of the ten children received an equal share.

Sarah Jane Adams continued to live on and operate the farm after the death of her husband. She retained a total of 460 acres plus the land the house, barns, and other out-buildings. As the remainder of her children grew up, married, and left home, Sarah Jane became dependent upon her youngest son, Robert Clyde Adams, to care for her and the home place. Robert Clyde married and continued to live on and work the farm, in addition to working the parcel he obtained following his father's death.

THE PARIS TOWNSHIP HOME OF JOHN QUINCY ADAMS

This picture, dated January 27, 1912, shows Sarah Jane (Wilson) Adams, seated, with her granddaughter, Juanita. Juanita's mother, Hattie (Mapes) Adams, is in the left rear. The girl in the right rear is probably a housekeeper.

Sarah Jane Adams died December 15, 1920. Although, through her will and a codicil to the will, Sarah Jane tried to direct a larger share of her estate to Robert Clyde and his wife, a civil action was successful in forcing division of her estate equally among her ten children.

John Quincy and Sarah Jane Adams are buried at the Wesley Chapel Cemetery between Centerville and Mound City on land immediately adjacent to some of their own land. The Wesley Chapel church is located on a corner of a quarter section owned at that time by John Quincy Adams. The church still occupies five acres retained in perpetuity for its use.

THE ADAMS HOUSE TODAY
Located about seven miles northwest of Mound City, Kansas
Picture taken by the author, August 28, 1991

THE TOMBSTONE OF JOHN QUINCY AND SARAH JANE ADAMS
Wesley Chapel Cemetery

SCHOOL EXAMINER'S CERTIFICATE.

The State of Ohio, Coshocton County---ss.

We, the Subscribers, Examiners of Common Schools in and for said County, having diligently examined *J. Q. Adams*, as to *his* qualifications to teach a Common School, do certify, that we find *him* qualified to teach Spelling, Reading, Writing, & Arithmetic,

And we do also certify, that *he* is proved to us to be of a good moral character.

Witness our hands and seals this *5th* day of *December* A. D. 18*48*.

This certificate to be valid for six months —

Wm Joseph **LS**

R. C. Bryan **LS**

Thos Campbell **LS**

SCHOOL EXAMINER'S CERTIFICATE

This is a copy of the first teaching certificate issued to John Quincy Adams on December 5, 1848, at Coshocton County, Ohio. It is of some interest that it was only valid for a period of six months and that it included language attesting to the moral character of the individual being certified.

J. W. [illegible]

Be it remembered, that on the 21st day of January in the year of our Lord one thousand eight hundred and fifty Six the following marriage license was issued by the Clerk of the Decatur Circuit Court, to=wit:

State of Indiana, Decatur County, Sct: The State of Indiana to any person empowered by law to solemnize marriages in said county, Greeting: You are hereby duly authorized to join together as husband and wife John Q. Adams and Sarah Jane Wilson

In testimony whereof, I, Henry A. Talbott clerk of the Decatur Circuit Court, have hereunto set my hand, and affixed the seal of said court, at Greensburg this 21st day of January A.D. 1856.

Henry A. Talbott Clerk.

And afterwards, to=wit: on the 25th day of January in the year of our Lord one thousand eight hundred and 56, W. W. Hibben returned to and filed in the office of the clerk of said court the following certificate, to=wit:

State of Indiana, Decatur county, Sct: I, W. W. Hibben Minister of the Gospel in said county, do certify that on the 22° day of January 1856, I joined together as husband and wife John Q. Adams and Sarah Jane Wilson

Given under my hand this 23° day of January 1856.

W. W. Hibben

MARRIAGE LICENSE FOR
JOHN QUINCY ADAMS AND SARAH JANE WILSON
WHO WERE MARRIED JANUARY 22, 1856, AT
GREENSBURG, INDIANA

THE STATE OF KANSAS, } ss.
LINN COUNTY.

In the Probate Court, in and for said County.

In the Matter of the Estate of

John Q. Adams

Late of said County, Deceased.

On this _27_ day of _October_, A. D. 18_93_, personally appeared before me, the undersigned, Judge of the said Court, _Ed J. Adams_, who, being by me duly sworn according to law, doth upon his oath depose and say, that _John Q. Adams_ died on the _13_ day of _October_ A. D. 18_93_, at _Linn_, County, and state aforesaid; that to the best of his knowledge and belief the names and places of residence of the heirs of said deceased, are as follows, to-wit:

Sarah J. Adams, widow. Paris Township   _Ira Guy Adams. Centerville Township Linn Co. Kans,_
John Q Adams Jr Dolores, Colorado   _Daisy Ashbaugh_   "   "   "   "   "
Ida B. Chitwood. Paris Township Linn Co. Kans, _Bruce Burns. Adams_   "   "
Mard. Melvin Adams. Kincaid. Anderson Co.   " _Don Leon Adams Paris Township_ "   "
Ed J. Adams   Paris Township Linn   "   _Myrtle May Adams_   "   "   "   "   "
                                                  Robert Clyde Adams   "   "   "   "   "

and that the deceased died without a will, as affiant verily believes.

                                                      Ed J. Adams

Subscribed and Sworn to before me, on the day and year first above written.

                                        Jacob Brynmore
Filed _October 27_ A. D. 18_93_   Probate Judge.

**PROBATE CERTIFICATE FOR
JOHN QUINCY ADAMS WHO DIED OCTOBER 13, 1893
This certificate is particularly helpful because
it provides the names and places of residence of all
the heirs of the deceased.**

Sarah Jane Wilson was the daughter of John Dickson and Sarah (Foster) Wilson. She married John Quincy Adams at Greensburg, Indiana, on January 22, 1856. Sarah Jane is believed to have met her husband while attending a girls school in Greensburg where John Quincy Adams was teaching.

Sarah Jane Wilson's known ancestry is illustrated here.

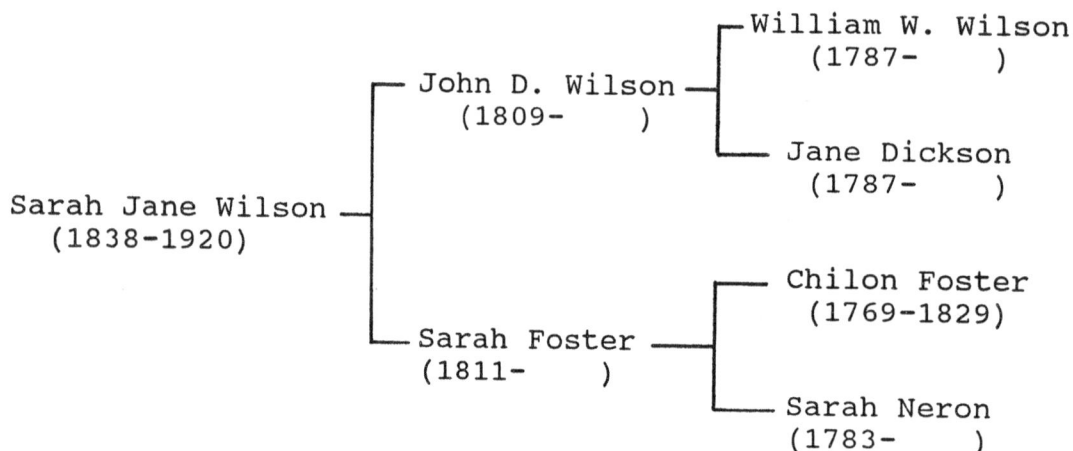

```
                                          ┌─William W. Wilson
                                          │     (1787-    )
                      ┌─ John D. Wilson ──┤
                      │      (1809-    )   │
                      │                    └── Jane Dickson
                      │                          (1787-    )
Sarah Jane Wilson ────┤
   (1838-1920)        │
                      │                    ┌── Chilon Foster
                      │                    │     (1769-1829)
                      └── Sarah Foster ────┤
                             (1811-   )    │
                                           └── Sarah Neron
                                                 (1783-    )
```

William W. Wilson, Sarah Jane Wilson's paternal grandfather, was born in Washington County, Virginia, September 24, 1787. While still in Washington County he married Jane Dickson on February 16, 1809. She was born July 2, 1787. William and Jane Wilson must have moved to Indiana shortly after marrying, as all ten of their children were born in Franklin County, Indiana.

(1) **John Dickson Wilson: born December 19, 1809, Married Sarah Foster on September 22, 1830.
  (2) **Catherine Wilson**: born August 20, 1811.
  (3) **Hannah Wison**: born October 27, 1812.
  (4) **Jane Wilson**: born August 17, 1815.
  (5) **Rachel Wilson**: born October 27, 1816.
  (6) **William D. Wilson**: born January 5, 1818.
  (7) **Edith Wilson**: born December 2, 1819.
  (8) **Darby Wilson**: born July 28, 1821.
  (9) **Arthur D. Wilson**: born September 24, 1823.
 (10) **Mahala D. Wilson**: born December 10, 1827.

Jane (Dickson) Wilson died sometime before 1840. On February 9, 1840, William Wilson married Serena Mock. William and Serena had two children.

(1) **Nancy Ann Wilson**: born August 7, 1841.
(2) **Desdemona Wilson**: born February 19, 1844.

No earlier information is offered on the history of the Dickson or Wilson families as the parents of William Wilson and Jane Dickson have not been identified.

John Dickson Wilson, the first child of William and Jane Wilson, was born in Franklin County, Indiana, and lived his entire life there. He is believed to be buried near his birthplace.

On September 22, 1830, John Dickson Wilson married Sarah Foster. Sarah was a native of Decatur County, Indiana. John and Sarah Wilson had eight children.

(1) **Serepta**: born September 12, 1831; married Thomas Lindsey Burke. Serepta and Thomas Burke had eleven children. One of these, daughter Ada May, married Edward Clark and had daughter Bertha Gladys Clark. Bertha Clark would become the second wife of Robert Clyde Adams, son of John Quincy Adams and Serepta's sister, Sarah Jane Wilson.
(2) **Chilon J.**: born October 2, 1833.
(3) **Milton Merrick**: born February 23, 1836.
(4) **Sarah Jane: born June 24, 1838; married John Quincy Adams on January 22, 1856.
(5) **William Leonidas**: born January 15, 1841.
(6) **Olney Foster**: born August 29, 1846.
(7) **Albert Franklin**: born February 18, 1850.
(8) **Leonora**: born March 6, 1857.

When John Dickson Wilson died has not been learned, but his wife survived him. Following her husband's death, Sarah Wilson moved to Linn County, Kansas, to live with her daughter, Sarah Jane (Wilson) Adams, who had married John Quincy Adams and moved west. Sarah (Foster) Wilson died sometime after 1893 and is buried in the Adams family plot at the Wesley Chapel Cemetery near Centerville, Kansas.

Sarah Foster's parents were Chilon and Sarah (Neron) Foster. Chilon Foster was living in Brookville Township, Franklin County, Indiana, in 1820. The census for that year lists his business to be manufacturing. Chilon Foster, born February 16, 1769, first married Hannah Lucas, who was born August 7, 1770. They had six children.

(1) **Samuel Foster**: born April 1, 1792.
(2) **Lydia Foster**: born September 7, 1794.
(3) **John M. Foster**: born January 19, 1797.
(4) **Elizabeth Foster**: born March 9, 1798.
(5) **Hannah Foster**: born January 18, 1801.
(6) **Louisa Foster**: born August 23, 1803.

What happened to Chilon Foster's first wife is not known, but he later married Sarah Neron. Chilon and Sarah Foster also had six children.

(1) **Mary Foster**: born February 29, 1808.
(2) **Rebecca Foster**: born August 14, 1809.
(3) **Sarah Foster: born April 21, 1811; married John Dickson Wilson; died after 1893.
(4) **Beulah Foster**: born November 28, 1813.
(5) **Chilon Foster**: born December 19, 1816.
(6) **John Lest Foster**: born September 27, 1818.

No earlier ancestry for Chilon Foster or Sarah Neron is known as their parents have not been identified. Chilon Foster's will has been obtained and a copy of a transcription is provided.

The biographical information concerning Sarah Jane Wilson, daughter of John D. Wilson and Sarah Foster and wife of John Quincy[8] Adams, is contained in the chapter for her husband.

STATE OF KANSAS
State Board of Health—Division of Vital Statistics

STANDARD
CERTIFICATE OF DEATH

Do not write

54 1474

in this space

1 PLACE OF DEATH: County _Linn_

Township
or _Paris_
City

Registered No. _____

No.
(If death occurred in a hospital or institution, give its NAME instead of street and number) St., _____ Ward

2 FULL NAME _Sarah Jane Adams_

(a) Residence. No. _____ St., _____ Ward.
(Usual place of abode)
Length of residence in city or town where death occurred _____ yrs. _____ mos. _____ ds. How long in U. S., if of foreign birth? _____ yrs. _____ mos. _____ ds.
(If nonresident give city or town and state)

PERSONAL AND STATISTICAL PARTICULARS

3 SEX	4 COLOR OR RACE	5 Single, Married, Widowed, or Divorced (write the word)
Female	_White_	_Widowed_

5a If married, widowed, or divorced
HUSBAND of
(or) WIFE of _J. L. Adams_

6 DATE OF BIRTH (month, day, and year) _____

7 AGE

Years	Months	Days	If LESS than 1 day, _____ hrs. or _____ min.
82	5	21	

8 OCCUPATION OF DECEASED
(a) Trade, profession, or particular kind of work _Housewife_
(b) General nature of industry, business, or establishment in which employed (or employer) _____
(c) Name of employer _____

9 BIRTHPLACE (city or town) _Greensburg_
Ind
(State or country)

10 NAME OF FATHER _J. D. Wilson_

11 BIRTHPLACE OF FATHER (city or town) _____
Indiana
(State or country)

12 MAIDEN NAME OF MOTHER _Sarah Foster_

13 BIRTHPLACE OF MOTHER (city or town) _____
Indiana
(State or country)

14 Informant _J. L. Adams_
(Address) _Mound City - Ks_

15 Filed _____ 19 _____ _Emory C. Oliver_
Registrar

MEDICAL CERTIFICATE OF DEATH

16 DATE OF DEATH (month, day, and year) _Dec. 15_ 19_20_

17 I HEREBY CERTIFY, That I attended deceased from
October 14/20, 19_20_, to _Dec. 15_, 19_20_,
that I last saw h___ alive on _Dec. 15_, 19_20_,
and that death occurred, on the date stated above, at _2 P.m._
The CAUSE OF DEATH was as follows:
Aortic Stenosis.

(79)

(duration) yrs. _1_ mos. _18_ ds.

CONTRIBUTORY
(Secondary) _____
(duration) yrs. _____ mos. _____ ds.

18 Where was disease contracted
if not at place of death? _____
Did an operation precede death? _____ Date of _____
Was there an autopsy? _none_
What test confirmed diagnosis? _____
(Signed) _Dr. C. L. Leeper_ M.D.
_____, 19 (Address) _Mound City Kansas_

* State the DISEASE CAUSING DEATH, or in deaths from VIOLENT CAUSES, state (1) MEANS AND NATURE OF INJURY, and (2) whether ACCIDENTAL, SUICIDAL, or HOMICIDAL. (See reverse side for additional space.)

19 PLACE OF BURIAL, CREMATION, OR REMOVAL	DATE OF BURIAL
Wesley Chapel	_Dec 17, 1920_
20 UNDERTAKER _Henry J. Woodcy_	ADDRESS _Mound City_

DEATH CERTIFICATE FOR
SARAH JANE (WILSON) ADAMS

THE WILL OF CHILON FOSTER

* *

The following transcription of the will of Chilon Foster was made from a copy of the original obtained from the Franklin Circuit Court in Brookville, Indiana. The will is recorded in Book B, Page 47, of the 1830 records.

* *

State of Indiana
Franklin County

        Be it remembered that on the 16th day of January AD 1830 Personally Appeared before me Enoch McCarty clerk of the Franklin Circuit Court for the county aforesaid William Sims Sue Simpson Jones and Andrew Carmichal the subscribing Witnefses to the Last Will and Testament of Chilon Foster and being duly sworn depose and say that the said Chilon Foster signed sealed and published and declaired the within and foregoing Will in writing in thier presence to be his true Last Will and Testament that the said Chilon Foster was the time of signing sealing publishing and declaring there of as aforesaid of sound mind memory and understanding and that they signed their names there to as subscribing witnefses in his presence and in the presence of each other In testimony where of I have hereunto set my hand the day of year first above written.

                                        Enoch Mc Carty clk FCC

        The record and copy of which will follow in these words and figures to with In the Name of God Amen I Chilon Foster of the County of Franklin State of Indiana being sick and weak in body but of sound mind memory and understanding praised be God for it an considering the certainty of death and the uncertainty of the time there of and to the end I may be the better prepared to leave this workld whenever it shall please God to call me hence, Do make and declare this my Last Will and Testament in manner and form following, that is to say, first and principally I commend my soul into the hands of almighty God who gave it, and my Body to the Earth at the discretion of my Executor herein after named - And as to the worldly Estate where with it has pleased God to Intrust me, I dispose of as follows to wit, first my will is that all my Just Debts as Shall be by me owing at my death together with my funeral Expenses and all things touching the proving of or any [   ] concerning the the carrying into complete effect this may Last Will and Testament be in the fist place out of my personal estate fully paid and satisfied and after payment there of and subject there unto, my will that all the residue of my personal estate be sold as the law directs and equally divided amongst my ten children that is to say that portion which would descend to Lyda Schofield I will and bequeath to her children in equal parts and not, to her, and my daughters.

Chilon Foster

Elizabeth Alyea, Loisey Patterson Hannah Morgan Mary Hammond Rebecca Foster Sarah Foster & Buley Foster to gether with my two sons Chilon Foster and John T. Foster Receive the balance in equal parts as they become of age reserving to my beloved wife Sarah Foster her Legacy in said personal estate allowed her by law of the said State of Indiana, and as to my Real Estate I will and bequeath to my beloved wife Sarah Foster my houses where I now live together with all the Lands to which I have the legal title on that side of Snail Creek where the house aforesaid stand and attached to said house together with all the Lands to which I have the legal title lying between my Mill Race and the West fork of White Water all during her Natural lifetime, And as to my Mills together with with all the rest of my Lands to which I may have the legal title at my death I wish sold and the proceeds thereof equally divided amongst all my children as aforesaid making the same reserve as to Lyda Schofield as aforesaid and making the same allowance to her children as aforesaid, Except that Quarter Section of Land which was formerly held equal between William Powers Decsd and myself high up on said Snail Creek which I give and bequeath unto my two Sons Chilon Foster and John T. Foster which shall descend to them for ever, and at the death of my wife Sarah

Chilon Foster

Foster all that portion left her by virtue of this my Last Will and Testament my Will is that it all be sold and equally divided as aforesaid amongst all by Children making the same reserve as to Lyda Schofield as aforesaid And allowing her children the same as aforesaid and lastly I do hereby Appoint John Adair and Joseph Meeks of Brookville my Executors to prove and to carry into complete effect this my Last Will an Testament hereby revoking and hereby making void all other Wills by me heretofore at any time made in testimony where of I have here unto Set my hand at the bottom of the first and Second Page of this my Last Will and Testament containing three pages and my hand and Seal at the bottom the third page this sixteenth day of December in the year of of Lord one thousand eight hundred and twenty nine

Chilon Foster   Seal

Signed sealed and published
and declared in the presence
of us who at the said Fosters
Request and in his presence
subscribed our names as
witnefses
                    his
        Simpson X Jones
                    mark

A Carmichall
Wm Sims Junr

Whereupon John Adair and Joseph Meeks the Executors in the said
Will named take upon themselves the Execution of Said Will (on the
18th day of January 1830) to whom Letters Testamentary (with a copy
of the Will annexed) are granted by the undersigned Clerk of the
Franklin Circuit Court they having executed Bond with Security
according to law and were also sworn as such Executors this 18th
day of January AD 1830
                              Enoch McCarty Clk
Recorded January 19th 1830   FCC
paid $3.50

NINTH GENERATION

ROBERT CLYDE[9] ADAMS

Robert Clyde[9] Adams was born on his family's farm near Mound City, Linn County, Kansas, on March 16, 1885. He was the youngest of ten children born to John Quincy[8] and Sarah Jane (Wilson) Adams.

Robert Clyde was only eight years old when his father died of a heart attack. Although he completed the eighth grade, Robert Clyde spent most of his effort working on the family farm. He loved to work with livestock and took great pride in the quality of the animals raised on the Adams farm.

**ROBERT CLYDE AND HATTIE (MAPES) ADAMS
WITH THEIR FIRST CHILD, JUANITA,
ABOUT 1912**

On September 16, 1909, in Iola, Allen County, Kansas, Robert Clyde (or Clyde, as he preferred to be called) married Hattie Mapes. Hattie's given name is Harriet, although she adopted the name Hattie and used it throughout her lifetime. Clyde met Hattie at home, as she worked for the Adams' as a housekeeper - or as they called her, the "hired girl". Hattie was born in Centerville, Kansas, on April 8, 1883. After her marriage, she reported her birthdate to be April 8, 1885, and she used that date or the date April 12, 1885, throughout the rest of her lifetime. She apparently did this to hide the fact that she was older than her husband.

Clyde and Hattie lived with his mother on the family farm. They cared for Sarah Jane Adams and operated the farm much as if it were their own. The farm had been divided by a court ordered partition following the death of his father, John Quincy Adams, and each of the ten children of Sarah Jane Adams owned a portion of the original farm. Clyde was an outstanding stockman. He raised some of the finest stock in the area and pioneered new crops to provide the best feed for his stock.

Through her will and a codicil to her will, Sarah Jane Adams attempted to have all her children deed their portions of the farm back to Clyde following her death. This did not happen because Clyde's brothers and sisters chose to retain the land rightfully given them under the court ordered partitioning that took place earlier. It is apparent that Sarah Jane wanted to keep from further dividing her half of the original farm into small pieces. This was, no doubt, also an attempt to reward Robert Clyde for caring for her in her later years.

Perhaps no one could have predicted the hard times to come in the 1920's and 1930's, but the dust bowl, the mortgage which Robert Clyde was forced to take on the property in order to continue farming after the death of his mother, and some bad business luck eventually contributed to the loss of the farm in 1939.

Hattie (Mapes) Adams died December 6, 1918, from complications arising from the flu during a flu epidemic. It is ironic that she had nursed Clyde and Sarah Jane through the flu only to succumb to it herself. The grief of this event is touchingly told by Madeline, Hattie's second child, in an essay written many years later. That essay is included in the chapter entitled "Tenth Generation, Madeline Adams".

Robert Clyde and Hattie (Mapes) Adams had three daughters.

(1) **JUANITA LENORE**[10]: born September 5, 1910; married Earnest W. Rigdon on December 25, 1933. They made their home in La Junta, Colorado. Earnest died on February 25, 1992. Juanita and Earnest have no children.

JUANITA AND EARNEST RIGDON
1933

HELEN AND CLYDE BEARLY
1939

(2) MADELINE[10]: born October 22, 1913; married Charles Edward Whitehead on July 26, 1936, at Kansas City, Missouri; died March 31, 1994, at Orcutt, California. Charles Whitehead died on October 4, 1991, at Santa Maria, California. Madeline (Adams) and Charles Whitehead have three daughters:

(1) **Emma Lou Whitehead**: born August 8, 1941; married, first, Thomas Addicks Webb on January 1, 1963, and second, Alan L. Bargerstock, on December 31, 1992, both at Las Vegas, Nevada.

(2) **Judy Lee Whitehead**: born January 30, 1945; married, first, John Lewis Chance, Jr. on May 25, 1964, at Las Vegas, Nevada, second, George Goss Wood on July 25, 1976, at Sheldon, Missouri, and third, Steven Knowles on October 16, 1993, in Santa Maria, California.

(3) **Jane Ann Whitehead**: born January 30, 1945; married Kenneth Lloyd Bosworth on February 8, 1964, at Las Vegas, Nevada.

(3) MYRTLE HELEN[10]: born November 19, 1915. Helen, as she has been known all her life, married Clyde L. Bearly on March 4, 1939, at Alta Vista, Kansas. Clyde was born September 22, 1911, on his parent's farm at Centerville, Kansas. His parents are Cowan and Elsie (Zimmerman) Bearly. Clyde Bearly died September 19, 1993, at Joplin, Missouri. He is buried at the Sheldon Cemetery. Helen and Clyde Bearly lived and farmed at Sheldon, Missouri. They have two children.

(1) **Mary Lynett Bearly**: born September 16, 1942, at a farm home northwest of Mound City, Kansas; married Earl Gene Bloesser on April 7, 1963. Lynett and Earl Bloesser have two children.

    (1) **Marti Jane Bloesser**: born June 7, 1966

    (2) **Brent Lee Bloesser**: born February 24, 1977.

(2) **Robert Cowan Bearly**: born June 9, 1945, in Garnett, Kansas; married, first, Beverly Sue Simmons on December 4, 1965, in Nevada, Missouri. Bob and Beverly were divorced December 9, 1978. Bob married, second, Elaine Jennifer Marshall (born November 24, 1959) on April 4, 1985, at Crown Center in Kansas City. Jeni has a daughter, Jessica, from a previous marriage. Jessica Lynn Graves was born November 9, 1979. Bob and Jeni have one daughter.

    (1) **Amanda Leigh Bearly**: born August 15, 1985.

Hattie is remembered by all three of her daughters as a beautiful and loving mother.

Robert Clyde Adams married, second, Bertha Gladys Clark on September 19, 1919. Bertha was born in a sod house near Preston, Pratt County, Kansas, on February 24, 1891. She is the daughter of Edward and Ada May (Burke) Clark.

Bertha had a difficult time adapting to life with the three daughters of Hattie Adams, as they were determined not to accept their new "mother". In time, Bertha would win this little battle. Bertha was a deeply religious woman and completely dedicated to her husband and to her duties as a wife and mother.

Following the loss of the farm in Linn County, Kansas, Clyde moved his family to Corvallis, Oregon. Here he maintained a large yard with a wonderful garden and worked at the University in Corvallis as a maintenance man. Clyde also worked as caretaker for his church, the First Methodist Church and Wesley Foundation in Corvallis.

Clyde and Bertha Adams had five children.

(1) ROBERT CLARK[10]: born July 22, 1920; died January 16, 1921.

(2) HOWARD MARVIN[10]: born February 18, 1922, near Mound City, Kansas; married Claire Eunice Luethe on March 20, 1943. Claire was born June 9, 1921, in Portland, Oregon, to parents Samuel and Matilda (Jennie M. Brooks) Luethe.

    Howard Marvin (he prefers to be called Marv) left college for the Army during World War II and landed at Normandy with the first unit of heavy trucks to support the Allied push thru France. He returned, finished school and operated a veterinary business for many years. He has also maintained an active hand in real estate and been successful in that venture. Claire trained in nursing and worked while Marv was in the service and while he completed his education following the war. After his business interests became successful, Claire devoted her time to raising the family and working as bookkeeper for the family businesses. Marv and Claire Adams have two children.

(1) **Jennifer Layne**[11]: born December 4, 1948; married Kraig Morton Saks on May 25, 1974, at Eugene, Oregon. Jennifer (Adams) and Kraig Saks have three children.

    (1) **Emilie Elisabeth Saks**: born September 4, 1979.
    (2) **Nathan Andrew Saks**: born October 6, 1981.
    (3) **Matthew Samuel Saks**: born May 8, 1984.

(2) **Gregory Marv**[11]: born April 30, 1950.

(3) BARBARA JANE[10]: born December 15, 1924, near Mound City, Kansas; married Robert Raymond Dargatz on March 10, 1951. Robert was born in Illinois on May 13, 1924, to parents Raymond Robert and Marjorie Helen (DeLind) Dargatz.

Barbara is an educator. She has worked as a school teacher, counselor, and principal, and while semi-retired serves as a university supervisor of student teachers. She was teacher of the year in Idaho. Bob is a structural engineer. He served as a first lieutenant in the Army during World War II. His latest project is the energy efficient home he designed and had built for them at Hailey, Idaho.

Both Bob and Barbara are outdoor enthusiasts and participate in backpacking, cross country skiing, bicycling, and other such activities.

Bob and Barbara have no children, but are joined in their outdoor lifestyle by Lady, a lovely siberian husky who is more a member of the family than a pet.

(4) MARY LOUISE[10]: born May 26, 1929; married James Stanley Buck on June 22, 1947. James was born June 8, 1929, in Starkweather, North Dakota. He is the son of John W. and Elizabeth Mae (Wright) Buck. John Buck was born June 17, 1898, at Starkweather, North Dakota; married Elizabeth on February 1, 1920; and died April 16, 1986. Elizabeth was born May 2, 1901, in Minnesota. Mary and James have three children.

(1) **Stephen Buck**: born October 15, 1949.
(2) **Gary Buck**: born June 4, 1952.
(3) **Wendy Buck**: born October 1, 1954.

(5) DAVID EDWARD[10]: born November 5, 1932; married Darlene (Ross) Munsen who was born August 7, 1934. David and Darlene have lived all their lives in the Corvallis, Oregon, area. David is a mechanic and a veteran of the Korean War. Darlene works in the drapery retail business. David and Darlene have three children.

(1) **David Leroy**[11]: born August 29, 1960; married Laura Hamilton.
(2) **Douglas E.**[11]: born December 13, 1963.
(3) **Teresa S.**[11]: born May 30, 1965; married Denny Cole on August 6, 1989.

Darlene Ross was previously married to Claude E. Munson (married March 21, 1951). She has one son, Neal (born June 18, 1952) from that marriage.

Robert Clyde Adams died on October 17, 1955. He is buried at the Oak Lawn Cemetery in Corvallis, Oregon. Bertha Adams later married Charlie Park and made her home in Taft, California. Following her death on September 17, 1973, she was buried with her first husband, Robert Clyde Adams, at the Oak Lawn Cemetery in Corvallis, Oregon.

The three daughters of Robert Clyde and Hattie (Mapes) Adams. Left to right: Juanita, Helen, and Madeline. The picture was taken about 1916.

The Wesley Chapel Church as it looked when the children of Robert Clyde Adams attended it. The church was destroyed by fire on January 31, 1945.

The church cemetery is the resting place of John Quincy Adams and his wife, Sarah Jane (Wilson) Adams, Hattie (Mapes) Adams, and a number of other family members.

Mrs. R. C. Adams Was Buried at Wesley Chapel Sunday.

Mrs. R. C. Adams died at her home six miles northwest of Mound City last Friday morning from influenza. The body was buried in Wesley Chapel cemetery Sunday afternoon after exercises at the grave conducted by Rev. E. N. Gause.

Hattie S. Mapes was born at Centerville April 8, 1885, and was married to R. C. Adams September 16, 1909. She leaves three children, Juanita, Mandalin and Helen. Besides her husband two sisters also survive, Mrs. W. McKeever of La Harpe and Mrs. H. J. Scheidts of Parsons, and one brother, Joe Mapes of Iola.

Mrs. Adam's husband had just recovered from the disease before her death.

Mrs. Adams was a woman who was universally loved by those who knew her and the community feels a distinct shock by her death.

Obituary for Hattie (Mapes) Adams from the
Mound City Republic, December 12, 1918.

Note the obituary gives Hattie's birth year as 1885.
Hattie started using this year of birth instead of the
correct year, 1883, when she married Robert Clyde Adams.
She apparently did this to hide the fact she was older
than her husband.

The picture of Hattie is undated.

Closing Out

Public Sale

As I am leaving the state, will sell at Public Auction at the farm known as the R. C. Adams farm, 5½ miles northwest of Mound City and 10 miles west of Pleasanton on the Pleasanton - Centerville gravel road, the following described property, commencing at 10 o'clock, on

Tuesday, September 19, 1939

66 — head of Livestock — 66

9 HEAD HORSES AND MULES

Grey mare, 6 years old, in foal by jack, season paid, weight 1600; sound and extra good.

Black mare, smooth mouth, weight 1500, in foal by jack, season paid.

Spotted mare, 8 years old; this mare is sired by government horse, Gordon Russell; splendid all-purpose mare, well broke to work and ride; sound, wt. about 1250, in foal by government horse, season paid.

Black gelding, 4 years old, wt. 1600, sound.

Black yearling gelding.

Yearling horse mule.

Suckling horse colt, extra good.

Two suckling mule colts, extra good.

HOUSEHOLD GOODS

Maytag washer with aluminum tub; Wyeth sewing machine, stitches perfectly; 6-lid wood cook stove; Banquet range; 3-burner oil stove with 2 ovens; 2 wood heating stoves, 1 a new Keep-Fire; Buffet, dining table, chairs, 2 rocking chairs, 2 beds, bed springs, day bed, 2 dressers, chiffonier, chest of drawers, 2 commodes, good Bush and Gerts piano, 9x12 Congoleum rug, National pressure cooker, 21 quart size, almost new. Some cooking utensils and tubs, dishes, stone jars in 1, 2, 3, 5 and 15 gallon capacity; pictures and some antiques; new shades and curtains; Kellog telephone; about 100 quarts of fruit, peaches, blackberries, pickles, vegetables and tomatoes; some potatoes and onions; ice cream freezer.

HARNESS

2 sets of harness and several collars, 19 to 22 inch.

22 HEAD OF CATTLE
MILKING SHORTHORNS

Red cow, 9 years old, freshen in October.

Two red cows, 8 years old, freshen in November.

Roan heifer, 3 years old, freshen in November.

Red cow, 7 years old, freshen in December.

Red heifer, 2 years old, freshen in March.

Roan heifer, 2 years old, freshen in February.

Roan heifer, 2 years old, freshen in March.

Red cow, 7 years old, freshen in May.

4 red yearling heifers, all bred, extra good.

5 heifer calves, 3 red and 2 roan.

2 steer calves.

Registered Shorthorn bull, Golden Pride II, number 1912413 calved September 20, 1936; extra good; sure breeder, wt. about 1600. This herd of cattle are descendants of two milking Shorthorn bulls one from an Iowa herd and the other from Wisconsin. A good clean herd of cows and all breeders raised 100 per cent calf crop last year. Nine of these cows are broke to milk and 8 are giving milk now.

Miscelaneous Articles

3 pumps, 2 4x10 cylinder and 1 smaller pump.

3 loads block wood and 3 or 4 loads wood in poles.

Pitchforks, scoops, spades, logchains, tank pump, etc.

No. 6 Sharples cream separator in good condition.

FEED AND GRAIN

12 acres Sargo with quite a lot of seed; 10 acres hygeria with plenty of seed; 3 acres of sowed cane, all in field. About 500 bushels good oats; few bushels of wheat.

25 HEAD OF SHEEP

11 head Shropshire ewes, all good ages.

9 Shropshire ewe lambs and 4 wether lambs.

Purebred Shropshire buck.

10 HEAD OF HOGS

5 good young white sows, weight about 350 pounds.

5 shoats, weight about 70 pounds.

FARM IMPLEMENTS

John Deere iron wheel wagon and extra good hay rack.

Wood wheel wagon with box.

John Deere low-down manure spreader.

Deering 6-foot mowing machine.

John Deere hay loader.

John Deere side delivery rake.

Deering 6-foot grain binder.

John Deere 16-inch riding plow.

12-inch walking plow.

Emerson disk cultivator.

New Century 4-shovel cultivator with 2 sets of shovels.

Overland 4-shovel cultivator.

Janesville corn planter and 80 rods check wire.

16-disc disk harrow.

12-foot harrow. 10-foot harrow.

16-tooth one-horse cultivator.

5-shovel one-horse cultivator.

Corn sheller.

International 6-Horse gas engine.

McCormick-Deering 8-inch feed grinder.

6-prong Louden hay fork.

150 feet good hay rope.

34-foot extension ladder.

20 foot ladder.

All implements have been kept in shed and all are in good condition, some like new.

155 CHICKENS

115 pullets, 40 New Hampshire Reds, 35 purebred Leghorns, 40 hybred chickens, 40 yearling hens, New Hampshire Reds and White Leghorns.

TERMS CASH; or see Your Banker Before Sale.

R. C. ADAMS, Owner

COLS. ED COFFEEN and ROSS HUCKABY, Auctioneers.

Lunch by Wesley Chapel Ladies Aid

J. O. DINGUS, Clerk.

DELAYED CERTIFICATE OF BIRTH

For use in cases where Birth Certificates cannot be supplied

54--949

PLACE OF BIRTH

County of ....Linn......

STATE BOARD OF HEALTH
Division of Vital Statistics

Township of.................................
or
City of....Mound City..... No....................,....................................street. Reg. No......

STATE OF KANSAS

Full Name of Child....................Robert Clyde Adams........................

☞ ALL DATA USED IN THIS CERTIFICATE MUST BE AS OF DATE OF BIRTH OF THIS CHILD

Sex of Child.	Twin, Triplet, or other?	Number in order of birth.		Date of birth........ March 16, 1885
Male		(To be answered only in event of plural births)		(Month) (Day) (Year)

FATHER	MOTHER
Full Name. John Quincy Adams	Full Maiden Name. Sarah Jane Wilson
Residence. (At time of birth of this child) Mound City, Kansas	Residence. (At time of birth of this child) Mound City, Kansas
Color. White Father's age 55 years. (At time of birth of this child)	Color. White Mother's age 47 years. (At time of birth of this child)
Birthplace. Boston, Massachusetts	Birthplace. Decatur County, Indiana
Occupation. (At time of birth of this child) Farmer	Occupation. (At time of birth of this child) Housewife

....................Winnie Simmons, midwife.....................
(Name of attending physician)

ABSTRACT OF EVIDENCE

......Affidavit of person living in community, H. W. Dingus...........
......Affidavit of sister, Mrs. Myrtle McRae...........
......Affidavit of person living in community, Ralph W. Moody...........
......Family Record, showing date of birth as March 16, 1885...........

I hereby certify that the above and foregoing facts relative to the birth of the above-named individual are true and correct, according to my best information and belief, and according to the application for delayed certificate of birth, duly completed, and on file in my office, and according to the substantiating documentary evidence viewed and examined by the state or local registrar.

Filed ......Mar 2 1942........, 19......

Minnie Fleming Registrar.

19-2680-s   2-12—100M

CERTIFIED COPY OF DELAYED CERTIFICATE OF BIRTH

Topeka, Kansas *April 1* 1942

I hereby certify that the above is a true and correct copy of the original delayed certificate on file in the office of the State Board of Health.

(Seal)

Minnie Fleming
State Registrar.

DELAYED CERTIFICATE OF BIRTH FOR
ROBERT CLYDE ADAMS

MARRIAGE LICENSE RECORD

State of Kansas, }
County of Allen, }

Office of the Probate Judge of Said County.

Be it Remembered, That on the _____16th_____ day of ___September___ A. D. 190_9_ there was issued from the office of said Probate Judge, a Marriage License, of which the following is a true copy:

Marriage License

ALLEN COUNTY, STATE OF KANSAS

Iola, Kansas, September 23th 190 9

To any Person Authorized by Law to Perform the Marriage Ceremony—Greeting:

You are hereby authorized to join in Marriage _Clyde Adams_ of _Mound City Ks_
aged _____24_____ years, and _Hattie S Mapes_ of _Centerville Ks_
aged _____24_____ years, and of this license you will make due return to my office within thirty days

(SEAL) _J. B. Smith_ Probate Judge.

And which said Marriage License was afterwards, to-wit: on the _20_ day of _September_ A. D. 190_9_ returned to said Probate Judge with the following certificate endorsed thereon, to-wit:

STATE OF KANSAS. COUNTY OF ALLEN, ss.

I, _John H. Price_ do hereby certify, that in accordance with the authorization of the within License, I did on the _16th_ day of _September_ A. D. 190_9_ at _Iola_ in said County, join and unite in Marriage the within named _Clyde Adams_ and _Hattie S. Mapes_

Witness my hand and seal the day and year above written.

ATTEST:

_____ Probate Judge.

John H. Price (Seal)
Pastor M. E. Church

MARRIAGE LICENSE FOR ROBERT CLYDE ADAMS
HATTIE S. MAPES

STATE OF KANSAS. 54 1139

STATE BOARD OF HEALTH—DIVISION OF VITAL STATISTICS.

County *Linn*

Township *Paris*

STANDARD CERTIFICATE OF DEATH.

City .... No. .... street .... Registered ward. No. 2 6

2Full Name *Hattie Adams*

[If death occurred in a hospital or institution, give its NAME instead of street and number.]

PERSONAL AND STATISTICAL PARTICULARS

MEDICAL CERTIFICATE OF DEATH

3Sex *Female*   4Color or Race *White*   5 Single, Married, Widowed, or Divorced (Write the word) *Married*

16Date of Death. *Dec 6th 1918*
Month Day Year

6Date of Birth. *April - 8 - 1885*
Month Day Year

17 I HEREBY CERTIFY, That I attended deceased from *Nov 26th 1918*, to *Dec 5th 1918*

7Age. *33* yrs *7* mos *28* ds   If LESS than 1 day, ... hrs. .... min.

that I last saw her alive on *Dec 5 1918* and that death occurred on the date stated above, at .... M.

8Occupation.
a) Trade, profession, or particular kind of work *Housewife*

The CAUSE OF DEATH was as follows: *Pneumonia*

b) General nature of industry, business or establishment in which employed (or employer)

1. 92.
(Duration) yrs .... mos .... ds

9Birthplace. (State or country) *Kansas*

Contributory (Secondary)
(Duration) .... yrs .... mos .... ds

10Name of Father. *Joseph Mapes*

(Signed) *D T Flewele* M D

11Birthplace of Father *Ind*

.... 191 (Address) ....

12Maiden name of Mother. *Nancy Cohran*

* State the Disease Causing Death or in deaths from Violent Causes state (1) Means of Injury and (2) whether Accidental, Suicidal, or Homicidal.

13Birthplace of Mother. (State or country) *Ohio*

18Length of Residence (for hospitals, institutions, transients, or recent residents).

14The above is true to the best of my knowledge.

At place of death .... yrs .... mos .... ds   In the State .... yrs .... mos .... ds

(Informant) *M. Adams*

Where was disease contracted, if not at place of death?

(Address) .... *Mound City*

Former or usual residence

15 *filed Dec 7 1918* *H S Brownlee* Registrar

19Place of Burial or Removal *Holy Chapel Cmly*   Date of Burial. *Dec 7 1918*

20Undertaker *A R Cole* Address *Mound City*

DEATH CERTIFICATE FOR
HARRIET "HATTIE" (MAPES) ADAMS

**ROBERT CLYDE AND BERTHA ADAMS
AND FAMILY**

Following the death of his first wife, Hattie, Robert Clyde
Adams married Bertha Gladys Clark. Robert Clyde and Bertha Adams
are shown here with all the Adams children. Back row, left to
right: Myrtle Helen, Madeline, and Juanita Lenore, all daughters
of Hattie (Mapes) Adams, and Howard Marvin. Front row, left to
right: Mary Louise, Robert Clyde, Bertha Gladys, David Edward, and
Barbara Jane. This picture was taken about 1933.

OREGON STATE HEALTH DIVISION
VITAL STATISTICS SECTION

STANDARD CERTIFICATE OF DEATH

STATE OF OREGON
BOARD OF HEALTH—PORTLAND
U.S. PUBLIC HEALTH SERVICE

STATE FILE NO. 11353

LOCAL REGISTRAR'S NUMBER 761

DATE RECEIVED 2 6 1955

1 NAME OF DECEASED (TYPE OR PRINT)	A. (First) Robert	(Middle) Cly_	c. (Last) Adams	420.1

2 PLACE OF DEATH		3 USUAL RESIDENCE

A COUNTY Benton — A STATE Oregon — B COUNTY Benton

B CITY OR TOWN Corvallis — C LENGTH OF STAY Yrs. — C CITY OR TOWN Corvallis

D FULL NAME OF HOSPITAL OR INSTITUTION 1216 Kings Road — D STREET ADDRESS 1216 Kings Road

4 DATE OF DEATH Oct. 17, 1955	5 SEX Male	6 COLOR OR RACE White	7A MARRIED, NEVER MARRIED, WIDOWED, DIVORCED Married	7B NAME OF HUSBAND OR WIFE Mrs. Bertha Adams

8 DATE OF BIRTH March 16, 1885	9 AGE (In years last birthday) 70	10 BIRTHPLACE Linn County, Kansas	11 CITIZEN OF WHAT COUNTRY U.S.A.

12 FATHER'S NAME John Q. Adams	13 MOTHER'S MAIDEN NAME Sarah Jane Wilson

14A USUAL OCCUPATION (Retired) Caretaker	14B KIND OF BUSINESS OR INDUSTRY Caretaker - Church	15 IF VETERAN NAME No	16 INFORMANT'S OWN SIGNATURE

17 SOCIAL SECURITY NO. 543-16-0883

MEDICAL CERTIFICATION ENTER ONLY ONE CAUSE PER LINE FOR (A), (B), AND (C)

I. DISEASE OR CONDITION DIRECTLY LEADING TO DEATH (A) _Coronary thrombosis_ — INTERVAL BETWEEN ONSET AND DEATH 1/2 hr.

ANTECEDENT CAUSES

18 CAUSE OF DEATH — Morbid conditions, if any, giving rise to the above cause (a) stating the underlying cause last. DUE TO (B) _Arteriosclerosis_

DUE TO (C)

II. OTHER SIGNIFICANT CONDITIONS — Conditions contributing to the death but not related to the disease or condition causing death

19A DATE OF OPERATION	19B MAJOR FINDINGS OF OPERATION	20 AUTOPSY? YES ☐ NO ☒

21A ACCIDENT SUICIDE HOMICIDE (Specify)	21B PLACE OF INJURY 21C CITY, TOWN, OR TOWNSHIP (COUNTY) (STATE)

21D TIME OF INJURY (Month) (Day) (Year) (Hour) m.	21E INJURY OCCURRED WHILE AT WORK ☐ NOT WHILE AT WORK ☐	21F HOW DID INJURY OCCUR?

22 I HEREBY CERTIFY THAT I ATTENDED THE DECEASED FROM Oct 1 1955 TO Oct 17 1955 THAT I LAST SAW THE DECEASED ALIVE ON 10/17 1955 AND THAT DEATH OCCURRED 10:30 A.M. FROM THE CAUSES AND ON THE DATE STATED ABOVE.

23A SIGNATURE	(Degree or title) M.D.	23B ADDRESS Corvallis, Ore.	23C DATE SIGNED 10/19/55

24A BURIAL, CREMATION, REMOVAL (Specify) Burial	24B DATE 10/21/55	24C NAME OF CEMETERY OR CREMATORY Oaklawn Memorial Park	24D LOCATION (City, town, or county) (State) Corvallis, Ore.

DATE REC'D BY LOCAL REG. 10-24-55	REGISTRAR'S SIGNATURE Esther Graves Dep	25 FUNERAL DIRECTOR'S SIGNATURE #137 Joe B. McHenry	ADDRESS Corvallis, Ore.

I CERTIFY THAT THIS IS A TRUE, FULL AND CORRECT COPY OF THE ORIGINAL CERTIFICATE ON FILE IN THE VITAL RECORDS UNIT OF THE OREGON STATE HEALTH DIVISION.

DATE ISSUED DEC 18 1989

EDWARD J. JOHNSON
STATE REGISTRAR

**DEATH CERTIFICATE FOR
ROBERT CLYDE ADAMS**

GRAVESTONE OF ROBERT CLYDE AND
BERTHA GLADYS (CLARK) ADAMS
AT THE OAKLAWN CEMETERY, CORVALLIS OREGON

LEFT TO RIGHT: MARV ADAMS, DAVID ADAMS,
MARY (ADAMS) BUCK, BARBARA (ADAMS) DARGATZ,
AND HELEN (ADAMS) BEARLY.
SEPTEMBER 1991

MAPES FAMILY

Harriet Surilda "Hattie" Mapes, the first wife of Robert Clyde Adams, was the daughter of Joseph Whitesel Mapes and Nancy Jane Cochran. The known Mapes lineage and ancestry is discussed here.

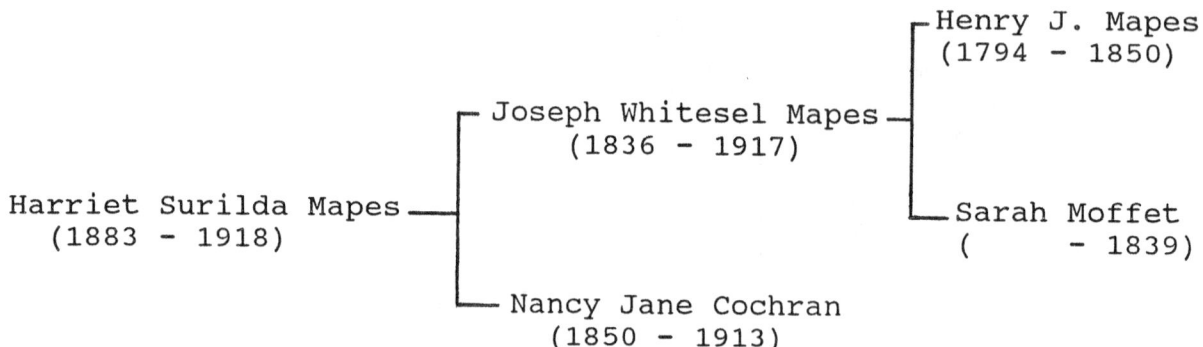

```
                                                          ┌─ Henry J. Mapes
                                                          │   (1794 - 1850)
                                    ┌─ Joseph Whitesel Mapes ─┤
                                    │    (1836 - 1917)     │
Harriet Surilda Mapes ─────┤                              └─ Sarah Moffet
   (1883 - 1918)           │                                 (      - 1839)
                           │
                           └─ Nancy Jane Cochran
                                (1850 - 1913)
```

Not much is known of Hattie's grandfather, Henry J. Mapes. From the birth places of his children, it is probably safe to assume he was an itinerant farmer. At the time of the 1850 census, he was farming and living in Lawrence County, Missouri. The 1850 census (taken October 25, 1850) gives his age as 56 and that he was born in New Jersey. The assumption that he was born in 1794 is drawn from this information. The assumption that he died in 1850 is drawn from a letter written for Joseph Whitesel Mapes during his efforts to obtain a Civil War pension. In that letter, it is stated that his (Joseph's) father died when he was fourteen years old.

Since Joseph was born in January 1836 and Henry J. Mapes was alive at the time of the 1850 census, this author has guessed that Henry died in late 1850. The same letter states that his mother died when he was only three years old. A Civil War report for the Adjutant General provides the name of Joseph's mother. A search of courthouse and cemetery records by the author in Lawrence County, Missouri, has failed to produce any clue as to the final resting place of either Henry J. or Sarah Mapes. No information has been found to identify the parents of either Henry J. Mapes or Sarah Moffet.

From letters by Joseph Mapes, the 1850 census, and marriage records in Lawrence County, Missouri, it is known that Henry and Sarah Mapes had at least three children.
   (1) **Harriet N. Mapes:** age 20 in 1850; born in Ohio; married George W. Sampsel March 31, 1853, in Lawrence County, Kansas.

(2) Joseph Whitesel Mapes: born January 16, 1836; born in Henry County, Indiana.

(3) **Ira L. Mapes**: age 12 in 1850; born in Illinois.

Hattie's father, Joseph Whitesel Mapes, was born in Henry County, Indiana, on January 16, 1837. There is much conjecture about the year of his birth. His tombstone gives his birth date as January 16, 1837, as do a number of Civil War records. The date on the tombstone probably comes about as a result of the fact the Civil War Pension Board finally accepted January 16, 1837, as his official birth date. This author fixes the actual birth date in 1936 as a result of an Adjutant General's report containing the date January 16, 1836, and a letter to the pension board written for Joseph Mapes (probably by his wife) which states clearly that he believed he was born in 1836 and that he was 25 years old when he enlisted in the Army on December 1, 1861.

Joseph Mapes probably did not have much formal education as he moved around with his parents and helped his father with the farming chores. In 1850 he lived with his father and step-mother, Barbara Mapes, in Lawrence County, Missouri. Following the death of his father, Joseph was without a home and is believed to have moved around, working as a farm laborer. He is believed to have lived and worked in the area of Centerville, Kansas, in about 1856.

Joseph married Cerilda Hornbeck, who was born March 10, 1838, on October 7, 1857, in Cooper County, Missouri. In the 1860 census, Joseph is reported living in Washington Township, Cedar County, Missouri, with his wife Cerilda Hornbeck and younger brother, Ira. They are farmers.

In all Mapes family records, Cerilda's name is spelled as given herein, "Cerilda Hornbeck". Cerilda's name in the 1850 census is given as "Zerilda". At that time she is listed as age 12, born in Missouri, and living in Cedar District, Cedar County, Missouri, with her father James Hornback and eight other family members.

Joseph Whitesel Mapes enlisted in the Union Army on December 1, 1861. He enrolled in Company K, 5th Kansas Volunteer Cavalry, 1st Brigade, 2nd Division, as a private. In the winter of 1861 he was ill with measles and was treated at Barnesville, Kansas. In 1862 he was taken prisoner in Texas County, Missouri, and was held at Black River Swamp, Arkansas, for fourteen days. In June 1862, Joseph Mapes deserted the army, possibly just after having been captured by the enemy. He remained absent without leave until August 1863, when he returned to his unit. His desertion was expunged by an action of a Court of Inquiry. The reason he left his unit has not been determined. It was not unusual for soldiers during this conflict to return home for periods of time, without permission.

With his Regiment, he took active part in the battles of Helena, College Bridge, Little Rock, Pine Bluff, Monticello, Mt. Eba, and Camden, Arkansas. He was honorably discharged December 19, 1864, at Little Rock, Arkansas. His brother, Ira L., also served during the war as a member of Company K, 5th Kansas Infantry.

Following the war, Joseph Mapes moved around a little, but eventually settled at Centerville, Kansas, and continued farming. An obituary for James H. Mapes in the Pilot and Graphic, a newspaper, dated July 13, 1894, reported that the family had moved to Kansas in 1867.

Joseph Whitesel and Cerilda Mapes had four children.
(1) **James H. Mapes**: born October 17, 1860, at Cedar County, Missouri; married Etta V. Mundell, daughter of Joseph and Millie (Read) Mundell of Linn County, Kansas, on February 19, 1888; was shot and killed by C.C. Conley at Parker, Kansas, July 4, 1894. James Mapes left his wife, father, and two children. He is buried at Goodrich Cemetery, near Goodrich, Kansas.
(2) **John M. Mapes**: age 21 in 1885 census; born in Missouri; resident of Centerville, Kansas, at time of death; died January 6, 1904; buried at Goodrich Cemetery, near Goodrich, Kansas.
(3) **William A. Mapes**: age 18 in 1885 census; born in Kansas.
(4) **Ira E. Mapes**

Cerilda Mapes died December 8, 1868, probably in the area of Centerville, Kansas.

On June 10, 1882, Joseph Mapes married Nancy Jane (Cochran) Lusk. Nancy was a widow, having lost her husband, James Lusk, on July 18, 1876. In the 1880 census, Nancy Jane Lusk is found living with her father, Henry Daniel Cochran, near Centerville.

Nancy Jane Cochran married her first husband, James Louis Lusk, who was born February 1, 1843, on January 22, 1868. James and Nancy Jane Lusk had five children, all born in Linn County, Kansas.
(1) **Catherine Ann (Kate) Lusk**: born September 30, 1868; died July 5, 1962; married George John Grunden on June 8, 1903. George was born August 15, 1862, near Decatur, Illinois, to Samuel Grunden and his second wife, Ann Whitehead. Ann Whitehead was a native of Scotland. Samuel Grunden's family had emigrated from the Alsace-Lorraine region of France. George Grunden had three sons, Clyde, Frank, and Harry, by his first wife, Rena, who had since died. Kate and George Grunden had three children.
   (1) **George Bernard Grunden**: born July 23, 1905, at Kansas City, Missouri; married Susan A. McClure in 1934; died

in 1990 at Warsaw, Missouri. Susan McClure was born in 1908 at Galena, Kansas, and died in 1961 at Kansas City, Kansas. George and Susan Grunden had one son.

(1) **Donald M. Grunden**: born in 1935 at Kansas City, Kansas. In 1957, Donald married Valeta M. Kohn, who was born in 1937 at Tipton, Kansas. Donald and Valeta had five children.

(1) **Michael L. Grunden**: born in 1958 at Kansas City, Kansas. In 1991, Michael married Lynette A. Pace who was born in 1963 in Kansas City, Missouri.

(2) **Christy S. Grunden**: born in 1963 at Kansas City, Kansas. In 1984, Christy married Rick J. Clarkston who was born in 1963 at Jefferson City, Missouri. Christy and Rick Clarkston have one daughter.

(1) **Jennifer L. Clarkston**: born in 1985 at Jefferson City, Missouri.

(3) **Terry L. Grunden**: born 1964; died in 1979 at Jefferson City, Missouri.

(4) **Scott P. Grunden**: born in 1966 at Kansas City, Kansas.

(5) **Tamara S. Grunden**: born in 1968 at Kansas City, Kansas.

George and Susan Grunden also adopted two sisters, Patricia J. and Shirley L. Warrington in 1947.

Left to right: Catherine Ann "Kate" (Lusk) Grunden, Mary Jane "Mada" (Mapes) Scheidts, Frances May "Fan" (Lusk) Hunter, and Sarah Jane "Sada" (Mapes) McKeever. Picture believed taken in the late 1950's.

(2) **Walter John Grunden:** born November 26, 1907; married Minnie Rice. Walter and Minnie had five children.
 (1) **Susan Grunden:**
 (2) **Walter Grunden, Jr.:**
 (3) **Elaine Grunden:**
 (4) **Brian Grunden:**
 (5) **Valerie Grunden:**
(3) **Mary Ann (Mabel) Grunden:** born May 2, 1911; married James LeRoy Markley on September 2, 1929. James Markley died January 7, 1937. Mabel and James Markley had four children.
 (1) **Patricia Ann Markley:** born June 19, 1930.
 (2) **John Eugene Markley:** born August 19, 1932.
 (3) **James Richard Markley:** born May 2, 1934.
 (4) **Joseph LeRoy Markley:** born July 4, 1937.
Mabel married Dan Ray Jones on June 13, 1941. Dan Jones was born in Kansas City, Missouri, on December 15, 1913, to Dennis Worth and Lucy Ray Jones. Mabel and Dan Jones had five children.
 (1) **Dennis William Jones:** born May 28, 1942.
 (2) **Jeaneane Marie Jones:** born May 26, 1947.
 (3) **Michael Ray Jones:** born July 2, 1949.
 (4) **Timothy Kevin Jones:** born November 2, 1952.
 (5) **Jerome Christopher Jones:** born July 13, 1956.
(2) **John Henry Lusk:** born February 3, 1870; died January 4, 1932. John had no children.
(3) **Polly Matilda Lusk:** born March 8, 1872; died November 4, 1930; did not marry.
(4) **Ingram Calvin Lusk:** born November 9, 1874; died October 26, 1903. Ingram Lusk was shot by an unidentified person.
(5) **Frances (Fannie) May Lusk:** born February 27, 1876; married a Mr. Hunter; had no children. Fannie May Hunter died December 8, 1952, in Long View, Washington.

Joseph and Nancy Jane Mapes had four children.
(1) **Harriet (Hattie) Surilda Mapes: born April 8, 1883; died December 6, 1918; married Robert Clyde Adams; lived near Mound City, Kansas.
(2) **Sarah Jane (Sada) Mapes:** born February 19, 1885; married William McKeever of La Harpe, Kansas; died February 16, 1978. Sada McKeever is buried at the La Harpe Cemetery, La Harpe, Kansas. Sada and William McKeever had one daughter.
 (1) **Winifred McKeever:** married Loren Barker. Loren Barker died December 8, 1985, and is buried at Clay Center, Kansas. Winifred and Loren had two children, one daughter and one son.
 (1) **Terry Lee Barker:** born February 20, 1943; teaches school in Anaheim California.
 (2) **William Franklin Barker:** born November 19, 1946; married Susan Jo Wilson on August 30, 1974. William

is an optometrist in the United States Air Force. William and Susan have one daughter.

  (1) **Christa Nicole Barker**: born September 18, 1979.

JOSEPH WHITESEL MAPES AND NANCY JANE (COCHRAN) LUSK
These pictures are believed to have been taken
on their wedding day, June 10, 1882

(2) **Mary Jane (Mada) Mapes**: born February 19, 1885; died November 16, 1958; married Herman John Scheidts of Parsons, Kansas, who was born April 21, 1877, and died April 20, 1954, on May 14, 1903. Herman's parents are Weimer Martin and Julia (Knepker) Scheidts. Wiemer Scheidts was born in Baden-Baden, Germany. Herman was a carpenter. Mada and Herman Scheidts had four children.

  (1) **Delphine Francis Scheidts**: born March 30, 1905; married, first, Paul Iden Kirk who was born September 8, 1891, on November 29, 1923. Paul Kirk, who was a farmer, died August 29, 1935. Delphine married, second, Clifford Charles Chase who was born July 8, 1885, in New Salem, Kansas. Clifford Chase, who as chief engineer of M.K.T., "Katy", (Missouri-Kansas-Texas) railroad power plants died May 13, 1964, and is buried at Parsons, Kansas. Delphine and Paul Kirk had one son.

    (1) **Kenneth Herman Kirk**: born February 26, 1926. Kenneth married, first, Colean Ann Guist on August 14, 1947. They were divorced December 14, 1980. Kenneth married, second, Betty Palmer Knott who was

born April 10, 1926, in San Diego, California, on March 12, 1982. Kenneth and Colean had four children.

> (1) **Paul Samuel Kirk**: born August 20, 1949; is an electrical engineer. Paul has an adopted daughter, Sara, and is the father of another daughter.
>> (1) **Alyssa Kirk**: born July 22, 1989.
>
> (2) **Katheryn Diane Kirk**: born December 23, 1950; married a Mr. Gilpin. Katheryn Gilpin has two children.
>> (1) **Chad Gilpin**: born October 9, 1985.
>> (2) **Kristen Gilpin**: born May 8, 1987.
>
> (3) **Kent Stewart Kirk**: born April 4, 1956; is a mechanical engineer. Kent Kirk has three daughters.
>> (1) **Amy Jo Kirk**: born July 28, 1978.
>> (2) **Samantha Kirk**: born July 20, 1988.
>> (3) **Natisha Kirk**: born July 20, 1988.
>
> (4) **Kyle Scott Kirk**: born May 27, 1963; manages a "Pier One" import store.

The children of Joseph Whitesel and Nancy Jane Mapes. Left to right: rear, Sarah Jane "Sada" and Harriet Surilda "Hattie"; front, Mary Jane "Mada" and Joseph Whitesel, Jr.

(2) **Genevieve Marguerite Scheidts:** born April 7, 1910; married Leo Martin Laska on January 3, 1930. Leo Laska was born June 6, 1898, in Polk County, Nebraska, and died March 5, 1982, at Columbus, Nebraska. Genevieve and Leo Laska had four children.

    (1) **Martha Ann Laska:** born December 14, 1935; married, first, Lou Krepel, and second Russell Aerni. Martha and first husband, Lou Krepel, had three children. There were no children from the second marriage.

        (1) **Debbie Krepel:**

        (2) **Sherie Krepel:**

        (3) **Terrie Krepel:** he works for a newspaper in Lincoln, Nebraska.

    (2) **James Norbert Laska:** born in 1937; retired Lt. Colonel. James and Karen Laska have four children.

    (3) **Bernard Laska:** married Candy _____; has two sons.

    (4) **Leo Laska, Jr.:** married Cindy _____; has twin sons.

(3) **Raymond Bernard Scheidts:** born December 19, 1916; married, first, Leonor Elliot, who died October 12, 1957. Ray married, second, Thelma Ealer on October 16, 1960, at San Jose, California. He is a retired electrical contractor.

(4) **LaVerne Marie Scheidts:** born January 30, 1920; married Kenneth C. McElwee on October 20, 1939. LaVerne and Kenneth McElwee had two children.

    (1) **Donald Raymond McElwee:** born May 26, 1941; married Connie Allum; has one son.

        (1) **Raymond McElwee:**

    (2) **Nancy J. McElwee:** born July 3, 1947; married Donald E. Deemer. Nancy served as an Ensign in the Navy Nurses Corps. Nancy and Don Deemer have one son and one daughter.

        (1) **Terrie Deemer:** born February 7, 1971.

        (2) **Kenneth Joseph Deemer:** born August 7, 1976.

(4) **Joseph Whitesel Mapes, Jr.:** born August 7, 1887, in Franklin County, Kansas; made his home in or near Iola, Kansas, at least until 1918; married Pansy Lipe at Iola, Kansas. Joseph was divorced and mysteriously disappeared about 1940. He was never heard from again. Joseph and Pansy Mapes had one daughter.

(1) **Pauline Mapes:**

Nancy Jane Mapes died July 15, 1913, at La Harpe, Kansas. Following the death of Nancy Jane, Joseph Mapes married a third time. On October 1, 1913, Joseph married Clarissa Boerstler at La Harpe, Kansas. Joseph was reported on the marriage license to be 70 years old. Clarissa was reported to be 42 years old. The marriage did not last and Joseph died alone on April 23, 1917, at his home in La Harpe, Allen County, Kansas. He apparently died of cerebral hemorrhage. The delivery boy who brought him milk found him lying dead on the kitchen floor of his home. Joseph Whitesel and Nancy Jane Mapes are buried in the Gas City Cemetery near Iola, Kansas.

JOSEPH WHITESEL AND NANCY JANE MAPES AND FAMILY
Left to right: Joseph, Jr., Mada, Nancy Jane,
Hattie, Sada, and Joseph, Sr. holding George,
son of Nancy's daughter Catherine.
Picture taken in late 1905.

STATE OF KANSAS. 1 1541

STATE BOARD OF HEALTH—DIVISION OF VITAL STATISTICS

STANDARD CERTIFICATE OF DEATH.

¹PLACE OF DEATH.

County _Allen_

Township _Elm_
or
City _La Harpe_ . No. _____ street _____ Registered ward. No. _85_

[If death occurred in a hospital or institution, give its NAME instead of street and number.]

²Full Name _Joseph W. Mapes_

PERSONAL AND STATISTICAL PARTICULARS.			MEDICAL CERTIFICATE OF DEATH.

³Sex. _Male_ ⁴Color or Race. _White_ ⁵Single, Married, Widowed, or Divorced. (Write the word.) _Married_

⁶Date of Birth. _Jan 15 - 1836_
(Month) (Day) (Year)

⁷Age. _81_ yrs. _3_ mos. _7_ da. | If LESS than 1 day, ____hrs. or ____min.

⁸Occupation.
(a) Trade, profession, or particular kind of work _Farmer retired_
(b) General nature of industry, business, or establishment in which employed (or employer) _____

⁹Birthplace.
(State or country). _New York, U.S.A._

¹⁰Name of Father. _Henry J. Mapes_

¹¹Birthplace of Father. (State or country). _U.S.A._

¹²Maiden name of Mother. _Sarah Whitesel_

¹³Birthplace of Mother. (State or country). _Ireland_

¹⁴The above is true to the best of my knowledge.
(Informant) _Mrs Jacob McKinzie_
(Address) _La Harpe Kans_

15 Filed _April 24_ 19_ _William Lambert_
Registrar.

¹⁶Date of Death. _April 23 1917_
(Month) (Day) (Year)

17 I HEREBY CERTIFY, That I attended deceased from _April 23_ 1917, to _April 23_ 1917,
that I last saw h__ alive on _April 23_ 1917
and that death occurred on the date stated above, at _8.9_ M.

The CAUSE OF DEATH was as follows: _Apparently Heart disease as he was in usual health and fell dying in a few mints_

____(Duration) ____yrs. ____mos. ____ds.

Contributory (Secondary.) _____

____(Duration) ____yrs. ____mos. ____da.

(Signed) _H E Dunlap_ M. D.
April 23 191_ (Address) _La Harpe Kas_

* State the Disease Causing Death, or in deaths from Violent Causes state (1) Means of Injury; and (2) whether Accidental, Suicidal, or Homicidal.

¹⁸Length of Residence (for hospitals, institutions, transients, or recent residents).

At place of death____yrs. ____mos. ____da. In the State____yrs. ____mos. ____da.

Where was disease contracted, if not at place of death? _____

Former or usual residence _____

¹⁹Place of Burial or Removal. _Moran Kansas._ Date of Burial. _April 24_ 1917

²⁰Undertaker. _A. C. Slater_ Address. _Moran Kan._

DEATH CERTIFICATE FOR
JOSEPH WHITESEL MAPES

-141-

STATE OF KANSAS.
STATE BOARD OF HEALTH—DIV. OF VITAL STATISTICS.

STANDARD CERTIFICATE OF DEATH.

¹ PLACE OF DEATH.

County *Allen.*

Township *Elm.*

City *La Harpe.* No. _____ street, _____ Ward. [If death occurred in a hospital or institution, give its NAME instead of street and number].

Registered No. *12*

² FULL NAME *Nancy J. Mapes.*

PERSONAL AND STATISTICAL PARTICULARS.	MEDICAL CERTIFICATE OF DEATH.
³ Sex *Female* **⁴ Color or Race** *white* **⁵ Single, Married, Widowed or Divorced** (Write the word.) *Married*	**16 Date of Death.** *July 15* 191*3* (Month) (Day) (Year)
⁶ Date of Birth. *Jan. 13th 1850* (Month) (Day) (Year)	**17 I HEREBY CERTIFY, That I attended deceased from** *June 14th* 191*3*, to *July 15* 191*3* that I last saw her alive on *July 15* 191*3* and that death occurred, on the date stated above, at *1* P. M.
⁷ Age *63* yr. *6* mos. *2* da. IF LESS than 1 day, ___ hrs. or ___ min.?	The CAUSE OF DEATH was as follows: *Carcinoma of stomach and liver*
⁸ Occupation. (a) Trade, profession, or particular kind of work. *Housewife* (b) General nature of industry, business, or establishment in which employed (or employer)	(Duration) *abt 40* yr. ___ mos. ___ da.
⁹ Birthplace. (State or country). *Iowa.*	Contributory (Secondary) (Duration) ___ yr. ___ mos. ___ da.
10 Name of Father. *Henry B. Cochran*	(Signed) *Jno. W. Fee* M. D. *July 16* (Address) *Iola Ks*
11 Birthplace of Father. (State or country). *Scotland*	* State the DISEASE CAUSING DEATH, or in deaths from VIOLENT CAUSES, state (1) MEANS OF INJURY; and (2) whether ACCIDENTAL, SUICIDAL or HOMICIDAL.
12 Maiden name of Mother. *Matilda McFarland*	**18 Length of Residence** (For hospitals, institutions, transients, or recent residents).
13 Birthplace of Mother. (State or country). *Ireland.*	At place of death ___ yrs. ___ mos. ___ da. In the State ___ yrs. ___ mos. ___ da.
14 The above is true to the best of my knowledge. (Informant) *H. Lusk* (Address) *Emporia Kans*	Where was disease contracted, if not at place of death? _____ Former or usual residence _____
15 Filed *July 16ms* *Anna Barker* Registrar.	**19 Place of Burial or Removal.** *Iola Kan.* **Date of Burial** *7—17* 191*3*
	20 Undertaker. *O. R. Sleeper* **Address** *Iola Kan.*

DEATH CERTIFICATE FOR
NANCY JANE (COCHRAN) (LUSK) MAPES

Left Card

_M._ | **5 Cav.** | **Kans.**

Joseph M. Mapes

............, Co. I, 5 Reg't Kansas Cavalry.*

Appears on

Company Muster Roll

for .... dated Dec 31, 1861.

Present or absent .... Present

Stoppage, $ .... 100 for ....

_____

Due Gov't, $ .... 100 for ....

_____

Valuation of horse, $ ...... 100 / 100

Valuation of horse equipments, $ 100

Remarks:

x Enlisted Nov. 25, 1861
at Ft. Lincoln
for 3 years.

_____

_____

x added by p m r Dec 4 1911

*This organization subsequently became Co. K, 5 Reg't Kans. Cav.

Book mark: ....

R. G. Clark

(358)   Copyist.

Right Card

_W._ | **5 Cav.** | **Kans.**

Joseph W. Mapes

...... Cu, Co. C I, 5 Reg't Kansas Cavalry.

Age ...21... years.

Appears on

Company Muster-in Roll

of the organization named above. Roll dated

............................, Feb 3, 1862.

Muster-in to date   Dec 1, 1861.

x Mustered in:
~~Joined for duty and enrolled~~:

When .... Dec 1 ...., 1861.

Where ...... Ft. Lincoln

Period ...3... years.

_____

Valuation of horse, $ ...... 100 / 100

Valuation of horse equipments, $ 100

Remarks: ....

_____

_____

_____

x Corrected by p m r Dec 4 1911

Book mark: 10697-D-1888

R. G. Clark

(356)   Copyist.

**MUSTER RECORDS FOR JOSEPH WHITESEL MAPES RECORDED BY
GOVERNMENT OFFICES AFTER THE END OF THE CIVIL WAR**
These documents record his enlistment and the date
he actually mustered in.

M. 5. Cav. Kans.

Joseph M. Mapes
, Co K, 5, Reg't Kans. Cav.

NOTATION.

Book mark: 10697. D. 1888.

~~Record and Pension Office~~

WAR DEPARTMENT, A.G.O.
Washington, Mch. 6, 1889.

The charge of desertion of June 13/62 against this man is removed under the provisions of the act of Congress approved July 5, 1884.

He was absent, without proper authority, from June 13/62 to Aug. 15/63, when he rejoined his company.

Roby
Copyist.

(438)

M | 5 Cav. Kans.

Joseph Mapes
, Co. K, 5 Reg't Kansas Cavalry.

Appears on Returns as follows:

July 1862 Absent without leave since Jan 1/62 Supposed to be at Ft Scott
Aug 1862 Loss Dropped
Nov 1863 Returned from desertion Oct 31/63, Pine Bluff
Nov 1863 Building Quarters
Dec 1863 to Mar 1864 Co Cook
Apl 1864 Post Carpenter
May to July 1864 Co Cook
Aug 1864 Absent on Ambulance Corps
Sept & Oct 1864 Co Cook
Dec 1864 Mustered out Dec 20/64, Little Rock

Book mark:

Austin
Copyist.

(546)

MUSTER RECORDS FOR JOSEPH WHITESEL MAPES RECORDED BY GOVERNMENT OFFICES AFTER THE END OF THE CIVIL WAR
These documents record the removal of the charge of desertion and the nature of his assignments when he returned to duty.

Joseph W Mapes

Prvt____, Co. K, 5 Reg't Kansas Cav.

Age 25 years.

Appears on a

Detachment Muster-out Roll

of the organization named above. Roll dated

Little Rock Ark., Dec 23, 1864.

Muster-out to date Dec 23, 1864.

Last paid to June 30, 1864.

Clothing account:

Last settled Dec 31, 1863; drawn since $_____100

Due soldier $_____100; due U. S. $_____100

Am't for cloth'g in kind or money adv'd $ 40 51/100

Due U. S. for arms, equipments, &c., $_____100

Bounty paid $_____100; due $ 100 100

Valuation of horse, $_____100

Valuation of horse equipments, $_____100

Remarks: Lost his horse & equipments at Cross Station Mo by being captured by the enemy the same being his own personal property, valued at $115 June 14/62. Mustered out by virtue of expira-

over

Book mark :_____

H White

(349)   Copyist.

tion of original term of service under circular 41, War Dept current series.
Muster out to take effect Dec 23/64.

JUN 13 10338066 018818

MUSTER RECORDS FOR JOSEPH WHITESEL MAPES RECORDED BY GOVERNMENT OFFICES AFTER THE END OF THE CIVIL WAR
This Muster-out Roll documents that Joseph Mapes was captured by the enemy and lost his personal property as a result.

ACT JUNE 27 1890.

3—402.

Certificate No. _553991_

Name _Joseph W. Mapes_

Department of the Interior,

BUREAU OF PENSIONS,

Washington, D. C., January 15, 1898.

SIR:

In forwarding to the pension agent the executed voucher for your next quarterly payment please favor me by returning this circular to him with replies to the questions enumerated below.

Very respectfully,

N. Clay Evans

Commissioner.

Centerville

Linn county

Kansas

First. Are you married? If so, please state your wife's full name and her maiden name.

Answer. _Moried nancy Jane cochran_

Second. When, where, and by whom were you married?

Answer. _July the 10 by the state Judg in the year 1882_ _Lyn county_

Third. What record of marriage exists?

Answer. _The records of marriges can bab found at_ _the county seat_

Fourth. Were you previously married? If so, please state the name of your former wife and the date and place of her death or divorce.

Answer. _Yes name of forme satilda hornbek died decembe the 8 1868_

Fifth. Have you any children living? If so, please state their names and the dates of their birth.

Answer. _yes Hattie Mapes aprile the 8. 1883_
Sarah J Mapes february th 18 1885 Mary J. Mapes
wosborn february th 18 1885 Joseph Mapes Jr wosborn auguste the 9 1887

Joseph W. Mapes
(Signature.)

Date of reply, _May the 4_, 189 _8_

REPORT FOR THE BUREAU OF PENSIONS

This report provides important information about the family of Joseph Whitesel Mapes. It is the only record located which documents the death of his first wife.

War Department,

ADJUTANT GENERAL'S OFFICE,

Washington, Feby 4'' , 188)

Respectfully returned to the Commissioner of Pensions.

Joseph W. Mapes , a Private of Company K .,
5 Regiment Kas. Cav. Volunteers, was enrolled on the
1 day of Dec , 1861 , at Ft. Lincoln 3 yrs .,
and is reported on rolls from muster in to April
30/62 present. May and June '62 absent on det. ser.
since June 14/62. July and Aug '62 deserted — date
not given. Not borne to Aug 31/63. Sept and Oct '63
present with remark: deserted June 13/62, re-
____ to Co. Aug 18/63. Restored to duty by ____
of inquiry. Present to Oct 31/64 Mustered out
with Detach'' Dec 23/64 at Little Rock Ark. a Pvt
____ remark, "Lost his horse and equipments at Crows
Station Mo by being captured by the enemy, the same
being his own personal property, valued at $115.00/100 June
19/62." Return for Sept 1863 does not report him
absent.

Prisoner of War Records furnish no information Over.

R C ____
Assistant Adjutant General.

326
22

REPORT FROM THE ADJUTANT GENERAL'S OFFICE
This report to the Commissioner of Pensions
summarizes Joseph Mapes' military service.

10,697-D- A. G. O. (E. B.), 1888.

War Department,

ADJUTANT GENERAL'S OFFICE,

Washington, March 12th 1889

To the

Commissioner of Pensions.

Sir :

I have the honor to inform you that the charge of desertion of June 13, 1862 —, standing against Joseph H. (or H.) Mapes ——, as of Co. "K", 5th Kansas Cavalry Vols., has been removed from his record in this office. He was absent without proper authority from June 13, 1862, to August 15, 1863.

Very respectfully,

Your obedient servant,

Theo Kilian

Assistant Adjutant General.
(325)

No. of Pension Claim unknown.

REPORT FROM THE ADJUTANT GENERAL'S OFFICE
This form letter removing the charge of desertion from Joseph Mapes' record provides some insight into the fact that many soldiers deserted and returned to service.

Centreville Kans
May 17 1907.
Dept of Interior
Dear sire
In reply to your letter I am
sorry to say that I have no
records, of my birth With the
exception of a record, Drawn
from the family Bible by
my oldest brother. Who is now
Dead. My mother died when
I was three years old my
father when I was 14. All such
records were of course destroyd
as after that we had no
home, & have neither Aunt
Uncle or any other relation
of either my father or

    The letter shown on this page and the page to follow was written by (or for) Joseph Whitesel Mapes in an attempt to establish his age for the purpose of qualifying for a Civil War Pension.

mother. And of our family
no living relation with
the exception of a brother
younger than myself Ira
L. Mapes. Who also enlisted
in the 5th Ks Cav Co K Vol.,
And is drawing a pension
under the new law, This
record that I have show
that I was born Jan 16 - 1836.
I know that I was born in
Henry co Ind, & that I was 25
yrs old when I enlisted on the
first Day of Dec. 1861 As my
discharge will show,

Joseph Whitesel Mapes signed affidavits stating his birth date
to be January 16, 1836, and January 16, 1837. Based upon his
insistence that he was 25 years old at the time he joined the 5th
Kansas Volunteer Cavalry and this letter, it must be assumed his
birth date was in 1836.

TO ALL WHOM IT MAY CONCERN:

Know ye, That Joseph W. Mapes, a Private of Lieut. J. M. Heddens Company, (K), Fifth Regiment of Kansas Cavalry Volunteers who was enrolled on the first day of December one thousand eight hundred and sixty-one to serve three years or during the war, is hereby DISCHARGED from the service of the United States, this twenty-third day of December, 1864, at Little Rock, Arkansas, by reason of expiration of term of service.

(No objection to his being re-enlisted is known to exist.)

Said Joseph W. Mapes was born in Henry County in the State of Indiana, is twenty-five years of age, five feet seven inches high, fair complexion, grey eyes, black hair, and by occupation, when enrolled, a Farmer.

Given at Little Rock, Arks. this Twenty third day of December 1864.

                                    Wm. S. Morse,
                                      Lt. 3 Minn.Vol.Infty.
                                        Commanding the Reg't.

J. M. Heddens,   A.C.M. Cav. Div. 7 A.C. ?
    1" Lt. Comdg. 5" Kansas Cav'l.   Act. Com. of Musters,
                                        Dept. of Arks.

The foregoing is a correct copy of the Certificate of Discharge this day returned to Joseph W. Mapes.

August 13, 1907.
                                            Chief Clerk.

(right margin, rotated text: Paid Dec. 24th /64 — John C. Pitzer, Pay M. USA)

JOSEPH WHITESEL MAPES' CERTIFICATE OF DISCHARGE FROM THE FIFTH REGIMENT OF THE KANSAS CAVALRY VOLUNTEERS

**THE GRAVE MARKER FOR JOSEPH W. AND
NANCY J. MAPES**
Located in the Gas City Cemetery
at Iola, Kansas

COCHRAN FAMILY

Hattie Mapes, the first wife of Robert Clyde Adams, was the daughter of Joseph Whitesel Mapes and Nancy Jane Cochran. Her known Cochran ancestry is discussed here.

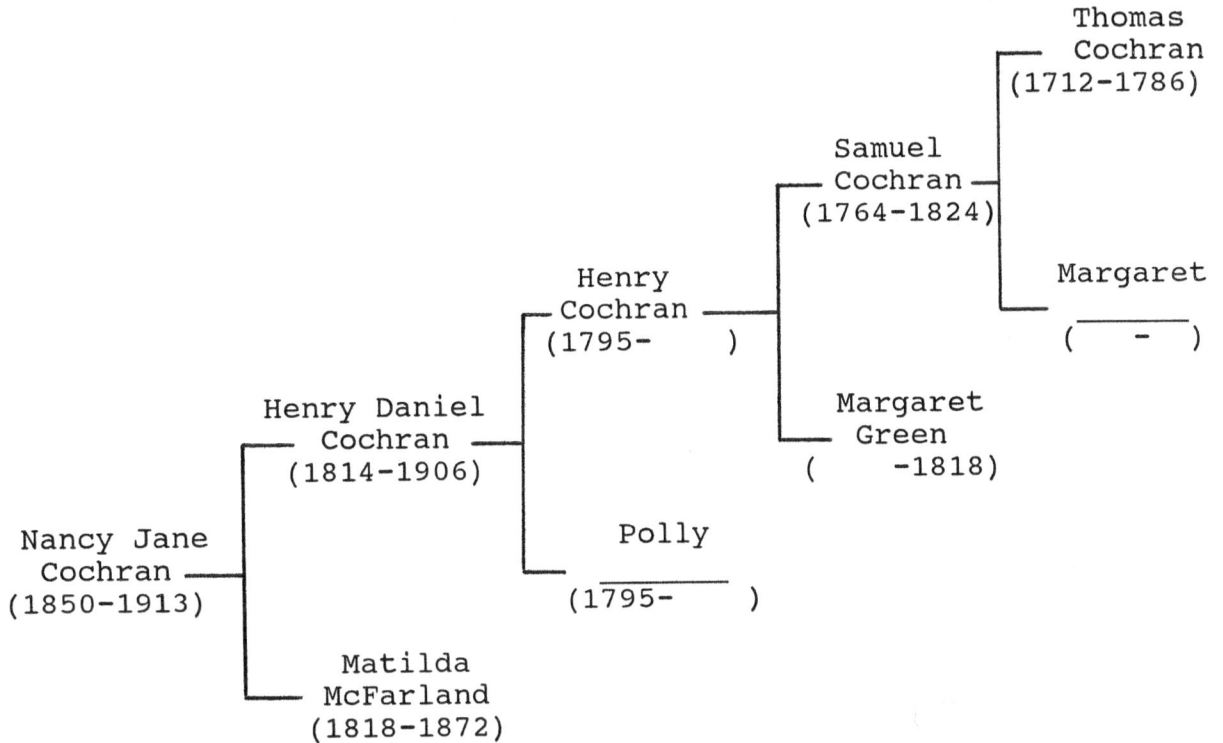

```
                                                              Thomas
                                                            ┌ Cochran
                                                            │ (1712-1786)
                                              Samuel ───────┤
                                            ┌ Cochran       │
                                            │ (1764-1824)   └ Margaret
                             Henry ─────────┤                 (    -    )
                           ┌ Cochran        │
                           │ (1795-    )     │ Margaret
                           │                └ Green
             Henry Daniel ─┤                   (    -1818)
           ┌ Cochran       │
           │ (1814-1906)   │ Polly
           │               └ (1795-    )
Nancy Jane ┤
 Cochran ──┤
(1850-1913)│ Matilda
           └ McFarland
             (1818-1872)
```

Nancy Jane Cochran's great-great-grandfather, Thomas Cochran, was born in Ireland in 1712. He married Margaret in about 1740. Nothing more is known of Margaret, wife of Thomas Cochran, as her maiden surname is not known and her parents have not been identified. Thomas moved to Pelham, Massachusetts, with his wife and some of his family about 1746. It is not known whether he moved there from Ireland or from some other location in America. From the records of the birth of his children, it is known he lived in Deerfield in 1744, then settled at some later date in Colrain, Massachusetts.

Thomas and Margaret Cochran had nine children.
(1) **Robert:** born February 1, 1741, at Pelham, Massachusetts; married Mary Gilmore on June 18, 1767.
(2) **Agnes:** born June 9, 1744, at Deerfield, Massachusetts; married Thomas Torrance on October 9, 1766.

(3) **Thomas, Jr.:** born July 6, 1746, at Pelham, Massachusetts.
(4) **Margaret:** born August 17, 1748, at Pelham, Massachusetts; married Silas White.
(5) **Martha:** born February 8, 1752, at Pelham, Massachusetts; married a Mr. Reisdel.
(6) **Rosanna:** born August 24, 1754, at Pelham, Massachusetts; married James Wilson on July 2, 1782.
(7) **John:** born August 5, 1759, at Pelham, Massachusetts.
(8) **Patience:** born January 25, 1762, at Pelham, Massachusetts.
(9) **Samuel: born July 1, 1764, at Colrain, Massachusetts; married Margaret Green in Colrain on July 5, 1785.

Thomas Cochran died in Colrain, Massachusetts, in February 1786. Where or when his wife Margaret died is not known.

Samuel Cochran, the youngest child of Thomas and Margaret Cochran, and the great-grandfather of Nancy Jane Cochran, was born in Colrain, Hampshire County, Massachusetts. In 1812 the name of the county was changed to Franklin. Samuel and his wife, Margaret, moved to Vermont shortly after they were married. There they made their home first in Bennington County, then Cambridge, and finally in Bakersfield Township, Franklin County.

Samuel and Margaret Cochran had ten children, all born in Vermont.
(1) **Elizabeth:** born September 29, 1785, in Bennington County, Vermont; married a Mr. Johnson.
(2) **Minerva:** born April 10, 1787, at Cambridge, Vermont; married, first, Mr. Main, and second, a Mr. Smith; died November 16, 1821.
(3) **Cynthia:** born February 4, 1789, at Cambridge, Vermont; married a Mr. Sherman.
(4) **David:** born March 8, 1791, at Cambridge, Vermont; married Polly _____; died in 1826.
(5) **Samuel:** born June 29, 1793, in Bakersfield Township, Franklin County, Vermont; married Deborah Powell.
(6) **Henry: born May 31, 1795, in Bakersfield Township, Franklin County, Vermont; married Polly (or Mary) _____.
(7) **Wilkinson:** born August 17, 1797, in Bakersfield Township, Franklin County, Vermont.
(8) **Frances:** born October 24, 1798, in Bakersfield Township, Franklin County, Vermont; married Abraham Courtright; died January 8, 1877.
(9) **Harriet:** born February 8, 1801, in Bakersfield Township, Franklin County, Vermont; married Thomas Miller on October 23, 1827; died August 27, 1881.
(10) **Nancy:** born December 17, 1803, in Bakersfield Township, Franklin County, Vermont; married Phineas Frary; died March 3, 1876.

Samuel and his family moved to Buffalo, New York, sometime around 1814. In Buffalo, Samuel built a boat and in 1816 traveled to the mouth of the Huron where he stayed for about three years. Here in 1818 his wife died. In 1819, Samuel relocated his family to a forested area at the present location of Sandusky, Ohio. He was the first white man to build a house in this area.

Samuel Cochran died in Sandusky County, Ohio, in January 1824. Nothing more is known of Margaret Green, wife of Samuel Cochran, as her parents have not been identified and no birth records have been located.

Samuel Cochran died intestate. In February 1824, Jane Cochran, identified as the widow of Samuel Cochran petitioned the Court of Common Pleas in Sandusky County, Ohio, for the rights to Samuel's estate. No records of a second marriage for Samuel Cochran have been found. The inventory of Samuel Cochran's estate and the division of assets makes it clear the probate records are for the Samuel Cochran of interest to this genealogy as the list of names of the heirs includes the surviving Cochran children, including the husband's names of Samuel's married daughters.

Henry Cochran, the sixth child born to Samuel and Margaret (Green) Cochran and grandfather of Nancy Jane Cochran, was born in Vermont on May 31, 1795. Henry married his wife, Polly, in Colrain, Massachusetts. Some records indicate that Henry's wife's name may have been Mary. If so it is likely that Polly was a nick-name, as it is the name most frequently found. Nothing more is known of Polly, as her maiden surname has not been found and her parents have not yet been identified.

Henry traveled with his father to New York and then to the area of Sandusky, Ohio, as previously described. While in the Sandusky area, both Henry and his son, Henry Daniel, must have hunted wolves for bounty money as Sandusky County records of 1823 indicate both received payment for wolf scalps. After the death of his parents, Henry moved his family to Delaware County, Iowa. The 1850 census records show that Henry and his son, Henry Daniel Cochran, were neighbors in District No. 7, Delaware County, Iowa. Both are listed as working as laborers.

Henry and Polly Cochran had at least two children.
(1) **Henry Daniel: born August 31, 1814; died July 25, 1906; married Matilda McFarland on September 17, 1842.
(2) **Mary J.**: born about 1834.

Several census records indicate that Henry Daniel Cochran was born in Sandusky County, Ohio. From the dates of the travels of his father, it is most likely he was born in Vermont, as already reported. The 1880 census reports he was born in Vermont. All other Federal Census records indicate he was born in Ohio. It is not known who provided the census information, but for Henry D. Cochran the records are extremely inconsistent.

Henry Daniel Cochran, father of Nancy Jane Cochran, was married to Matilda McFarland in Sandusky County, Ohio, on September 17, 1842.

Matilda McFarland was born June 19, 1818, in County Tyrone, Ireland. Family information indicates that Matilda left Ireland with her parents within a few days after her birth. It is believed her father faced imprisonment or execution by the English, if captured, because he had participated in Irish rebellion against them. Nothing more is know of Matilda's ancestry. The names of her parents have not been learned. Matilda's name is frequently used with the middle initial "E". Records show the "E" to stand for "Easter" or "Ester".   Which is correct is not known.

HENRY DANIEL AND MATILDA (McFARLAND) COCHRAN

From the birth records for their children, we know that Henry and Matilda lived at different times in Sandusky and Delaware Counties, Ohio, and Delaware and Clayton Counties, Iowa.

Information provided in the obituary for their son, Cyrus C. Cochran, establishes that Henry and Matilda moved their family to Kansas in March 1869. After that time, they operated a farm in the area of Centerville, Kansas.

Henry and Matilda Cochran had six children.

(1) **Robert**: born August 13, 1843, in Sandusky County, Ohio; died November 10, 1844, in Sandusky County, Ohio.

(2) **George Leonard**: born January 30, 1845, in Sandusky County, Ohio; married Mary Jane Husted on March 1, 1868, in Centerville, Linn County, Kansas; died March 8, 1899; buried at the Oakwood Cemetery near Centerville.

(3) **Cyrus C.**: born October 28, 1847, in Sandusky County, Ohio; married, first, Rebecca Jane Jones March 24, 1869, at Mound City, Linn County, Kansas, and second, Allie Edwards in 1913; died April 3, 1915, at Selma, Anderson County, Kansas; is buried at the Oakwood Cemetery near Centerville, Kansas.

(4) **Nancy Jane: born January 13, 1850, in Delaware County, Iowa; married, first, James Louis Lusk and second, Joseph Whitesel Mapes; died July 15, 1913.

(5) **Polly Anvilla**: born February 13, 1852, at Clayton County, Iowa; married Moses Jones on February 3, 1870, at Mound City, Linn County, Kansas; died in 1846; buried at the Pleasant View Cemetery, Linn County, Kansas.

(6) **William James**: born July 15, 1854, in Clayton County, Iowa.

Henry Daniel Cochran died July 25, 1906, near Centerville, Kansas. Matilda E. (McFarland) Cochran died April 3, 1872, near Centerville, Kansas. Both Henry Daniel and Matilda Cochran are buried at the Oakwood Cemetery, near Centerville, Kansas.

Nancy Jane Cochran traveled with her parents to the area of Centerville, Kansas, where they farmed. Here Nancy Jane met and married her first husband, James Louis Lusk. Nancy and James Lusk had five children. Following the death of her first husband, Nancy Jane Lusk lived with her father for awhile. On June 10, 1882, Nancy Jane Lusk married Joseph Whitesel Mapes, a farmer and Civil War veteran. The remaining biographical information about Nancy Jane can be found in the Mapes portion of this genealogy.

It is believed that Nancy Jane's father objected strenuously to her marriage to Joseph Whitesel Mapes, possibly because he expected her to continue to live at home and to care for him. After all, he took in her entire family after the death of her husband. The strongest evidence of some unhappiness comes from the will of Henry D. Cochran. In his will, Henry D. Cochran leaves $50.00 to each of Nancy's children and the balance of the estate is ordered divided into equal thirds going to Nancy's surviving two brothers and sister. Nancy is left the sum of one dollar. A transcription of the will is provided on the following page.

THE WILL OF HENRY DANIEL COCHRAN

****

The following transcription of the will of Henry Cochran has been made from a copy obtained from the Lynn County Courthouse, Mound City, Kansas. Punctuation has been altered.

****

County of Linn and State of Kansas.

I Henry D. Cochran, of County and State aforesaid, being of lawful age, and sound mind, Do hereby will and bequeath my property personal and real as follows. To my grand children, each and in full viz Katy Lusk, $100.00; John H. Lusk, $50.00; Polly Lusk, $50.00; Ingraham C. Lusk, $50.00; Fanny Lusk, $50.00. Then to the heirs of my son George L. Cochran (deceased); to my son Cyrus C. Cochran, and my daughter Anvilla Jones, each and equal one third, being one third to George L. Cochran's heirs, one third to Cyrus C. Cochran or heirs, and one third to Anvilla Jones or heirs, the remaining property after the above specified amounts, to grand children, and necessary debts, sickness, and burial expenses have been fully paid, and one dollar paid to my daughter Nancy J. Mapes, mother of aforesaid named grand children, to whoom amounts specified has been made, The distribution of my property to be made without recourse to law, differences to be settled by arbritation in a peacable manner, and any or either heir going to law in the matter of my Estate, to be by that act disinherited from any benefit therein, and as administrator I empower my son Cyrus C. Cochran to act.

Henry D. Cochran, Testator

Witnessed by us whoo saw testator sign his name there to.

J.D. Trear, Witness   W.E. McIntyre, Witness
   Oakwood, Kansas   Oakwood, Ks

I W.B. Scott, Notary Public, In and for Linn County, State of Kansas Hereby certify that I wrote the foregoing will of Henry D. Cochran, Saw him sign the same, and the witnesses put their names thereto, this sixth day of March AD 1901.

W.B. Scott, Notary Public

A codicil to a will made by me on the sixth day of March AD 1901. As follows, the alowence of $100.00 to Katy Lusk to be $50.00, instead of $100.00. And the amount to Ingraham C. Lusk of $50.00 to revert to the Estate, proper, as Ingraham C. Lusk has died since the making of the will in 1901.

Witnessed this 24th of July 1905,
   by N.K. Scott
      Alma S. Howard   H.D. Cochran
   and written by
      W.B. Scott

****

```
***********************************************
```
OBITUARY FOR CYRUS C. COCHRAN
from the
BLUE MOUND SUN
April 16, 1915

Cyrus C. Cochran died at his home in Selma last Sat. evening, following an illness of 12 day pneumonia. He was born in Ohio 28 Oct 1847 and came to Kans with his parents March 1869. He was married to Rebecca J. Jones (no date) who died 8 years ago. Five of their seven children survive him. He settled in Rich Twp (Anderson Co) about 1870 and has been a resident there ever since. On Dec 2, 1913, he married Miss Allie Edwards. About 21 years ago he united with the Methodist Church. He died April 3, 1915. He was buried in the Oakwood Cemetery (Linn Co.)
```
***********************************************
```

THE GRAVE MARKER OF HENRY D. AND MATILDA E. COCHRAN
Located at the Oakwood Cemetery near
Centerville, Kansas

TENTH GENERATION

MADELINE[10] ADAMS

Madeline[10] Adams was born in Paris Township, Linn County, Kansas, on October 22, 1913. She was the second daughter born to Robert Clyde[9] Adams and his first wife, Hattie Mapes.

Madeline was five years old when her mother died December 6, 1918, during a flu epidemic. Nothing could describe her feelings as she grew up better than an undated letter found in her papers many years later. The following is a transcription of that letter probably written sometime before 1960. The punctuation and spelling in the text has been edited a little to improve continuity. No attempt has been made to correct the entire text. The title has been added.

RECOLLECTIONS

There is so much I remember I hardly know where to start. I was one of three little girls beginning my life on a Kansas farm. And like so many other little girls; lived, played, and loved.

My earliest recollections of life and my surroundings was when my mother lay dying in the big walnut bed in the west bedroom of the old farm house. For a while she was delirious and would say funny things. My two sisters and my self thought it great fun to race into her bedroom and hear all the funny things she'd say to us. We were duly scolded and shooed out of the room by grandmother, who with my daddy took care of us. Then came the day when grandmother ran to the barn to get daddy and I heard them say she was gone. I didn't realize then what it meant, but was soon to know, when my daddy held us up to see mother for the last time and we were allowed to kiss her good-by.

After mother's death, there followed a period of one housekeeper after another and we three little girls were allowed to do as we pleased, without much discipline. Daddy and grandmother felt sorry for us, as indeed it was quite a tragedy for three little girls ages 7 - 4 - 2 to lose their mother so young. We were spoiled rotten.

Several of my aunts and cousins came to visit us and with them a strange woman I didn't pay much attention to at the time, but this strange woman was soon to become my step-mother. In those days the word step-mother was something to abhor, so instead of looking upon her kindly, we learned to look upon her as some kind of a monster. These thoughts were due to the gossip of all my relatives, neighbors, and my grandmother, who thought no one could love or take care of us like she did.

The day finally came when daddy told us we were going to have a new mother, and that he was going to get her and would be gone for awhile.

While daddy was gone, we three gathered all the big sticks we could find and hid them in his closet. We were determined this monster was not to invade our household and that we would use the sticks to whip daddy when he came home. Our sticks were discovered by granny who took them out of the closet and tried to prepare us for our new mother.

I don't remember when they came home as time didn't mean very much to me. I do remember of our new mother trying to get us to call her mother, and all three of us stubbornly refused and called her Bertha which was her first name. My own mother died in December of 1918 and daddy remarried in September of 1919. The following spring my beloved grand-mother died and it seemed to me everything I had known or loved suddenly disappeared. I was a lonesome forlorn little girl and took to crying a lot. My parents were exasperated with my crying. My step mother tried to love me and comfort me, but I would have none of it. I think this would probably have gone on, if it hadn't of been for one of my aunts, who hid in the old peach orchard and every time I cried, would mimic me. I began to believe there was a ghost in the orchard, and soon stopped crying.

This summer, we were due to have a new arrival, and in July, my two sisters and myself were hastily hurried upstairs with my uncle, there we awaited the arrival of my new baby brother. What he did to entertain us during those lonely hours while the doctor was there I'll never know. When I went downstairs I saw an ugly, red, squalling infant. That September I started to school and can remember walking the mile and half to school on the hot dusty road. I don't think I learned very much as I was allowed to sit with my older sister and she did most of my work for me. My school clothes consisted of button shoes, long black stockings, a dark calico dress which hung loosely, and braided hair. My hair was naturally curly, so it frizzed all over my head. I went to school in a one room school house. In those days we bought all our own books, pencils, and tablets, carried our lunch in a tin pail, drank water from a well and used an outside privy. I remember my teacher had a long nose, wore a black skirt, white blouse and had her hair combed in a pompadour. I was terribly afraid of her. After school was out we trudged home again, swinging our empty lunch pail. We arrived home starved to death. We all had a certain amount of chores to do. I had to fill the wood box behind the kitchen stove and pick up corn cobs. It seemed the wood box was always empty and the bushel basket held a million cobs. After all our chores were done we would all gather around the family table for supper and as usual daddy would say, "Did you wash your hands?" The answer would be all of us hastily jumping up to wash, that is give ourselves a lick and a promise, most of the dirt went on the towels.

About that time I had a birthday. I was six and had never had a birthday cake. Mother told me to go into the pantry to get something. There sat one of the most glorious cakes I had ever seen, with six candles all aglow. I ran and cried to daddy that the cake was on fire, everyone laughed at me and wished me a happy birthday. It was about that time that I began to call my step-mother, mother. I thought someone who could do something that wonderful to me wasn't so bad after all.

THE NUMBER 9 SCHOOL HOUSE
Located at Kossuth when Madeline Adams attended,
it is now located in a historical park in
Mound City, Kansas.

Madeline's sisters remember her name to be Nettie. During most of her young life at home Madeline was called Nettie. This nickname, which she hated, stuck until she left home.

As a young woman, Madeline Adams moved to Kansas City and stayed with her aunt Kate, Catherine Grunden. Madeline worked as a maid for wealthy families in Kansas City, Missouri, and later as a waitress, also in Kansas City. Later she worked as a "Harvey Girl" at an inn in Needles, California.

From Needles, by mail, Madeline kept up correspondence with a boyfriend she had met in Kansas City. The boyfriend was Charles Edward Whitehead. Their love blossomed, and they arranged to get married in Kansas City on July 26, 1936. The "arrangement" necessary to get Madeline back to Kansas City from Needles involved a little larceny. Neither Madeline or Charlie had very much. Charlie had a car, but not two dimes to rub together. Madeline had about a hundred dollars saved. In order to save what they had, they decided to take advantage of a Fred Harvey Company policy. Madeline could be allowed a trip home at the expense of her employer if there was a serious emergency at home.

Madeline and Charlie cooked up a plan whereby Charlie would telegram Madeline that one of her family members was dying and she was needed at home. They planned the ruse for a night when they knew there was a train from Needles to Kansas City the very next day. On cue, Charlie's telegram arrived and Madeline was packed off by her understanding employer. Once in Kansas City, she married Charlie, resigned her job, and headed off to California to pursue their dreams.

Madeline and Charlie in 1936. The picture was taken in La Junta, Colorado, as they visited Madeline's sister Juanita on the way to California.

Madeline and Charlie first went to San Francisco to enjoy the end of their honeymoon and to look for jobs. Work was not to be found so they continued on to Los Angeles, California. There they were able to find work in restaurants. Charlie cooked and Madeline was a waitress. Madeline continued to work until she became a mother then she stayed home to raise her children. Charlie worked at a number of locations, including the Brown Derby, before he settled into a career with United Airlines. At United, Charlie worked himself into a position as a supervising chef and ran one of the largest kitchens in the country.

Madeline and Charles Whitehead had three daughters.
(1) **EMMA LOU WHITEHEAD**: born August 8, 1941; married, first, Thomas Addicks Webb (born August 24, 1937) on January 1, 1963, and second, Alan L. Bargerstock on December 31, 1992, both at Las Vegas, Nevada. Emma and Alan Bargerstock live, work, and operate a horse ranch at Payson, Utah. Emma and Tom Webb had two sons.
> (1) **Colin Eaton Webb**: born January 1, 1964.
> (2) **Ronald Addicks Webb**: born December 20, 1965; married Rae Ellen (Smith) Lui on November 5, 1990. Ronald and Rae have two sons, both born at Fountain Valley, Calif.
> > (1) **Christian Addicks Webb**: born June 4, 1991.
> > (2) **James Thomas Webb**: born September 20, 1995.

(2) **JUDY LEE WHITEHEAD** : born January 30, 1945; married, first, John Lewis Chance, Jr. on May 25, 1964, second, George Goss Wood on July 25, 1976, and third, Steven Knowles on October 16, 1993, at Santa Maria, California. John Chance died following a long bout with multiple Sclerosis. Judy and Steven Knowles live in Tulare, California. Judy has one daughter from her marriage to George Wood.
> (1) **Heather Dawn Wood**: born March 17, 1978, in Kansas City, Missouri.

(3) **JANE ANN WHITEHEAD**: born January 30, 1945; married Kenneth Lloyd Bosworth on February 8, 1964. Kenneth and Jane Bosworth have twin sons.
> (1) **Thomas Lloyd Bosworth**: born July 3, 1972; married Abha Malhotra (born October 11, 1973, at Toronto, Ontario, Canada), daughter of Anand Kishore and Shashi Kiron (Kapoor) Malhotra, on July 11, 1993, at Knott's Berry Farm, Buena Park, California.
> (2) **Charles Floyd Bosworth**: born July 3, 1972; married Rain Christine Grant (born January 6, 1972, at San Francisco, California), daughter of Robert John and Jane Christine (Omark) Grant, on August 21, 1993, aboard the sternwheeler William D. Evans on Mission Bay, San Diego, California.

Ken and Jane Bosworth live in Mission Viejo, California. Jane is a special education tutor and a mystery writer. Ken manages a power plant for the City of Los Angeles.

About three years following his retirement from United Airlines, Charles and Madeline Whitehead relocated to Santa Maria, California. Here, in 1977, they began their real retirement.

Charlie planted a large garden each year and Madeline canned fruits, vegetables, and jellies enough for the entire year with some to share with their children and grandchildren.

CHARLES AND MADELINE   **JUDY, EMMA, AND JANE**
These pictures of the Whitehead family were taken in 1963 at their home in Los Angeles, California

In 1986, all the children and grandchildren gathered in Santa Maria, California for a celebration of Madeline's and Charlie's fifty years of marriage.

Charles Whitehead died as a result of congestive heart failure on October 4, 1991. Madeline died March 31, 1994, at Orcutt, California. Charles and Madeline Whitehead are buried at the Rose Hills Memorial Park in Whittier, California.

STATE OF KANSAS. 54 702

STATE BOARD OF HEALTH—DIV. OF VITAL STATISTICS.

STANDARD CERTIFICATE OF BIRTH.

PLACE OF BIRTH	
County of _Lynn_	Registered No. _119_
Township of _Lewis_	
City of _____ No. _____ street.	

FULL NAME OF CHILD _Madeline Adams_ † If child is not yet named, make supplemental report, as directed

Sex of Child _f_	Twin, triplet, or other? (To be answered only in event of plural births.)	Number in order of birth.	Legitimate. _yes_	Date of birth _Oct 22_ 191_3_ (Month) (Day) (Year)

FATHER.	MOTHER.
Full Name. _Clyde Adams_	Full Maiden Name. _Hettie Majors_
Residence. _Mound City Kan_	Residence. _Mound City Ks_
Color. _W_ Age at last birthday _23_ (Years.)	Color. _W_ Age at last birthday _22_ (Years.)
Birthplace. _Kans._	Birthplace. _Kans._
Occupation. _Farmer_	Occupation. _Housewife_
Number of children born to this mother, including present birth _2_	Number of children of this mother now living _2_

CERTIFICATE OF ATTENDING PHYSICIAN OR MIDWIFE.*

I hereby certify that I attended the birth of this child, who was _Born Alive_ at _9:00_ M., on the date above stated (Born alive or stillborn.)

(Signature) _____ M.D.

*When there was no attending physician or midwife, then the father, householder, etc., should make this return. A stillborn child is one that neither breathes nor shows other evidence of life after birth.

Given name added from supplemental report _9-24-42_ 191_

Address _Mound City Ks_

Filed _Oct 31_ 191_   _____

Registrar.   Registrar.

MADELINE ADAMS' BIRTH CERTIFICATE
She was born on the Adams farm near
Mound City, Kansas

MARRIAGE LICENSE.

No.
A 63693

OFFICE OF

· RECORDER OF DEEDS ·
JACKSON COUNTY, MISSOURI.
AT KANSAS CITY,

STATE OF MISSOURI } ss.
COUNTY OF JACKSON.

This License authorizes any Judge, Justice of the Peace, licensed or ordained Preacher of the Gospel, who is a citizen of the United States, or other person authorized under the laws of this State to solemnize marriage between _Charles E Whitehead_ of the County of Jackson and State of Missouri, who is _over_ the age of twenty-one years and _Madeline Adams_ of the County of Jackson and State of Missouri, who is _over_ the age of eighteen years

Witness my hand as Recorder, with the seal of office hereto affixed, at my office in Kansas City, Missouri, this _20th_ day of _July_ 1936

JOSEPH S. CRISP
RECORDER.

By _J A Kilmer_
DEPUTY RECORDER.

STATE OF MISSOURI } ss.
COUNTY OF JACKSON.

This is to certify that the undersigned, an _Ordained Minister_ did in said County and State on the _26_ day of _July_ A.D. 1936 unite in marriage the above named persons.

J. R. Thomas, Pastor
Oakhurst Meth. Epis. Church.

The person performing the marriage ceremony will please insert after his signature the place of his Office, Church or Residence.
This License must be returned to the office of Recorder of Deeds by the person solemnizing the marriage, within ninety days from the issuing thereof.

MADELINE ADAMS' MARRIAGE LICENSE
Madeline Adams and Charles Whitehead were married
in Kansas City, Missouri

CERTIFICATE OF DEATH
STATE OF CALIFORNIA
USE BLACK INK ONLY/NO ERASURES, WHITEOUTS OR ALTERATIONS
VS-11 (REV. 7/93)

STATE FILE NUMBER		LOCAL REGISTRATION NUMBER

	1. NAME OF DECEDENT—FIRST (GIVEN)	2. MIDDLE	3. LAST (FAMILY)
	MADELINE	A.	WHITEHEAD

DECEDENT PERSONAL DATA	4. DATE OF BIRTH MM/DD/CCYY	5. AGE YRS.	IF UNDER 1 YEAR — MONTHS / DAYS	IF UNDER 24 HOURS — HOURS / MINUTES	6. SEX	7. DATE OF DEATH MM/DD/CCYY	8. HOUR
	10/22/1913	80			F	03/31/1994	1757

	9. STATE OF BIRTH	10. SOCIAL SECURITY NO.	11. MILITARY SERVICE	12. MARITAL STATUS	13. EDUCATION —YEARS COMPLETED
	KS	562-16-5319	19___ To 19___ [X] NONE	Widowed	12

	14. RACE	15. HISPANIC—SPECIFY		16. USUAL EMPLOYER
	White	[ ] YES	[X] NO	Self Employed

	17. OCCUPATION	18. KIND OF BUSINESS	19. YEARS IN OCCUPATION
	Homemaker	Own Home	54

USUAL RESIDENCE	20. RESIDENCE—STREET AND NUMBER OR LOCATION
	24702 Pallas Way

	21. CITY	22. COUNTY	23. ZIP CODE	24. YRS IN COUNTY	25. STATE OR FOREIGN COUNTRY
	Mission Viejo	Orange	92691	16	California

INFORMANT	26. NAME, RELATIONSHIP	27. MAILING ADDRESS (STREET AND NUMBER OR RURAL ROUTE NUMBER, CITY OR TOWN, STATE, ZIP)
	Jane A. Bosworth - Daughter	24702 Pallas Way, Mission Viejo, CA 92691

SPOUSE AND PARENT INFORMATION	28. NAME OF SURVIVING SPOUSE—FIRST	29. MIDDLE	30. LAST (MAIDEN NAME)	
	-	-	-	
	31. NAME OF FATHER—FIRST	32. MIDDLE	33. LAST	34. BIRTH STATE
	Robert	Clyde	Adams	KS
	35. NAME OF MOTHER—FIRST	36. MIDDLE	37. LAST (MAIDEN)	38. BIRTH STATE
	Hattie	Surilda	Mapes	KS

DISPOSITION(S)	39. DATE MM/DD/CCYY	40. PLACE OF FINAL DISPOSITION
	04/06/1994	Rose Hills Memorial Park, 3900 S. Workman Mill Rd., Whittier, CA 9060

FUNERAL DIRECTOR AND LOCAL REGISTRAR	41. TYPE OF DISPOSITION(S)	42. SIGNATURE OF EMBALMER	43. LICENSE NO.
	Burial	▶ Daryl Vanderlyn	6867
	44. NAME OF FUNERAL DIRECTOR	45. LICENSE NO.	46. SIGNATURE OF LOCAL REGISTRAR	47. DATE MM/DD/CCYY
	Rose Hills Mortuary	FD-970	▶ Mid Schacher	04/04/1994

PLACE OF DEATH	101. PLACE OF DEATH	102. IF HOSPITAL, SPECIFY ONE:	103. FACILITY OTHER THAN HOSPITAL:	104. COUNTY
	Residence	[ ] IP [ ] ER/OP [ ] DOA	[ ] CONV. HOSP. [X] RES. [ ] OTHER	Santa Barbara
	105. STREET ADDRESS—STREET AND NUMBER OR LOCATION			106. CITY
	263 Crescent Avenue			Santa Maria

CAUSE OF DEATH	107. DEATH WAS CAUSED BY: (ENTER ONLY ONE CAUSE PER LINE FOR A, B, C, AND D)		TIME INTERVAL BETWEEN ONSET AND DEATH	108. DEATH REPORTED TO CORONER
	IMMEDIATE CAUSE (A)	Arteriosclerotic Cardiovascular Disease	Years	[XX] YES [ ] NO
				REFERRAL NUMBER C94-131
	DUE TO (B)			109. BIOPSY PERFORMED [ ] YES [XX] NO
	DUE TO (C)			110. AUTOPSY PERFORMED [ ] YES [XX] NO
	DUE TO (D)			111. USED IN DETERMINING CAUSE [ ] YES [ ] NO
	112. OTHER SIGNIFICANT CONDITIONS CONTRIBUTING TO DEATH BUT NOT RELATED TO CAUSE GIVEN IN 107			
	---			
	113. WAS OPERATION PERFORMED FOR ANY CONDITION IN ITEM 107 OR 112? IF YES, LIST TYPE OF OPERATION AND DATE.			

PHYSICIAN'S CERTIFICATION	114. I CERTIFY THAT TO THE BEST OF MY KNOWLEDGE DEATH OCCURRED AT THE HOUR, DATE AND PLACE STATED FROM THE CAUSES STATED.	115. SIGNATURE AND TITLE OF CERTIFIER	116. LICENSE NO.	117. DATE MM/DD/CCYY
	DECEDENT ATTENDED SINCE MM/DD/CCYY	DECEDENT LAST SEEN ALIVE MM/DD/CCYY	▶ ---	---	---
	---	---			
			118. TYPE ATTENDING PHYSICIAN'S NAME, MAILING ADDRESS + ZIP		

CORONER'S USE ONLY	I CERTIFY THAT IN MY OPINION DEATH OCCURRED AT THE HOUR, DATE AND PLACE STATED FROM THE CAUSES STATED.	120. INJURY AT WORK	121. INJURY DATE MM/DD/CCYY	122. HOUR	123. PLACE OF INJURY
		[ ] YES [X] NO	----	--	----
	119. MANNER OF DEATH	124. DESCRIBE HOW INJURY OCCURRED (EVENTS WHICH RESULTED IN INJURY)			
	[XX] NATURAL [ ] SUICIDE [ ] HOMICIDE				
	[ ] ACCIDENT [ ] PENDING INVESTIGATION [ ] COULD NOT BE DETERMINED	----			
	125. LOCATION (STREET AND NUMBER OR LOCATION AND CITY AND ZIP CODE)				
	----				
	126. SIGNATURE OF CORONER OR DEPUTY CORONER	127. DATE MM/DD/CCYY	128. TYPED NAME, TITLE OF CORONER OR DEPUTY CORONER		
	▶ Dennis Prescott	04/01/1994	Dennis Prescott, Deputy Coroner		

STATE REGISTRAR	A	B	C	D	E	F	G	H	FAX AUTH. #	CENSUS TRACT

MADELINE ADAMS' DEATH CERTIFICATE
Madeline was living in a board and care home in
Orcutt, California, at the time of her death

WHITEHEAD FAMILY

Charles Edward Whitehead, husband of Madeline Adams, is the son of William Henry Whitehead and Blanche Eaton. His Whitehead ancestry is discussed here.

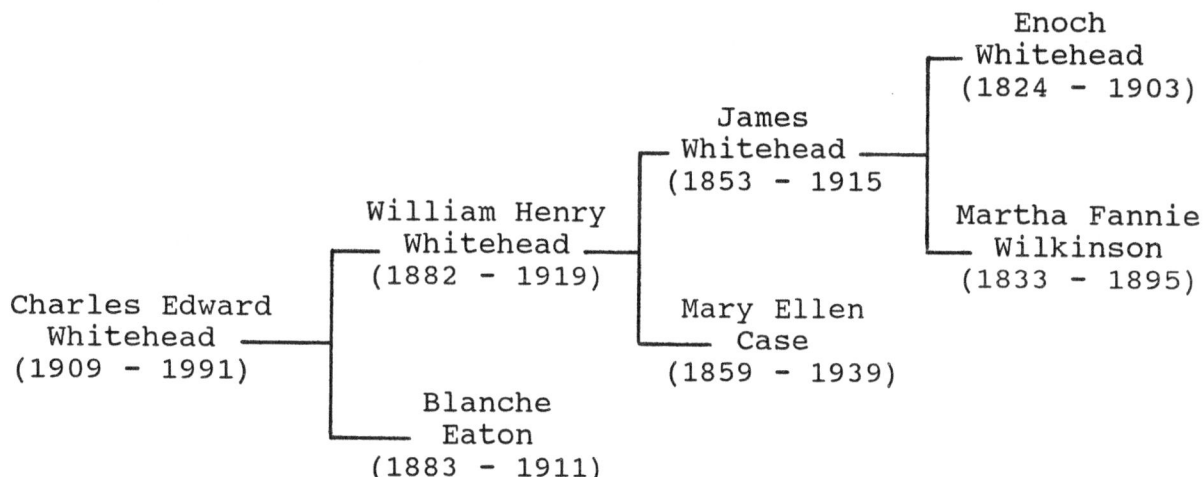

```
                                                                    Enoch
                                                                  ┌ Whitehead
                                                                  │ (1824 - 1903)
                                                      James       │
                                                    ┌ Whitehead ──┤
                                                    │ (1853 - 1915│
                                  William Henry     │             │ Martha Fannie
                                ┌ Whitehead ────────┤             └ Wilkinson
                                │ (1882 - 1919)     │               (1833 - 1895)
            Charles Edward      │                   │
            Whitehead ──────────┤                   │ Mary Ellen
            (1909 - 1991)       │                   └── Case
                                │                       (1859 - 1939)
                                │ Blanche
                                └── Eaton
                                    (1883 - 1911)
```

Charles Whitehead's great-grandfather, Enoch Whitehead, was born in England, October 6, 1824. Enoch's father was James, but nothing more is known of Enoch's parents. Enoch Whitehead married Martha Fannie Wilkinson on April 2, 1850, at Masbro, Rotherham, York, England. Their marriage licence identified him as a joiner and her as a spinster. It's hard to imagine Miss Wilkinson to be considered a spinster, since she was not yet 17 years old at the time she married. She was born April 4, 1833. The marriage license identifies John Wilkinson to be her father. Nothing more is known of her parents.

According to the 1900 census, Enoch traveled to the United States in 1853. He was accompanied on the voyage by his wife and his first two children, Martha and James.

Enoch settled in Illinois and spent his years farming. He lived in McKee Township, Adams County, Illinois, for most of the 50 years he lived in America.

Enoch and Martha Whitehead had nine children.
(1) **Martha Ellen Whitehead**: born July 25, 1851, in England; died March 26, 1854.
(2) **James Whitehead: born January 24, 1853, in England; died August 12, 1915, in Chariton County, Missouri; married Mary Ellen Case on January 13, 1876.

(3) **Mary Sue Whitehead**: born May 8, 1855; married a Mr. Whitaker.
(4) **Emma Jane Whitehead**: born September 18, 1857; died August 27, 1903; married a Mr. Triplett.
(5) **John Will Whitehead**: born February 18, 1859; died October 30, 1859.
(6) **Ada Elizabeth Whitehead**: born September 21, 1860; died March 9, 1929; married Thomas Lane.
(7) **Catherine Whitehead**: born September 3, 1862; died May 24, 1893; married a Mr. Perrigo.
(8) **Martha Fannie Whitehead**: born March 3, 1864; died February 24, 1932; married a Mr. Likes.
(9) **Anna May Whitehead**: born June 13, 1868; died July 13, 1882.

MARRIAGE RECORD FOR ENOCH WHITEHEAD AND
MARTHA FANNY WILKINSON
Although the license states that Miss Wilkinson was 19 years old, her birth record from a family bible clearly establishes her age at the time of her marriage to be two days less than seventeen years.

Martha Fannie Whitehead died June 5, 1895. Enoch Whitehead died September 13, 1903, near McKee Township, Illinois. He is buried at the Whitaker cemetery.

As a young man James Whitehead, eldest son of Enoch Whitehead, worked on his father's farm. In the 1870 census, James is reported to be 16 years old and living at home. Only a short distance away, also in McKee Township, lived the family of Daniel Case. Daniel's second daughter, Mary, who would become the wife of James Whitehead six years later, is reported to be 11 years old and going to school.

Daniel Case was born in Kentucky sometime after 1830. Nothing is known of his family or how he came to live in Illinois. Daniel

Case married Lovicie Catherine Lane, a native of Illinois, and the only child of Noah and Mary Richard (Ramey) Lane. Noah Lane was the father of 11 other children from a first marriage to Lovicie Tylor. Lovicie (Tylor) Lane died in 1838 following the birth of her eleventh child.

Lovicie Catherine Lane was born March 21, 1841, and died April 7, 1881. She married Daniel Case on August 31, 1856.

Daniel and Lovicie Catherine Case had five children.
(1) **Sarah Case**: married a Mr. Hull.
(2) **John Case:**
(3) **Mary Ellen Case: born December 5, 1859; died February 3, 1939; married James Whitehead January 13, 1876.
(4) **Lizzie Case**: married a Mr. Thomas.
(5) **Anna Case**: married a Mr. Martin.

James Whitehead farmed and acquired land in Chariton and Carroll Counties, Missouri. James Whitehead married Mary Ellen Case on January 13, 1876. As his sons married he gave each of them 50 acres of farm land as wedding presents.

James and Mary Ellen Whitehead had seven children whose histories are well documented. Some family accounts indicate they may have had as many as eleven children, although no documentation has been located to verify this. The seven children known to have been born to James and Mary are:
(1) **Minnie May (Mary) Whitehead**: born January 11, 1877; died December 19, 1950; married Isaac Cooper; had two children, Walter (born June 1896) and Amy (born November 1897).
(2) **Martha Irene Whitehead**: born October 25, 1878; died October 10, 1950; married Charles Edward Croco on January 20, 1897.
(3) **Julia Ann Whitehead**: born March 20, 1880; died August 22, 1962; married Nathan David Baldry on March 21, 1904.
(4) **William Henry Whitehead: born January 19, 1882; died July 19, 1919; married, first, Blanche Eaton on February 17, 1906, and second, Mary Steele on December 22, 1911.
(5) **James E. Whitehead**: born September 26, 1884; killed on September 28, 1908, while trying to break a wild horse. The horse had been sold to James by a friend who apparently knew the animal was dangerous. The bitterness of the family is apparent by the inscription on the gravestone: "Betrayed by those who he thought were his friends.:
(6) **Walter Whitehead**: born November 8, 1889; died March 7, 1963; married March 7, 1913, to Iona Likes.
(7) **Edwin Earl Whitehead**: born December 7, 1894; died August 9, 1968; married Cecil Parks; had two sons, Leroy and Ralph.

Some family records indicate that other children named Katie, Charles, Enoch, and Eric, may have been born to James and Mary

Whitehead. This information has not been substantiated by this author. The will of James Whitehead, made on March 27, 1909, names three daughters and three sons. The second son of James and Mary Whitehead, James, preceded his parents in death. A transcribed copy of the will follows the text of this chapter.

James Whitehead died on August 12, 1915. Following his death his wife, Mary, married Mr. Post and made her home in Hale, Missouri. She was living in Hale at the time of her death. Mary is buried with her first husband, James Whitehead, in the Lakeside Cemetery, about one mile south of Sumner, Missouri.

WILLIAM AND BLANCHE (EATON) WHITEHEAD ON THEIR WEDDING DAY, FEBRUARY 17, 1906

William Henry Whitehead grew up on his father's farm. Most of the lands were in Chariton County, Missouri, although some of the land was in Carroll County, just across the Grand River. Both William and his father were also joiners, a skill passed down from William's grandfather. They did finish work on many of the buildings in the area.

William Whitehead was born January 19, 1882. He married Blanche Eaton, daughter of John Eli and Mary Louisa (Smith) Eaton, on February 17, 1906. Blanche Eaton was born April 23, 1883, in Grand River Township, Livingston County, Missouri. William and Blanche made their home on their own 50 acres of farm land, given them by William's father as a wedding gift. The land given to William spanned the Grand River and as such was partly in Chariton County and partly in Carroll County, Missouri.

William and Blanche Whitehead had three sons.
(1) **Rollie Elsworth Whitehead**: born February 26, 1907; died May 23, 1953, of wounds received in battle during WWII. Rollie is buried at Fort Sam National Cemetery, Fort Sam Houston, Texas. Rollie married Marguerite E. Koch on September 22, 1937. Marguerite was born June 14, 1916, at Hamburg, Iowa. Following Rollie's death, Marguerite remarried. Marguerite Hovel, widowed for the second time, lives in San Antonio, Texas. Marguerite and Rollie Whitehead had one son and one adopted daughter.
   (1) **Lloyd Arnold Whitehead**: born August 28, 1938; married Phyllis Masonhall (born November 17, 1941) on April 26, 1958. Lloyd and Phyllis Whitehead have four children.
      (1) **Candy Whitehead**: born July 7, 1959; married Jay McCraw. Candy and Jay McCraw have two children.
         (1) **Jermey McCraw**: born January 4, 1983.
         (2) **Jessica McCraw**: born August 14, 1987.
      (2) **Cindy Whitehead**: born October 26, 1960; married Robert Buford. Though now divorced, Cindy and Robert Buford have two children.
         (1) **Shannon Buford**: born March 17, 1981.
         (2) **Sabrina Buford**: born July 5, 1984.
      (3) **Lloyd Arnold Whitehead, Jr.** : born February 22, 1963; married Dena Jurey, who was born August 4, 1963. Lloyd and Dena Whitehead have four children.
         (1) **Jessica Whitehead**: born July 31, 1985.
         (2) **Brookie Whitehead**: born August 12, 1987.
         (3) **Brandi Whitehead**: born January 14, 1989.
         (4) **Brian Whitehead**: born May 29, 1990.
      (4) **Randy Allen Whitehead**: born January 17, 1966.
   (2) **Linda Whitehead**: born April 30, 1944; adopted when she was one month old; married John Elizando, Jr. Linda and John Elizando have two children.
      (1) **Timothy Scott Elizando**: born March 9, 1964.
      (2) **John David Elizando**: born January 13, 1968.

Rollie and Marguerite Whitehead. The picture was taken shortly after they were married in 1937. The following article appeared in a 1935 edition of the Hale Leader, published at Hale, Missouri.

Rollie Whitehead and Marguerite Koch were auto riding out in these parts Saturday afternoon. Rollie stopped at Lakeside cemetery to view his father's and mother's graves and at the Eaton home to bid his aunt and uncle goodbye before departing for the "Gems of the Pacific."

**(2) Charles Edward Whitehead: born August 11, 1909; died October 4, 1991; married Madeline Adams on July 26, 1936. Charles and Madeline Whitehead had three daughters.

(1) **Emma Lou Whitehead:** born August 8, 1941; married, first, Thomas Addicks Webb (born August 24, 1937) on January 1, 1963, and second, Alan L. Bargerstock on December 31, 1992, in Clark County, Nevada. Emma and Alan Bargerstock live and raise horses at Payson, Utah. Emma and Thomas Webb had two sons.

(1) **Colin Eaton Webb:** born January 1, 1964.

(2) **Ronald Addicks Webb:** born December 20, 1965; married Rae Ellen (Smith) Lui on November 5, 1990. Rae was born April 20, 1962 in West Covina, California. Her parents are Eldon Frank and Sandra Rae (Stone) Smith. Ronald and Rae have two sons, both born in Fountain Valley, California.

(1) **Christian Addicks Webb:** born June 4, 1991.

(2) **James Thomas Webb:** born September 20, 1995.

(2) **Jane Ann Whitehead:** born January 30, 1945; married Kenneth Lloyd Bosworth (born April 2, 1942) on February 8, 1964. Kenneth is the son of Lloyd Omer and Carol Rose (Colburn) Bosworth. Jane and Kenneth Bosworth have twin sons.

(1) **Thomas Lloyd Bosworth**: born July 3, 1972, married Abha Malhotra on July 11, 1993.
(2) **Charles Floyd Bosworth**: born July 3, 1972, married Rain C. Grant on August 21, 1993.
(3) **Judy Lee Whitehead**: born January 30, 1945; married, first, John Lewis Chance, Jr. (born May 14, 1944) on May 25, 1964, second, George Goss Wood on May 25, 1976, and third, Steven Knowles on October 16, 1993, at Santa Maria, California. John Chance died February 21, 1983, following a long bout with multiple sclerosis. Judy and George Wood had one daughter.

(1)**Heather Dawn Wood**: born March 17, 1978, in Kansas City, Missouri.

CHARLES WHITEHEAD ABOUT 1936

(3) **Henry Raymond Whitehead**: born March 7, 1911. In his adult life, Henry always signed his name "Ray" or "Raymond". In a letter to Charles and Madeline Whitehead congratulating them upon their marriage in 1936, Ray indicated his wife was dead and he had a daughter named Ula Mae, who was born in September 1931. Raymond was working in the area near Eugene, Oregon, as a lumberjack in 1936. Ray Whitehead married, second, Martha (Tolva) Chopard, in about 1944. Martha Copard had three children from a previous marriage: a son, Robert Eugene, and twin daughters, Etta Fay and Ella May, who were born April 4, 1933. Ray and Martha Whitehead were divorced in 1946. Ray was later married to Virginia (Johnson) Kelly. Ray Whitehead is living in Brookings, Oregon, with his adoptive daughter, Etta Fay (Chopard) Waite. Henry Raymond Whitehead is the father of one daughter.

(1) **Ula Mae Whitehead**: born September, 1931. Ula Mae is married and living near Seattle, Washington.

Henry "Ray" Whitehead with second wife, Martha (Tolva) Chopard. This picture was taken about the time they were married in 1944.

Blanche Whitehead died of blood poisoning on March 21, 1911, shortly after the birth of her third son, Henry.

William Whitehead married, second, Mary Steele of Dean Lake, Missouri, on December 22, 1911. Mary was born August 23, 1896, the daughter of William and Martha (Meekum) Steele. William and Mary Whitehead had two children.

(1) **Lorea Ellen Whitehead**: born October 28, 1912; married Robert Henry Dickinson January 31, 1931, at Winner, South Dakota. Robert Dickinson died June 18, 1978. Lorea lives in Hot Springs, South Dakota. Lorea and Robert Dickinson did not have any children.

(2) **Harry Earl Whitehead**: born February 17, 1915.

William Whitehead died of heat stroke while working on his farm on July 19, 1919. He is buried in the Whitehead family plot at the Lakeside Cemetery, about one mile south of Sumner, Missouri.

Mary (Steele) Whitehead was not able to care for all five children, so the three sons of William and Blanche were sent to live with other relatives. Mary retained custody of her own two children and eventually moved to Martin, South Dakota. At Martin she met and married Roy Pierce. Mary and Roy Pierce had three children; Marie Iva, Roy, Jr., and Marrion. Mary Pierce died on March 14, 1983, at Hot Springs, South Dakota.

Charles Whitehead was only ten years old when he went to live with his aunt and uncle, Charles Edward Decatur Pultz and his wife Emma in Hale, Missouri. Emma was Charles' aunt, born Emma Eaton, a sister to Charles' mother, Blanche Eaton. The Pultz's had one daughter, Emma Christina, who was considered by Charlie to be his sister.

Charles was an honor student at Hale High School and an outstanding basketball player. He worked at the Pultz's Drug Store in Hale. One of Charles' early passions was duck hunting at Swan Lake, near Sumner. As Charles grew older, he attended business college and worked odd jobs in Kansas City. In Kansas City he met and eventually married Madeline Adams.

Most of his adult life, Charles worked as a cook. Among his more interesting career stops was a period of about five years when he worked at the Brown Derby Restaurant in Hollywood. He worked for 25 years for United Air Lines. He attained the position of supervising chef and operated one of the largest kitchens in the country. Charles retired from United Air Lines in 1974 and relocated to Santa Maria, California in 1977. Charles spent his retirement years tending his garden and canning almost his entire years supply of vegetables and fruits each summer.

Charles Edward Whitehead died in Santa Maria on October 4, 1991, and was buried at Rose Hills Memorial Park in Whittier, California. Madeline (Adams) Whitehead died March 31, 1994, at Orcutt, California, and is buried beside Charles at Rose Hills Memorial Park.

THE WILL OF JAMES WHITEHEAD

****

The following transcription of the will of James Whitehead is made from a copy obtained from the Circuit Court of Chariton County, at Keytesville, Chariton County, Missouri.

****

I, James Whitehead, of Chariton County, Missouri, being of sound and disposing mind and memory do make, publish and declare this to be my last will and testament in manner and form following;

1st I direct that all my just debts, the expenses of my last illness and my funeral expenses be first paid.

2nd I give, bequeath and devise all of my property of whatsoever kind and nature to the same real, personal or mixed and wheresoever found or situate to my beloved wife Mary E. Whitehead, to have and to hold the same the said Mary E. Whitehead for and during her natural life and at her death I direct that all of the rest, residue and remainder of my estate go to my Six children, namely Minnie May Cooper, wife of Isaac Cooper, Martha Irene Croco, wife of Charles Croco, Julia Ann Baldry, wife of Edward Baldry, William H. Whitehead, Walter Whitehead, and Earl Whitehead, the said children to share and share alike.

3rd I hereby revoke any and all former wills by me made.

4th The bequests in the second paragraph of this my last will to my wife shall be in lieu of all dower interest.

5th I hereby nominate, constitute and appoint, my wife Mary E. Whitehead, executrix of this my last will and testament, she to act without bond.

In witness whereof I have hereunto subscribed by name this the 27 day of March, 1909.

James Whitehead

****

MISSOURI STATE BOARD OF HEALTH
BUREAU OF VITAL STATISTICS
CERTIFICATE OF DEATH

1 PLACE OF DEATH

County _Chariton_

Township _Cunningham_   Registration District No. _176_   File No. _____

Village   Primary Registration District No. _5244_   Registered No. _____

City _____ (NO. _____ St. _____ Ward)

2 FULL NAME _James Whitehead_

PERSONAL AND STATISTICAL PARTICULARS	MEDICAL CERTIFICATE OF DEATH

3 SEX _Male_   **4 COLOR OR RACE** _White_   **5 SINGLE MARRIED WIDOWED OR DIVORCED** (Write the word) _Married_

16 DATE OF DEATH _Aug 12 1915_ (Month) (Day) (Year)

6 DATE OF BIRTH _Jan 26 1852_ (Month) (Day) (Year)

17 I HEREBY CERTIFY, that I attended deceased from _Jan 1913_ to _July 1 1915_ that I last saw h____ alive on _July 1 1915_ and that death occurred, on the date stated above, at _____

7 AGE _63_ yrs. _6_ mos. _16_ da.   **If LESS than 1 day ...hrs. or ...min.?**

The CAUSE OF DEATH was as follows:
Senility. Was paralyzed - Right Hemplegia in Jan 1913. Gradually got weak mentally + physically until death (Duration) _2 yrs. 6 mos. 16_

8 OCCUPATION
(a) Trade, profession, or particular kind of work _Farming_   82D   75B
(b) General nature of industry business or establishment in which employed (or employer) _Farm Labor_   197

CONTRIBUTORY (Secondary) _Arterio Sclerosis Great drinker. Had Keely cure_ (Duration) _____ mos. _____ da.

9 BIRTHPLACE (City or town, State or foreign country) _England_

(Signed) _J M Hardy_ M. D.
Aug 13 191 (Address) _Sumner Mo._

*State the Disease Causing Death, or, in deaths from Violent Causes, state (1) Means of injury; and (2) whether Accidental, Suicidal or Homicidal.

10 NAME OF FATHER _Enoch Whitehead_

11 BIRTHPLACE OF FATHER (City or town, State or foreign country) _England_

12 MAIDEN NAME OF MOTHER _Wilkinson_

18 LENGTH OF RESIDENCE (For Hospitals, Institutions, Transients, or Recent Residents)

At place of death _____ yrs. _____ mos. _____ da.   In the State _____ yrs. _____ mos. _____ da.

Where was disease contracted if not at place of death? _____

13 BIRTHPLACE OF MOTHER (City or town, State or foreign country) _England_

Former or usual residence _____

14 THE ABOVE IS TRUE TO THE BEST OF MY KNOWLEDGE

(Informant) _Mary E. Whitehead_

(Address) _Sumner Mo_

19 PLACE OF BURIAL OR REMOVAL _Lakeside Cemetery_   **DATE OF BURIAL** _Aug 14 1915_

15 Filed _Aug 13. 1915_ _J W Hardy_ Registrar

20 UNDERTAKER _Wash F Thorne_   **ADDRESS** _Sumner Mo._

DEATH CERTIFICATE FOR JAMES WHITEHEAD
James Whitehead was survived by his wife,
Mary, who remarried and was known to her
grandchildren as Grandma Post.

MISSOURI STATE BOARD OF HEALTH
BUREAU OF VITAL STATISTICS
CERTIFICATE OF DEATH

Mar 16 1939

Registration District No. 137
Primary Registration District No. 4057
File No.
Registered No. 3

1. PLACE OF DEATH
County Carroll
Township
(City) Hale

2. FULL NAME Mary E. Post
(a) Residence, No.
(Usual place of abode)
Length of residence in city or town where death occurred yrs. mos. ds. How long in U. S., if of foreign birth? yrs. mos. ds.

PERSONAL AND STATISTICAL PARTICULARS

3. SEX Female
4. COLOR OR RACE White
5. SINGLE, MARRIED, WIDOWED, OR DIVORCED Widow
5A. IF MARRIED, WIDOWED, OR DIVORCED HUSBAND OF OR WIFE OF Mr. Post
6. DATE OF BIRTH (MONTH, DAY, AND YEAR) Dec. 5 1859
7. AGE YEARS 79 MONTHS 1 DAYS 28

Birthplace (City or Town) (State or Country) Illinois
13. NAME David Case
14. BIRTHPLACE (City or Town) (State or Country)
15. MAIDEN NAME Nathanni Lang
16. BIRTHPLACE (City or Town) (State or Country)
17. INFORMANT Earl Whitehead Hale mo
18. BURIAL, CREMATION, OR REMOVAL DATE Feb 5 1939
19. UNDERTAKER Frank E. Slater Hale mo
20. FILED Feb 4 1939 Registrar 132

MEDICAL CERTIFICATE OF DEATH

21. DATE OF DEATH (MONTH, DAY, AND YEAR) Feb 3 1939
22. I HEREBY CERTIFY, That I attended deceased from Jan 27 1939 to Feb 3 1939 I last saw her alive on Feb 3 1939. Death is said to have occurred on the date stated above, at ... m. The principal cause of death and related causes of importance were as follows:
Hemmorage of Brain 1-27-39

Name of operation ... Date ...
What test confirmed diagnosis? ... Was there an autopsy? ...
23. If death was due to external causes (violence), fill in also the following:
Accident, suicide, or homicide? ... Date of injury ... 19 ...
Where did injury occur? ...
Manner of injury ...
Nature of injury ...
24. Was disease or injury in any way related to occupation of deceased? No
(Signed) ... M.D.
(Address) Hale Mo.

DEATH CERTIFICATE FOR MARY E. POST
Mary Post was born Mary E. Case, and was
the wife of James Whitehead

MARRIAGE LICENSE.

STATE OF MISSOURI,
COUNTY OF LIVINGSTON.

This License Authorizes any Judge of a Court of Record, or Justice of the Peace, or any Licensed or Ordained Preacher of the Gospel who is a citizen of the United States, to SOLEMNIZE MARRIAGE between _William H Whitehead_ of _Sumner_ in the County of _Chariton_ and State of _Missouri_ who is _Over_ the age of twenty-one years; and _Miss Blanche Eaton_ of _Hale_ in the County of _Carroll_ and State of _Missouri_ who is _Over_ the age of eighteen years.

Witness my hand as Recorder of Deeds, with the seal of office hereto affixed, at my office in Chillicothe, this _Chillicothe_ Mo, _14th_ _Feby_, 190.6.

By _S H Taylor_ Deputy. _R Randolph_ RECORDER OF DEEDS.

STATE OF MISSOURI,
County of _Livingston_ ss.

This is to certify that the undersigned _an ordained minister_ did at _home of the brides father_ in said County, on the _17th_ day of _February_ A. D. 190.6, unite in marriage the above named persons. And I further certify that I am a citizen of the United States, and legally qualified under the laws of the State of Missouri to solemnize marriage.

Henry Neighbors

The foregoing License and Certificate of Marriage was filed for record in my office on the _20_ day of _February_ 19.?.?.

By _S H Taylor_ Deputy. _R Randolph_ Recorder of Deeds.

**MARRIAGE LICENSE FOR WILLIAM HENRY WHITEHEAD
AND BLANCHE EATON**
William and Blanche Whitehead were married
on February 17, 1906, at her father's home.

DEATH CERTIFICATE FOR BLANCHE (EATON) WHITEHEAD
Blanche Whitehead died of infection from complications
following the birth of her third son, Henry.

DEATH CERTIFICATE FOR WILLIAM HENRY WHITEHEAD
William Whitehead died of heat stroke while working
on his farm.

MISSOURI STATE BOARD OF HEALTH
Bureau of Vital Statistics

CERTIFICATE OF BIRTH

1. PLACE OF BIRTH
State _Missouri_
County _CARROLL_
City _____
Street No. or
Name of Hosp. _____

Certificate No. _97894_

2. Full Name _CHARLES EDWARD WHITEHEAD_
3. Sex _MALE_ 4. Twin, triplet or single _____ 5. Date of birth _AUG. 11 1909_
Month Day Year

FATHER	MOTHER
6. Full name _WILLIAM WHITEHEAD_	11. Full maiden name _BLANCHE EATON_
7. Color _WHITE_ 8. Age at time of this birth _27 yrs_	12. Color _WHITE_ 13. Age at time of this birth _____
9. Birthplace (city or county) _CARROLL_ (State or country) _MISSOURI_	14. Birthplace (city or county) _LIVINGSTON_ (State or country) _MISSOURI_
10. Occupation at time of child's birth _FARMER_	15. Occupation at time of child's birth _HOUSEWIFE_

CERTIFICATE OF ATTENDING PHYSICIAN, MIDWIFE, PARENT OR RELATIVE

I hereby certify that I attended the birth of this person, who was born alive at the place and date above stated.

DO NOT USE THIS SPACE
Confirmed by.
Affidavit ✓
Baptismal Certificate _____
Other Documentary Evidence _____
Accepted and Filed _APR 1919_
By _R. L. Gilmore_
(Name of Clerk)

*Signature _J. W. Hardy M.D._
Dated _Mar. 9 1942_ _____
(Physician, Midwife, Friend, Father, etc.)
Address _Skinner MO_
Approved and Accepted _James Stewart M.D._
State Registrar.

(SEE INSTRUCTIONS ON PAGE 4)

BIRTH CERTIFICATE FOR CHARLES EDWARD WHITEHEAD
Charles was born on his parent's farm. Although the
birth is recorded in Carroll County, Missouri, the
farm was mostly in Chariton County.

CERTIFICATE OF DEATH
STATE OF CALIFORNIA
USE BLACK INK ONLY

3-91-42

STATE FILE NUMBER			LOCAL REGISTRATION DISTRICT AND CERTIFICATE NUMBER

DECEDENT PERSONAL DATA

1A. NAME OF DECEDENT—FIRST (GIVEN)	1B. MIDDLE	1C. LAST (FAMILY)	2A. DATE OF DEATH—MO, DAY, YR	2B. HOUR	3. SEX
CHARLES	EDWARD	WHITEHEAD	October 4, 1991	2000	M

4. RACE	5. HISPANIC—SPECIFY	6. DATE OF BIRTH—MO, DAY, YR	7. AGE IN YEARS	IF UNDER 1 YEAR — MONTHS / DAYS	IF UNDER 24 HOURS — HOURS / MINUTES
White	☐ YES ☒ NO	August 11, 1909	82		

8. STATE OF BIRTH	9. CITIZEN OF WHAT COUNTRY	10A. FULL NAME OF FATHER	10B. STATE OF BIRTH	11A. FULL MAIDEN NAME OF MOTHER	11B. STATE OF BIRTH
MO	USA	William James Whitehead	MO	Blanche Eaton	MO

12. MILITARY SERVICE?	13. SOCIAL SECURITY NO.	14. MARITAL STATUS	15. NAME OF SURVIVING SPOUSE (IF WIFE, ENTER MAIDEN NAME)
19 __ TO 19 __ ☒ NONE	565-12-1526	Married	Madeline Adams

16A. USUAL OCCUPATION	16B. USUAL KIND OF BUSINESS OR INDUSTRY	16C. USUAL EMPLOYER	16D. YEARS IN OCCUPATION	17. EDUCATION—YEARS COMPLETED
Chef	Food Service	United Airlines	40	14

USUAL RESIDENCE

18A. RESIDENCE—STREET AND NUMBER OR LOCATION	18B. CITY	18C. ZIP CODE
1128 North Hal Street	Santa Maria	93454

18D. COUNTY	18E. NUMBER OF YEARS IN THIS COUNTY	18F. STATE OR FOREIGN COUNTRY	20. NAME, RELATIONSHIP, MAILING ADDRESS AND ZIP CODE OF INFORMANT
Santa Barbara	15	California	Jane A. Bosworth (Daughter) 24702 Pallas Way Mission Viejo, California 926

PLACE OF DEATH

19A. PLACE OF DEATH	19B. IF HOSPITAL, SPECIFY ONE: IP, ER/OP, DOA	19C. COUNTY
Marian Extended Care	--	Santa Barbara

19D. STREET ADDRESS—STREET AND NUMBER OR LOCATION	19E. CITY	TIME INTERVAL BETWEEN ONSET AND DEATH	22. WAS DEATH REPORTED TO CORONER? REFERRAL NUMBER
1530 Cypress Way	Santa Maria		☐ YES ☒ NO

CAUSE OF DEATH

21. DEATH WAS CAUSED BY: (ENTER ONLY ONE CAUSE PER LINE FOR A, B, AND C)		
IMMEDIATE CAUSE (A) *Ischemic Cardiomyopathy*	12 yrs	23. WAS BIOPSY PERFORMED? ☐ YES ☒ NO
DUE TO (B) *and severe congestive* ▶		24A. WAS AUTOPSY PERFORMED? ☐ YES ☒ NO
DUE TO (C) *heart failure* ▶		24B. WAS IT USED IN DETERMINING CAUSE OF DEATH? ☐ YES ☒ NO

25. OTHER SIGNIFICANT CONDITIONS CONTRIBUTING TO DEATH BUT NOT RELATED TO CAUSE GIVEN IN 21	26. WAS OPERATION PERFORMED FOR ANY CONDITION IN ITEM 21 OR 25? IF YES, LIST TYPE OF OPERATION AND DATE.
Hypertension & Ao Stenosis	*open heart surgery in 1983*

PHYSICIAN'S CERTIFICATION

I CERTIFY THAT TO THE BEST OF MY KNOWLEDGE DEATH OCCURRED AT THE HOUR, DATE AND PLACE STATED FROM THE CAUSES STATED.	27B. SIGNATURE AND DEGREE OR TITLE OF CERTIFIER	27C. CERTIFIER'S LICENSE NUMBER	27D. DATE SIGNED
	[signature] M.D.	A 32982	10/7/91

27A. DECEDENT ATTENDED SINCE MONTH, DAY, YEAR	DECEDENT LAST SEEN ALIVE MONTH, DAY, YEAR	27E. TYPE ATTENDING PHYSICIAN'S NAME AND ADDRESS
1-11-80	9-25-91	Ram K. Setty, M.D., 206 South Stratford Avenue, Santa Maria, CA

CORONER'S USE ONLY

I CERTIFY THAT IN MY OPINION DEATH OCCURRED AT THE HOUR, DATE AND PLACE STATED FROM THE CAUSES STATED.	28A. SIGNATURE AND TITLE OF CORONER OR DEPUTY CORONER	28B. DATE SIGNED

29. MANNER OF DEATH—specify one: natural, accident, suicide, homicide, pending investigation or could not be determined	30A. PLACE OF INJURY	30B. INJURY AT WORK ☐ YES ☐ NO	30C. DATE OF INJURY MONTH, DAY, YEAR	31. HOUR

32. LOCATION (STREET AND NUMBER OR LOCATION AND CITY)	33. DESCRIBE HOW INJURY OCCURRED (EVENTS WHICH RESULTED IN INJURY)

FUNERAL DIRECTOR AND LOCAL REGISTRAR

34A. DISPOSITION(S)	34B. PLACE OF FINAL DISPOSITION—NAME AND ADDRESS	34C. DATE MO, DAY, YEAR	35A. SIGNATURE OF EMBALMER	35B. LICENSE NUMBER
CR-BU	Rose Hills Memorial Park 3900 So. Workman Mill Rd., Whittier, CA	10-8-91	Not Embalmed	----

36A. NAME OF FUNERAL DIRECTOR (OR PERSON ACTING AS SUCH)	36B. LICENSE NO.	37. SIGNATURE OF LOCAL REGISTRAR	38. REGISTRATION DATE
Dudley-Hoffman Mortuary	56	▶ Sarah L. Miller	10-07-91

STATE REGISTRAR

A.	B.	C.	D.	E.	F.	CENSUS TRACT

DEATH CERTIFICATE FOR CHARLES EDWARD WHITEHEAD
Charles Whitehead died on October 4, 1991, at
Santa Maria, California.

EATON FAMILY

Blanche Eaton was the wife of William Henry Whitehead and mother of Charles Edward Whitehead (husband of Madeline Adams). She was the daughter of John Eli and Mary Louisa (Smith) Eaton. Her known Eaton ancestry is discussed here.

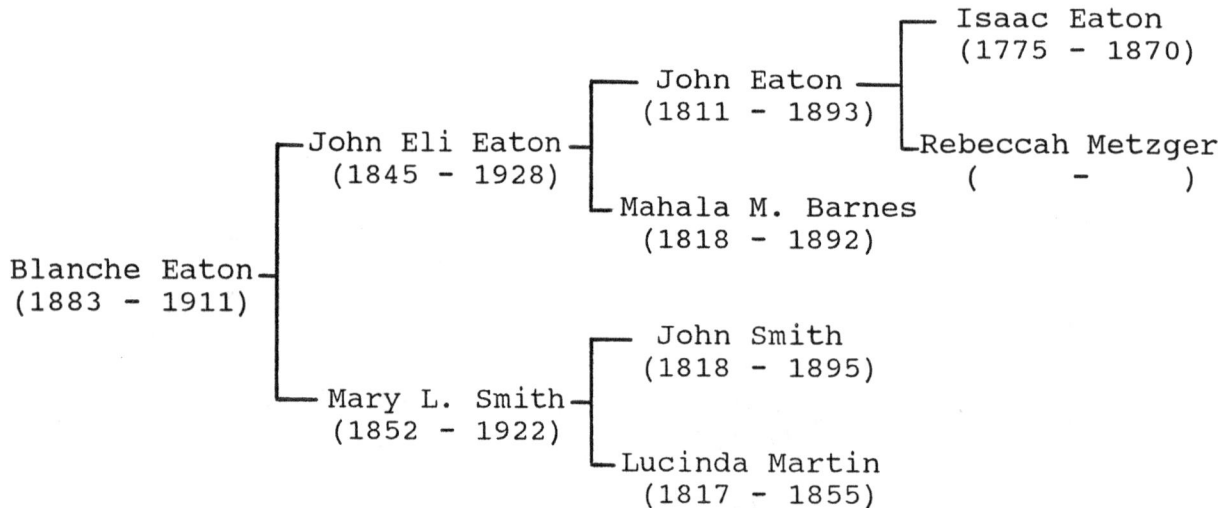

```
                                                        ┌─ Isaac Eaton
                                                        │  (1775 - 1870)
                                      ┌─ John Eaton ────┤
                                      │  (1811 - 1893)  │
                  ┌─John Eli Eaton────┤                 └─Rebeccah Metzger
                  │  (1845 - 1928)    │                   (    -    )
                  │                   └─ Mahala M. Barnes
                  │                      (1818 - 1892)
  Blanche Eaton───┤
  (1883 - 1911)   │
                  │                   ┌─ John Smith
                  │                   │  (1818 - 1895)
                  └─ Mary L. Smith────┤
                     (1852 - 1922)    │
                                      └─Lucinda Martin
                                        (1817 - 1855)
```

As a young man Isaac Eaton moved from Loudoun County, Virginia, to Maryland. His exact birth place in Virginia and the names of his parents have not been discovered. He was raised in Maryland, near Antietam. He married Rebeccah Metzger on September 13, 1806, in Frederick County, Maryland. Isaac Eaton moved to Indiana sometime shortly after 1830. Nothing has been learned of the ancestry of Rebeccah Metzger.

The 1830 census shows that Isaac Eaton lived in Frederick County, Maryland, District No. 3. The census indicates that living with Isaac and Rebeccah were five free white males and one free white female. The ages of the males are: one between ages 5 and 10; one between ages 10 and 15; two between ages 15 and 20; and one between ages 20 and 30. The female is between ages 10 and 15. This information indicates that Isaac and Rebeccah Eaton had at least six children living at the time of the census. One of those was John Eaton, who would have been 18 or 19 years old at the time of the census.

At the time of the 1840 census Isaac Eaton lived in Clay Township, St. Joseph County, Indiana. Living with him was his wife and two free white males, one between the ages of 20 and 30 and one between the ages of 30 and 40.

In the 1850 and 1860 census records, Isaac is reported living and farming in Clay Township, St. Joseph County, Indiana with his wife, Margaret. We can only presume that his first wife died and he remarried. When this may have happened has not been learned.

John Eaton, grandfather of Blanche Eaton, was born in Frederick County, Maryland, on August 4, 1811. He married Mahala Metsker Barnes, who was born in Maryland on February 16, 1818, in Maryland. They moved to Indiana, probably at about the same time as his father, and lived at different times in South Bend and then Porter County, near Valpariso. John Eaton was a farmer and a brick maker.

The middle name given Mahala is too much like the maiden name of Rebeccah, wife of Isaac Eaton, to be a coincidence. If Mahala is daughter to a Mr. and Mrs. Metscar, as reported in a family document, she must have been married to a Mr. Barnes before marrying John Eaton. It appears that Rebeccah and Mahala may have some common ancestry. The three spellings (Metzker, Metsker, and Metscar) are enough alike to be variations of a single original family name. Family records indicate the parents of Mahala, a Mr. and Mrs. Metscar, were a wealthy Dutch family and had come from the old country with ten children. Nothing more about this lineage is known.

John and Mahala Eaton had at least nine children, all born in Indiana. The years of birth given are approximate, extracted from information in the 1850, 1860 and 1870 census records.

(1) **Isaac N. Eaton:** born about 1843.
(2) **Franklin Eaton:** born about 1844; made his home in Boone Grove, Indiana.
**(3) John Eli Eaton: born March 31, 1845; died January 1, 1928; married Mary Louisa Smith on December 2, 1873.
(4) **Ann B. Eaton:** born about 1846.
(5) **Amelia L. Eaton:** born about 1849.
(6) **Samuel E. Eaton:** born February 19, 1851, near Boone Grove, Indiana; married Mary Shipp; had eleven children, seven of whom grew to adulthood. Samuel and Mary owned 40 acres about four and one-half miles north of Hale, Missouri.
(7) **Ada E. Eaton:** born about 1856; married a Mr. Bissett.
(8) **Hanna M. Eaton:** born about 1859; married a Mr. Foster and made her home in Nampa, Idaho.
(9) **Candes E. Eaton:** born about 1862.

John Eaton moved his family to Missouri in 1863, traveling by covered wagon from Indiana. In Missouri he settled on unfenced land along Vinegar Creek about three miles north of Hale. This area in Livingston County later became known as Grand River Township.

Mahala Eaton died December 31, 1892, and John Eaton died May 2, 1893. They are buried together at the Cameron Cemetery located in Livingston County, Missouri, about a mile and a half north of Hale. Hale is in Carroll County.

GRAVE MARKER FOR JOHN AND MAHALA EATON

John Eli Eaton was born in Indiana in part of what is now known as South Bend on March 31, 1845. He traveled with his parents and family to Livingston County, Missouri, as a young man. Until he married, he worked with his father on the family farm.

On December 2, 1873, John Eli Eaton married Mary Louisa Smith, daughter of John and Lucinda (Martin) Smith of Livingston County, Missouri. Mary Smith was born on her parents farm in Livingston County, Missouri.

John Smith was born about 1818 in Kentucky. Lucinda Martin was born August 15, 1817, also in Kentucky. They were married on August 21, 1845, in Howard County, Missouri. Later, about 1851, they moved to Livingston County, where John Smith was to become one of the areas most successful farmers and business men.

Lucile Midyett wrote in a book entitled <u>Hale, Missouri, One Hundred Years Since the Beginning, 1884-1984</u>, that "John Smith built a residence for his family, about two and one-half miles north of Hale. It became known as 'Smith's Tavern' as the stage coach between Chillicothe and Brunswick would stop there for noon meals or overnight accommodations. It was also a place of mail exchange." Lucile Midyett is a grand daughter of Lucy Jane (Smith) Dougherty.

MARRIAGE LICENSE FOR JOHN ELI EATON
AND MARY LOUISA SMITH

John and Lucinda Smith had four children.
(1) **Lucy Jane Smith**: born about 1846; married John Dougherty.
(2) **Nathaniel Smith**
(3) **Mary Louisa Smith: born February 16, 1852; died June 12, 1922; married John Eli Eaton on December 2, 1873.
(4) **James Smith**

Lucinda (Martin) Smith died on October 12, 1855. John Smith married, second, Evaline, a woman twenty years his junior. John and Evaline Smith had 14 children. Not all the children have been identified, but include Oscar J., Flora B., John H., Laura E., Daniel B., Charles A., Emma L., Minnie A., George E., Maggie F., and Ettie N.

No earlier history of the John Smith ancestry is known. If any reader has ever tried to trace the name John Smith, the difficulty is well known. No earlier history of the ancestry of Lucinda Martin is known, as her parents have not yet been identified.

John Eli Eaton and wife Mary made their home in Livingston County where they established their own farm. John Eli Eaton was known as Eli all his adult life.

Eli and Mary Eaton had six children.
(1) **Selene A. Eaton:** born November 21, 1874; died November 30, 1875.
(2) **Oscar Samuel Eaton:** born February 11, 1876; he was a school teacher and a prominent area Minister of the Methodist Church; died February 12, 1938. Oscar Eaton married Marie Johnson on December 24, 1921. She was killed in an automobile accident on December 8, 1923.
(3) **Ella A. Eaton:** born April 15, 1878, died at San Antonio, Texas, on July 15, 1967.
(4) **Mary J. Eaton:** born October 1, 1879; died August 7, 1935; married Charles Edgar Bedell on September 19, 1902. Mary and Charles Bedell had one son, Ralph, who was to become a prominent educator.
    (1) **Ralph C. Bedell**
(5) **Emma C. Eaton:** born July 31, 1881; died September 2, 1966; married C.W.D. Pultz. Mr. Pultz died June 1, 1963. Emma and Charlie Pultz had one daughter.
    (1) **Emma Christina Pultz:** born August 15, 1911; married Harold Alter on April 23, 1929. Harold Alter died December 17, 1987. Christina and Harold Alter had no children.
As detailed in the Whitehead section of this book, Charlie and Emma Pultz raised Charles Whitehead as their son following the death of his parents. Charles Whitehead always considered "Tina" to be his sister.
(6) **Blanche Eaton: born April 23, 1883; died March 21, 1911; married William Henry Whitehead on February 17, 1906; had sons Rollie, Charles, and Henry.

Mary Eaton, wife of John Eli Eaton, died June 12, 1922. Eli Eaton died January 1, 1928. They are buried together at the Cameron Cemetery in Livingston County, Missouri.

Blanche Eaton was born April 23, 1883, in Grand River Township, Livingston County, Missouri. Blanche married William Henry Whitehead and they made their home on land given them as a wedding present by William's father. The details of this union are offered in the Whitehead section of this book.

MISSOURI STATE BOARD OF HEALTH
BUREAU OF VITAL STATISTICS
CERTIFICATE OF DEATH

1783

1. PLACE OF DEATH

County _Livingston_ Registration District No. _1076_ File No.

Township _Grand River_ Primary Registration District No. _5684_ Registered No. _1_

City _____

2. FULL NAME _John Eli Eaton_

(a) Residence. No. _____ St. _____ Ward. _____ (If nonresident give city or town as State)

Length of residence in city or town where death occurred _Many years_ mos. _____ da. _____ How long in U.S., if of foreign birth? yrs. _____ mos. _____ da.

PERSONAL AND STATISTICAL PARTICULARS	MEDICAL CERTIFICATE OF DEATH

3. SEX _Male_ | 4. COLOR OR RACE _White_ | 5. SINGLE, MARRIED, WIDOWED OR DIVORCED (write the word) _Widowed_

16. DATE OF DEATH (month, day and year) _Jan 1_ 19 _28_

5a. IF MARRIED, WIDOWED, OR DIVORCED HUSBAND of (or WIFE of)

17. I HEREBY CERTIFY, That I attended deceased from _Dec 20, 1927_ to _Jun 1, 1928_ that I last saw him alive on _Dec 26, 1927_, and that death occurred, on the date stated above, at _____

6. DATE OF BIRTH (month, day and year) _Mar. 31, 1845_

7. AGE Years _82_ | Months _9_ | Days _1_ | If LESS than 1 day, _____ hrs. _____ min.

THE CAUSE OF DEATH was as follows:

Interstitial Nephritis Chronic Several years.

8. OCCUPATION OF DECEASED
(a) Trade, profession, or particular kind of work _Retired farmer_
(b) General nature of industry, business, or establishment in which employed (or employer)
(c) Name of employer

CONTRIBUTORY (SECONDARY) _Senility_

9. BIRTHPLACE (CITY OR TOWN) _South Bend_
(STATE OR COUNTRY) _Indiana_

WHERE WAS DISEASE CONTRACTED IF NOT AT PLACE OF DEATH

10. NAME OF FATHER _John Eaton_

DID OPERATION PRECEDE DEATH? _no_ Date of _____
WAS THERE AN AUTOPSY? _No_

11. BIRTHPLACE OF FATHER (CITY OR TOWN)
(STATE OR COUNTRY) _Maryland_

WHAT TEST CONFIRMED DIAGNOSIS? _Physical signs_

12. MAIDEN NAME OF MOTHER _Adelia Barnes_

(Signed) _J. W. Hand, M.D._
Jan 1. 1928 (Address) _Sumner Mo_

13. BIRTHPLACE OF MOTHER (CITY OR TOWN)
(STATE OR COUNTRY) _Maryland_

*State the Disease Causing Death, or in deaths from Violent Causes, state (1) Means and Nature of Injury, and (2) whether Accidental, Suicidal, or Homicidal. (See reverse side for additional space):

14. INFORMANT _Ellis Eaton_
(Address) _Hale, Mo._

19. PLACE OF BURIAL, CREMATION, OR REMOVAL _Emerson Cemetery_ | DATE OF BURIAL _Jan 2 1928_

20. UNDERTAKER _N. J. Horne_ _Sumner Mo._ | ADDRESS

15. Filed _Jan 31 1928_ _Mrs. Geo. Cox_ Registrar

DEATH CERTIFICATE FOR JOHN ELI EATON

-191-

BIBLIOGRAPHY

While it is not possible to list every document which has been of some assistance in compiling this work, it is necessary to offer special thanks to some wonderful people. The staff at the National Archives, Pacific Southwest Region, Laguna Niguel; the Mission Viejo Family History Center and the Family History Library in Salt Lake City, Utah, operated by the Church of Jesus Christ of Latter-Day Saints (The Mormons); the fine people at the Los Angeles Central Library; and the numerous family members who have provided documents, photographs, and information have truly made this book possible.

History of the Adams Family, with Biographical Sketches of Distinguished Descendants of the Several American Ancestors, Including Collateral Branches. Compiled by Henry Whittenmore. Published in New York, Willis McDonald & Co., Publishers, 39-43 Gold Street, 1893.

The Ancestry of Thomas Lloyd and Charles Floyd Bosworth. Written and published by Kenneth L. Bosworth, 1990.

The Boston Transcript, 1902 - 1914.

Genealogical and Family History of the State of New Hampshire. Compiled under the Editorial Supervision of Ezra S. Stearns, assisted by William F. Whitcher and Edward E. Parker. The Lewis Publishing Company, New York/Chicago.

The History and Genealogy of the Knowltons of England and America. Author, Rev. Charles Henry Wright Stocking, D.D. Published in New York by The Knickerbocker Press, 1897.

Elisha S. and Lavina (Locke) Andrus...Their Ancestors and Descendants. Published by John V. Beck, 906D Maxwell Terrace, Bloomington, Indiana, 1985.

Lawrence Leach of Salem, Massachusetts and some of His Descendants. Volume I. Author, F. Phelps Leach. Printed by The Messenger Press, St. Albans, Vermont, 1924.

Genealogies of the Families and Descendants of the Early Settlers of Watertown, Massachusetts. Author, Henry Bond, M.D., Volume I, Genealogies. Published in Boston by Little, Brown, and Company, 1855.

The Record of My Ancestry, by Charles L. Newhall. Published in Southbridge by the Herald Power Print, 1899.

<u>History of Sandusky County, Ohio, with Portraits and</u> <u>Biographies of Prominent Citizens and Pioneers</u>. 1812 to 1882. Published in Cleveland, Ohio, by H.Z. Williams and Bro.

<u>Watertown Records</u>, Town Proceedings, Lands Grants and Possessions, The Proprietors' Book, the First Book and Supplement of Births, Deaths, and Marriages. Prepared for publication by the historical society. Published in Watertown, Massachusetts by Press of Fred G. Barker, 1894.

<u>Book of the Lockes</u>. A Genealogical and Historical Record of the Descendants of William Locke, of Woburn, by John Goodwin Locke. Published in Boston and Cambridge by James Munroe and Company, 1853.

<u>Vital Records of Reading, Massachusetts, to the Year 1850</u>. Compiled by Thomas W. Baldwin, A.B., S.B., Member of the New England Historic Genealogical Society. Published in Boston, Massachusetts, 1912.

<u>Genealogical History of the Town of Reading, Massachusetts</u>, Including the Present Towns of Wakefield, Reading, and North Reading, with Chronological and Historical Sketches, from 1639 to 1874, by Hon. Lilley Eaton. Published in Boston by Alfred Mudge & Son, Printers, 34 School Street, 1874.

<u>Early Settlers of Rowley, Massachusetts</u>, by George Brainard Blodgette and Amos Everett Jewett. A reprinting by the New England History Press, Somersworth, 1981.

<u>Rowley, Massachusetts, "Mr. Ezechi Rogers Plantation" 1639-</u> <u>1850</u>, by Amos Everett Jewett and Emily Mabel Adams Jewett. Published by the Jewett Family of America, Rowley, Massachusetts, 1946.

<u>History of Lynn, Essex County, Massachusetts</u>, Including Lynnfield, Saugus, Swampscot, and Nahant, by Alonzo Lewis and James R. Newhall. Printed for James R. Newhall in Lynn, 1865.

<u>The History of New Ipswich, New Hampshire, 1735-1914, with</u> <u>Genealogical Records of the Principal Families</u>. Compiled and written by Charles Henry Chandler with the assistance of Sarah Fiske Lee. Published at Fitchburg, Massachusetts, by the Sentinel Printing Company, 1914.

<u>The Essex Antiquarian</u>. Volume II, No. 6, Salem Massachusetts, June 1898.

<u>A History of Colrain, Massachusetts, With Genealogies of Early</u> <u>Families</u>, by Lois McClellan Patrie.

Eliot Family, by Walter Graeme Eliot. Published at New York, New York, by Press of Livingston Middleditch, 1887.

A Family Record of Dr. Samuel Adams, United Empire Loyalist of Vermont and Upper Canada, compiled by Robert Train Adams and Douglass Graem Adams, 1995.

The History of Woburn, Middlesex County, Mass., by Samuel Sewall, M.A., of Burlington, Mass., sometime pastor of the church there. Published at Boston, Massachusetts, by Wiggin and Lunt, 1868.

A Genealogical Dictionary of the First Settlers of New England, in four volumes, by James Savage. Published at Boston, Massachusetts, by Little, Brown and Company, 1860.

Pioneers of Massachusetts, by Charles Henry Pope. A facsimile reprint by Heritage Books, Inc., 1991.

INDEX

The following alphabetical index contains all the names of all the persons listed in this work. With only a few exceptions, female family members are indexed only by their maiden names. Those persons with the surname ADAMS and the same given names are also indexed by their birth or baptism year, where known, due to the large number of persons with the same given names.

ADAMS,CONT'D: Joel,14,28;John,6,7,87;
John(1631),4,7,10;John(1668),7;
John(1704),8;John(1719),17;John
(1722),17;John(1731),12;John
(1742),13;John(1762),4,48;John
(1763),32;John(1764),4,32,48;
John(1781),46;John(1799),49;John
(1857),4,86,99,109;John(1870),
81;John(1894),90;John(1918),90;
John(1921),81;John(1970),91;
John(1974),88;John(1977),92;
John Q.(1800),1,4,50,67,80,83-
85;John Q.(1830),1,4,80,85,86,
99,103-112,117,118,123;Jonathan,
18;Joseph(1702),4,13,14,26,29,
30,33,34;Joseph(1733),4,26,33;
Joseph(1752),33;Joseph(1765),33;
Juanita,4,103,105,117-119,123,
124,129,163;Kendall,92;Lance,88;
Lanette,88;Lemuel(1734),16;
Lemuel(1751),16;Lemuel(1760),15,
28;Lester,98;Leta,94;Lisa,88;
Lloyd,94;Lois,92;Lorna,81;
Lucienne,88;Lucinda,46;Lucy
(1740),14,27;Lucy(1754),31;
Lydia,17,31;Lydia(1704),4,14,27,
29;Lydia(1730),13,27;Lydia
(1750),14,27;Lydia(1756),15,28;
Lydia(1757),32,47,51;Lydia
(1777),46;Lydia(1789),47;Lyle,
92;Mable,87;Madeline,1,2,4,103,
119,123,124,129,160,162-169,174,
177,186;Margaret,81;Margery,89;
Maria,4,50,67;Marjorie,99;Maro,
4,87,99,109;Martha,17;Marvin,88;
Mary,4,7,9,31;Mary(1667),8;Mary
(1670),7;Mary(1675),6;Mary
(1701),8;Mary(1708),16;Mary
(1714),13;Mary(1717),12;Mary
(1733),13,27;Mary(1739),13;Mary
(1742),14,27;Mary(1744),14,27;
Mary(1745),16;Mary(1748),17;
Mary(1758),33;Mary(1929),103,
121,129,131;Matthew,88;Mehitabel
(1700),15;Mehitable(1665),8;
Melinda,46;Melvin,90;Mercy
(1674),4,9,15;Mercy(1680),4,9,
16;Mercy(1704),13;Mercy(1747),
14,27;Merril,87;Milo,82;Milvin,
93;Moses(1735),13;Moses(1759),
31;Moses(1760),17;

ADAMS,CONT'D: Myrtle(1881),4,99,100,
109;Myrtle"Helen"(1915),4,103,
119,123,124,129,131;Nathaniel,
13,17;Nathaniel(1641),4,9,10,
12,18,19,21;Nathaniel(1670),4,
9,12;Nathaniel(1695),12;Nathaniel
(1712),17;Nathaniel(1717),8;
Nathaniel(1727),12;Nathaniel
(1756),17;Nathaniel(1989),90;
Nehemiah,32;Owen,90;Patrician,
92;Paul,99;Pauline,91;Persis
(1732),14,27;Persis(1742),14,27;
Priscilla(1712),7;Priscilla
(1729),13,26,33;Priscilla(1753),
33;Quincy(1775),4,32,49,50,51,
66,67,70-73,76-78,80,84;Ralph,
95,96,103;Randal(1950),90,91;
Randall,5;Rebecca(1736),14,27;
Rebecca(1767),4,32,49,51;Rebekah
(1782),46;Renda(1960),92;Renda
(1980),88;Robbie,88;Robert,87,
103;Robert(1705),13;Robert(1885),
4,99,103,105,109,111,117,118,
120,122-127,129-132,136,153,160;
Robert(1914),81;Robert(1920),
120;Roscoe(1901),93;Russel
(1900),92;Russell(1926),92;Ruth
(1739),14,27;Ruth(1746),17;Ruth
(1906),81;Ruth(1933),93;Samuel,
17;Samuel(1635),4,8,10;Samuel
(1670),8;Samuel(1682),4,9,16;
Samuel(1706),15,16;Samuel(1710),
8;Samuel(1711),16;Samuel(1726),
16;Samuel(1730),16;Samuel(1742),
16;Samuel(1791),47;Sarah,6,7;
Sarah(1675),4,9,15;Sarah(1676),
9;Sarah(1697),4,13,26,29;Sarah
(1699),8;Sarah(1710),16;Sarah
(1729),12;Sarah(1732),13;Sarah
(1739),16;Sarah(1746),14,27;
Sarah(1754),17;Sarah(1755),33;
Sarah(1756),31;Sarah(1768),33;
Sarah(1784),46;Sarah(1787),47;
Sarah(1833),4,81;Sharilyn,88;
Silas(1733),14,27;Silas(1738),
14,27;Simon,6;Simon(1694),6;
Stacy,92;Stanley(1921),90;
Stanley(1953),90;Stephen,32;
Stephen(1712),8;Stephen(1753),
32,47,50;Stephen(1779),47;
Susanna(1785),46;

ADAMS,CONT'D:Teresa(1965),122;Thomas(1672),4,9,13,26,28,29;Thomas(1699),4,13,26,29-31,33-36,41,42,44,45,66;Thomas(1723),4,26,31,34,35;Thomas(1751),31,46,47,50;Thomas(1757),31;Thomas(1785),47;Timothy,46;Veronica,90;Wayne,88;William,4,6;William(1594),1,4-6,10,12;William(1650),6,7;William(1673),9;William(1678),4,9,15;William(1679),6;William(1696),12;William(1722),12;William(1783),47;Zella,93

AERNI: Russell,139

AGGELER: Clayton,91;Luke,91;Rachel,91;Ted,91

AIKEN: John,49

AKERS: Ada,68

ALLEN: David,96;Eric,96;Helen,96;Mark,96;Mathew,96;Morris,96;Susan,96

ALLUM: Connie,139

ALTER: Harold,190

ANDREWS: George,18

ANDRUS: Elisha,56

ANNABLE: Wilbur,81

APPLETON: Aaron,33;Daniel,31;Isaac,14,27;John,7;Samuel,39

AYERS: Doris,90;Ellen,98

BABBAGE: Hester,73

BAGLEY: Elizabeth,8

BAHR: Judith,88

BALCH: Elizabeth,73,75,76;Freeborn,73

BALDRY: Edward(sic),178;Nathan,171

BALDWIN: Susannah,68

BARGERSTOCK: Alan,119,164,174

BARKER: Christa,137;Loren,136;Terry,136;Thomas,23;William,136,137

BARNES: Clara,68;Edwin,68;John,94;M.A.,68;Mahala,186-188;Olive,68

BARTLETT(E): Anna,67;Obediah,14,27

BARTLEY: Gary,92;Jon,92;Stanley,92

BATCHELDER: Abigail,40

BEACH: Ruth,15

BEARLY: Amanda,120;Clyde,103,119;Cowan,119;Mary,120;Robert,120

BECHTEL: Stephanie,92

BEDELL: Charles,190;Ralph,190

BELCHER: Jer.,38

BEMIS: Sybil,14,28

BERGEMAN: Aaron,98;Cara,98;Marvin,98

BIRGE: Carmen,69

BISHOP: Josiah,13,26;Lydia,41

BISSETT: Mr.,187

BLACK: Andria,101;Ariel,101;Cassandra,101;David,101;Devin,101;Kinberly,101;Shannon,101;Tiara,101;William,101

BLACKMAN: Ann,16;Ebenezer,15

BLANCHARD: Bethia,4,13,26,29

BLODGETT: Samuel,57

BLOESSER: Brent,120;Earl,120;Marti,120

BOERSTLER: Clarissa,139

BOGAN: Willamena,87

BOLLES: Joseph,12;Ruth,12

BOND: John,58

BONNER: Brenda,98

BOOTH: Eunice,16

BOSWORTH: Charles,2,11,164,175;
    Kenneth,2,119,164,174;Lloyd,2,
    174;Nancy,2;Richard,2;Thomas,2,
    164,175

BOWLES: John,34

BRADFORD: Alice,6

BRADSTREET: Elizabeth,6

BRASSFIELD: Franklin,100;Lois,101;
    Louise,101

BREWER: Daniel,58

BRIGHAM: Sebastian,23

BROCKLEBANK: John,7;Samuel,24

BROOKS: Brenda,93;Carter,93;Freda,93;
    Janice,93;Lenna,93;Lynnette,93;
    Mary,86;Matilda,120;Robert,93;
    Sharon,94;Shelia,94;Sherlyn,93;
    Solomon,51;Timothy,94;Ward,94;
    Wilber,94;William,93;Williard,93

BROWN(E) (BROUNE): Dorothy,81;
    Elizabeth,31;Ester,12;Francis,
    73-75;John,38;Mary,73-75;Samuel,
    31;Sarah,61,62;Thomas,7;
    William,31

BROWNBACK: Chad,102;Christopher,102;
    Herbert,102;John,102;Leo,102;
    Lois,102;Loyd,102;Mable,1;
    Michelle,102;

BRYAN: Frances,15

BUCHOLZ: Kimberly,89;Lyle,89;Walter,88

BUCK: Gary,121;James,103,121;John,
    121;Stephen,121;Wendy,121

BUFORD: Robert,173;Sabrina,173;
    Shannon,173

BURKE: Ada,111,120;Thomas,111

BURKHEAD: Hattie,94

BURLEY: Andrew,16;Mary,16

BURNAP: Benjamin,61,62,65;David,62;
    Dorcas,62,63;Easter,63;Elizabeth,
    48,55,58,59,61-63;Hannah,63;
    Isaack,62;John,62;Jonathan,62;
    Joseph,62;Lydia,62;Mary,62,63;
    Rebecca,62;Robert,61,62;Samuel,
    62;Sarah,62

BURNHAM: Phebe,7

BURNITT: Donna,100

BURNS: William,76

CANADA: John,75

CARR: Dorothy,8

CARTER: John,57

CASE: Anna,170;Daniel,170,171;John,
    170;Lizzie,170;Mary,169-172,
    178,180,190;Sarah,170

CHAMBERLAIN: Edna,87

CHANCE: John,119,164,175

CHANDLER: Charles,45;Joseph,14,27

CHAPMAN: Nathan,7

CHASE: Clifford,137;Delphine,1

CHITWOOD: Avis,87;Edna,87;William,87

CHOATE: Daniel,7

CHOPARD:Ella,175;Etta,175;Robert,175

CLARK(E): Bertha,103,111,120,122,129,
131;Edward,111,120;Mary,55-57;
Rose,61;Sarah,32,47;William,55,
56,59

CLARKSON: Jennifer,135;Rick,135

CLOVER: Mable,69

COCHRAN: Agnes,153;Cynthia,154;Cyrus,
156-159;David,154;Elizabeth,154;
Frances,154;George,157,158;
Harriet,154;Henry,153-155;
Henry D.,134,153,155-159;John,
154;Margaret,154;Martha,154;
Mary,155;Minerva,154;Nancy,154;
Nancy J.,132,134,137-140,142,
146,152-158;Patience,154;Polly
(Anvilla),157,158;Robert,153,
157;Rosanna,154;Samuel,153-155;
Thomas,153,154;Wilkinson,154;
William,157

COCKS: Thomas,75

COGGSWELL: William,38

COKER: Sarah,8

COLBURN: Carol,2,174

COLBY: Carrie,68;Charles,67,68;
Christopher,67;Clara,67;Frank,
67;Harry,68;Helen,67;Henry,68;
Herbert,68;John,67;Leora,68;
Norman,67;Samuel,50,67

COLE: Denny,122

COLEMAN: Jess,91

COLLINS: Joseph,68;Lucy,68

COLYER: Della,94

CONANT: John,59;Ruth,32;49;Sarah,9

CONLEY: C.C.,134

CONVERSE: James,57

COOK: Norman,100

COOPER:Amy,171;Gleason,69;Isaac,171,
178;Joseph,68;Mary,69;Walter,171

COUNCIL: Jeffrey,69;Matthew,69;
Wendy,69

COURTRIGHT: Abraham,154

COWEE: Dorothy,68,69;Edwin,68;Emily,
68;Frank,68;James,50,68;John,68;
Lucy,68;Merrill,68

CRADDOCK: Gov. Matthew,42,77

CRAGIN: Francis,49,66,80

CROCO: Charles,171,178

CROSBY: Constance,23

CROSS: Mr.,46

CULVER: Regina,92

CUMMINGS: Donald,97;Isaac,34;Moses,
13;Vickie,97

CUNNINGHAM: Joyce,89

CURTIS: Martha,16

CUTTER: Richard,55,58;Samuel,55,58;
Sarah,55,58,59

DAKEN (DAKIN): Hannah,76;Justus,76

DALAND: Samuel,39

DANE: Elizabeth,17;Mr.,18

DARGATZ: Raymond,121;Robert,103,121

DAVENPORT: Merla,81

DAVIS: Ivor,101

DAVISON: Margaret,12

DAWSON: Abba,82;Clyde,82;Effie,82;

DAWSON,CONT'D: James,82;John,82;Kate, 82;Merrill,82;Ora,82;Perly,82; William,82

DAY: John,43

DEEMER: Donald,139;Kenneth,139; Terrie,139

DeFOREST: Hezekiah,16

DeLECHE: John,42

DeLIND: Marjorie,121

DICKINSON: James,21,23,24;Martha,21; Mary,21;Mercy,4,9,12,19,21; Robert,176;Samuel,22;Sarah,21, 24;Thomas,9,12,19,21-24

DICKSON: Jane,110

DILLARD: April,69;Bill,69;Crystal,69; Melisa,69

DODGE: Israel,75;Joanna,17;Nehemiah; 34,35

DONALD: Amy,89;Ashley,90;Dale,90; Dana,89;Dee,89;Dwight,89;Howard, 89;Karen,89;Laura,89;Mable,1; William,90

DOUGHERTY: John,189

DOW: Mercy,8

DREHER: Jason,94;Kristen,94;Stanley, 93;Steven,93;Teresa,94

DRINKWATER: Emerenza,68

DRISKILL: Glenna,100

DUDERSTADT: Eric,93;Stacey,93;Wayne,93

DUVALL: Gerrie,91

DWIGHT: Timothy,7

EALER: Thelma,139

EATON: Ada,187;Amelia,187;Ann,187; Blanche,169,171-173,176,177,181, 182,186,187,190;Candes,187;Ella, 190;Emma,177,190;Franklin,187; Hanna,187;Isaac,186,187;John, 186-188;John E.,173,186-191; Jonathan,62;Mary,190;Oscar,190; Samuel,187;Selene,190

EDWARDS: Allie,157,159;Benjamin,41; Bethia,36,37,40,41;Elizabeth,41; John,41;Mary,41;Rice,40,41; Sarah,41;Thomas,41

ELIOT (ELLIOT): Abigail,75,76;Andrew, 73-76,79;David,76,78;Dolly,4,32, 49,50,67,70,72,73,77-80,84;Elcy, 78,79;Elizabeth,75,77;Emma,74, 75;Francis,75;Hannah,75;Israel, 77;Jesse,78,79;John,73,75-77; Joseph,77,79;Judith,75;Julia,78, 79;Leonor,139;Mary,74,75;Mel,78; Molly,77;Nathaniel,75,76; Rebecca,78;Samuel,78,79;Sarah, 76,77;Seth,77,79;Skipper,75,76; Susan,78,79;Walter,74;William, 49,67,73-79

ELIZANDO: John,173;Timothy,173

ELLINGTON: Ella,95;Isaac,95

ELWELL: Robert,44

EMENS: Barbara,101

EMERSON: John,38;Martha,17;Nathaniel,7

EMORY: Lucy,76

ENDICOTT: John,42,76,77;Mary,73,76,77; Zerubbabel,76

EVANS: Sarah,95

EVERETT: David,26,33

FAIRCHILD: Mary,15,16;Samuel,15

FAIRFIELD: Benjamin,15;Daniel,15; Nathaniel,15;Samuel,15;Sarah,15; Tabitha,15;Walter,15

FARNSWORTH: Hannah,59;Molly,31,46

FARRAR: Mr.,78;Susanna,64

FASSETT: Hiram,46

FINLAY: Dorothy,82;Grace,82;Hugh,82

FLEMMING: Eric,100;Joe,100;John,100

FLETCHER: Peter,14,27

FOSDICK: Sarah,65

FOSKET: John,43

FOSTER: Beulah,112,115;Chilon,110-112,
    115;Elizabeth,111,115;Emma,41;
    Hannah,111,115;John,111,112,115;
    Louisa,111,115;Lydia,111,115;
    Mary,112,115;Mr.,187;Rebecca,
    112,115;Samuel,111;Sarah,85,
    110-112,115

FRANKLIN: Ruby,92

FRARY: Phineas,154

FRENCH: Abigail,9;Hannah,9;Hester,9;
    John,9;Mary,9;Thomas,9;William,9

FRINK: Alice,32,48

FROST: John,47

GARDNER: Henry,57;Persis,68;Samuel,7

GARTRELL: Janice,87;Milton,87

GAY: Rebecca,65

GIBSON: Elizabeth,76

GIDDINGS: Isaac,39

GILMORE: Mary,153

GILPIN: Chad,138;Kristen,138;Mr.,138

GINTER: Frederick,68

GLEASON: Edwin,82;John,82;Maud,82;
    Olivia,81

GOLDTHWAIT: Ezekiel,17

GOODALL: Bonnie,91

GOODHUE: Margery,30;William,12

GORGES: Ferdinando,30

GRAMMAGE: John,6

GRANT: Deborah,37;Georgia,100;Rain,
    164,175;Robert,164

GRAVES: Jessica,120

GREELEY: Alice,68

GREEN(E): Margaret,153-155;Rebecca,
    61-64;Thomas,61,64

GREENSTREET: Richard,102

GROUT: Daniel,17

GRUNDEN:Brian,136;Christy,135;Clyde,
    134;Donald,135;Elaine,136;Frank,
    134;GeorgeB.,134,135,140;George
    J.,134;Harry,134;Mary(Mabel),
    136;Michael,135;Samuel,134;Scott,
    135;Susan,136;Tamara,135;Terry,
    135;Valerie,136;Walter,136

GUIST : Colean,137,138

HACK: Andrea,89;David,89;Ed,89;
    Garrett,89;Kelsey,89;Steven,89

HALE: Eunice,14,27;Joanna,14,28

HAMILTON:Hugh,69;James,69;Laura,122;
    Patricia,69;Quincy,69

HAMM: Elizabeth,67;Peter,67

HAMMON: Eleanor,87;Marjorie,87;Percy,87

HAMMOND: Chad,92;Jared,92;Michael,92

HARPER: Donna,98

HARRINGTON: Mary,17

HARTWELL: Ephraim,51;Isaac,58

HATCH: Margaret,100;Phebe,47

HAYS: Kasey,94;Paul,94;Stephanie,94

HECK: Rosalyn,101

HENDERSON: Mary,81;Paul,81

HERNDON: Mark,89

HERRMANN: Cathy,93;Delbert,93;Nancy,93

HILDRETH: Oliver,77;Rebecca,76,77

HILL(S): Joseph,61,64;Mary,67;Rebecca,
  61,64

HOBSON: Ferne,100

HOCK: Rosalind,82

HOOK: Keziah,68

HOPKINSON: Mighill,23

HORNBECK (HORNBACK): Cerilda,133,134,
  146;James,133

HOSLEY: Ashley,88;Crystal,88;David,88;
  Kevin,88;Paul,88

HOWARD: Alma,158

HOWE: Increase,7

HUBBARD: Sarah,31

HUBBLE: Christina,90;David,90;Mr.,90

HULL: Mr.,170

HUNT: Elizabeth,17;Mary,17

HUNTER: Mina,95;Mr.,136

HUSEBY: Mark,92

HUSTED: Mary,157

HUTTON: Susanna,40

INFRANCAS: Annie,101;Frank,101

JENKS: Scott,101

JEWETT:Jeremiah,21;Joseph,23;Luther,
  32,49;Maximilian,23

JOHNSON: Emma,96;John,68;Josiah,57;
  Marie,190;Mary,73-75;Matthew,57;
  Mr.,154;Virginia,175

JONES: Dan,136;Dennis,136;Jeaneane,
  136;Jerome,136;Junior,97;Michael,
  136;Moses,157;Olive,17;Rebecca,
  157,159;Timothy,136;William,58

JOSLYN: Joseph,46

JUREY: Dena,173

KAPOOR: Shashi,164

KIMBALL: Abigail,12;Caleb,12

KINARD: Fred,97;Karen,98;Rachel,98

KINSMAN: Lydia,26,31,45,46;Paletiah,
  34;Robert,38

KIPER: Katherine,89

KIRK: Alyssa,138;Amy,138;Katheryn,
  138;Kenneth,137,138;Kent,138;
  Kyle,138;Natisha,138;Norman,100;
  Paul,137,138;Samantha,138;Sara,
  138

KNEPKER: Julia,137

KNIGHT: Aaron,46;Asa,46

KNOTT: Betty,137

KNOWLES: Steven,119,164,175

KNOWLTON: Benjamin,37; Charles,28;
    Deborah,4,13,26,30,31,34,36,41,
    42,44,45;Ezekiel,30,31,36,40-42,
    44;John,36,37,39-41;Mary,37,39;
    Nathaniel,37;Rice,14,27,39;
    Robert,40,41;Samuel,37;Sarah,41;
    Thomas,30,37-40;William,36-40

KOCH: Marguerite,173,174

KOHN: Valeta,135

KREPEL: Debbie,139;Lou,139;Sherie,
    139;Terrie,139

LALLY: David,91;Dustin,91;Gregory,91;
    Kate,91;Lacey,91;Norman,91;
    Scott,91;Toby,91;Victoria,91

LAMB: Barry,88;Kendra,88;Kyla,88;
    Merril,88;William,88

LAMSON: Hannah,12;Joseph,65;Mary,12;
    Peter,14,27;Thomas,13

LANE: Lovicie,170;Mr.,78;Noah,170

LANGLEY: Abel,21

LARCOM: C.,75

LASKA: Bernard,139;James,139;Leo,139;
    Martha,139

LEACH: Abigail,43; Ambrose,43;Ann,44;
    Bethiah,43;Charles,44;Clement,
    43;Edmund,43;Elizabeth,43,44;
    Giles,43;Hannah,44;James,43;
    John,43,44;Joseph,44;Lawrence,
    42,43;Margaret,43;Mary,43,44;
    Paul,44;Rachel,43;Richard,43;
    Robert,41-44;Samuel,43;Sarah,
    30,31,36,40-44

LEAKE: Sherry,90

LEATHERHEAD: Elizabeth,55,58

LEWIS: Alonzo,63

LINHART: Dorothy,81;Edward,81;Lois,
    81;Samuel,81

LIPE: Pansy,139

LOCKE: David,59;Ebenezer,57,59;
    Elizabeth,57,59;Hannah,58;James,
    48,55,57-63;John,45,55,57,59;
    Jonathan,58-60;Joseph,57;Lavina,
    56;Martha,59;Mary,57,58;Phebe,
    58;Rebecca,4,26,31,32,48,50,55,
    59-61,71,73;Rebeckah,58;Ruhannah,
    58;Samuel,57;Sarah,47,58,59;
    William,45,55-57,59

LONG: Quincy,101

LONGLEY: William,63

LORD: Robert,7

LOUR: Michael,88;Tina,88

LOVETT: Vicky,98

LOW: Jacob,12

LUCAS: Hannah,111

LUETHE:Claire,103,120,121;Samuel,120

LUSK: Catherine,134,135,140,158,162;
    Frances,135,136,158;Ingram,136,
    158;James,134,157;John,136,158;
    Polly,136,158

LUTZ: Mary,81

MAHAFFIE: Cynthia,97

MAIN: Mr.,154

MALHOTRA: Abha,164,175;Anand,164

MANIGONIA: Joyce,93

MANNING: Mary,6

MANWEILER: Gladys,69

MAPES: Harriet (Hattie),4,103,105,117,
    118,120,123,124,127-129,132,133,
    136,138,140,146,153,160;Harriet
    N.,132;Henry,132;Ira E.,134;

MAPES,CONT'D: Ira L.,133,134;James,
    134;Joe,124;John,134;Joseph,
    132-134,137-141,143-153,157;Mary
    Jane (Mada),124,135,137,138,140,
    146;Pauline,139;Sarah Jane
    (Sada),124,135,136,138,140,146;
    William,134

MARCH: Hugh,8

MARIN: Rosa,88

MARKLEY: James,136;John,136;Joseph,
    136;Patricia,136

MARSHALL: Elaine,120

MARTIN: Eunice,96;Lucinda,186,188,
    189;Mr.,170

MASCALL: John,73;Sarah,73,76

MASON: John,30

MASONHALL: Phyllis,173

MATTOX: Charles,96

MATTSON: Gretchen,91

McCLAIN: Steven,101,102;Tammie,101

McCLURE: Susan,134,135

McCRAW: Jay,173;Jeremy,173;Jessica,173

McDOWELL: Cathie,101;Harold,101;Homer,
    101;Peggie,101

McELWEE: Donald,139;Kenneth,139;Nancy,
    139;Raymond,139

McGEE: Andrea,98;Andrew,98;Anna,98;
    Brenda,97;Candy,98;Carl,97;
    Charoletta,97;Earl,97;Gary,98;
    Jane,98;Larry,98;Lauren,98;
    Rettie,97;Richard,97;Stephanie,
    98;Vernon,97;Wayne,98

McGINNIS: Nellie,81

McGREW: Emmet,96;Ethel,96

McFARLAND: Matilda,153,155-157,159

McINTYRE: W.E.,158

McKEEVER: William,136;Winifred,136

McKILLOP: John,67;Katherine,67

McNABB: Mary,102

McRAE:Alice,101;Althea,102;Anna,101;
    Avis,102;Carl,100;Hilma,100;
    Larry,100;Leo,100;Mable,102;
    Ricky,100;Roy,100;Ruby,101;
    Timothy,100;Velma,100;Vicky,
    100;Walter,100,101;Wanda,100

MEEKS: Joseph,115,116

MEEKUM: Martha,176

MELTON: Judith,96

MERRIAM: Dorothy,13,14,26;Lucy,17

MERRILL: Dorothy,49,67,76-78;
    Nathaniel,77

MESHKAT: Siavash,96

METZGER (METSCAR): Rebeccah,186

MIDYETT: Lucile,188,189

MILLER: Clarence,82;Thomas,154

MINOTT: Beulah,32,48

MIRICK: Hannah,37

MOCK: Serena,110

MOFFET: Sarah,132

MOORE: Sophie,81

MORRILL: Israel,8

MORSE: Anna,13

MOULTON: Elizabeth,10;Eunice,14,28;

MOULTON,CONT'D: James,9;John,9;
        Jonathan,9;William,10

MUDDLE: Henry,38

MUNCEY: Francis,9;John,9;Samuel,9

MUNDELL: Etta,134;Joseph,134

MUNROE: William,58

MUNSON: Claude,122;Neal,122

MURDOCK: Thomas,49

NELSON: Thomas,23

NERON: Sarah,110-112,115

NEWHALL: Charles,63;Daniel,65;Elisha,
        64,65;Elizabeth,61-65;Hannah,
        65;James,63;John,63,64;Joseph,
        64;Lydia,65;Martha,65;Mary,63,
        64;Nathaniel,64;Rebecca,64,65;
        Samuel,64,65;Susanna,63;Thomas,
        61-65

NEWTON: Beulah,59

NORMAN: Alice,92

NORRIS: Grace,81

NORTON: Mehitable,8;William,38

OLNEY: Mercy,47

OMARK: Jane,164

O'NEAL: Etta,68

OSBORNE: John,8

OVIATT: Abigail,15;Thomas,15

PACE: Lynette,135

PADDOCK: Elma,101

PARK(S): Cecil,171;Charlie,122

PARKER: Joseph,48;Mary,75;Nathan,75

PARSONS: Jennifer,89;Justin,89

PATCH: John,34,35

PEARSON: Claude,81;James,8

PERKINS: Mary,15,28;William,46

PERRYMAN (PERRIMAN): Frances,55,58

PICKARD: John,24

PIERCE: Marie,177;Marrion,177;Phebe,
        58;Roy,177;Thomas,58

PILLSBURY: Paul,21

PIPER: Alice,8

PITMAN: Joseph,44

PLUMB: Jemima,16

POLLARD: Benjamin,14,27

PORTER: Anna,31,75

POST: Mr.172

POTTER: Anthony,10;Elizabeth,61,63,64;
        Hannah,17;Nicholas,63;Persis,
        14,27

POWELL: Deborah,154

PRESTON: Judith,26,32

PRICE: William,31

PULTZ: Charles,177,190;Emma,177,190

PYGAN: Lydia,6

QUARLES: William,21

RALPH: Stephen,33;Susannah,26,33

RAMEY: Mary,170

RAMSDEN: John,9

RAND: Solomon,17

RAWIE: Mary,94;T.J.,94

RAYMOND: Susan,47

READ: Millie,134

REISDEL: Mr.,154

REMINGTON: John,23

REYNER: Humphrey,23

RHODES: Dennis,92;Derek,92;Jaci,92;
    Kayla,92

RICE: Minnie,136

RICHARDS: Nicholas,46

RICKERS: Della,97

RIGDON: Angela,97;Earnest,103,118,119;
    Edna,96;Ethel,97;Harry,97;Jacob,
    97;JoAnn,97;Keith,96;Ralph,96,
    103;Scott,96;Sheiliy,96;Verl,96;
    William,96

ROBERTS: Linda,102

ROBINS (ROBBINS): Abram,79;Jacob,81;
    John,70,77,80

ROBINSON: Kathleen,90

ROGERS: Ada,90;Daniel,39;Elizabeth,13;
    Ezekiel,19,23

ROOK: Lola,98

ROSCELLI: Alan,69

ROSS: Darlene,103,121,122;Mae,90;
    Thomas,31

SAKS: Emilie,121;Kraig,121;Matthew,
    121;Nathan,121

SARGEANT (SARGENT): Elizabeth,77;
    Sarah,65

SAVORY: Thomas,13

SAWTELLE: Sarah,47

SAWYER: William,62

SCHEIDTS:Delphine,137;Genevieve,139;
    Herman,137;LaVerne,139;Raymond,
    139;Weimer,137

SCOTT: Janet,93;N.K.,158;W.B.,158

SCRIBNER: Susanna,80

SHANK: William,82

SHATTUCK: Mercy,74

SHEDD: Abel,32,49

SHERMAN: Mr.,154

SHIPP: Mary,187

SIMMONS: Beverly,120

SMITH: Abijah,31,47,48;Ann Elizabeth,
    36,37;Anna,89;Charles,189;
    Daniel,189;Eldon,174;Emma,189;
    Ephraim,31;Ettie,189;Flora,189;
    George,189;James,189;John,16,
    186,188,189;Laura,189;Lucy,189;
    Maggie,189;Mary,173,186-189;
    Minnie,189;Mr.,154;Nathaniel,
    189;Oscar,189;Rae,164,174;
    Richard,16

SPANGLER: Ella,81;Emma,81;George,82;
    Sam,81

SPEAR: Joseph,46

SPIEKER: David,93;Dustin,93;Evan,93

STACE: Thomas,7,10

STACEY: Elizabeth,6;Simon,6,10

STANLEY: Rachel,87

STAPLETON: Gladys,92

STARKEY: Christopher,102;Jean,102;
    Marvin,101

STEARNS: Elizabeth,31,46;Johas,46;
    Thomas,46

STEELE: Mary,171,176,177;Tracy,91;
    William,176

STEVENS: John,59;Remember,15;Silas,
    14,27

STILES: Isaac,15

STONE: Sandra,174

STOW: Abner,16;Joseph,14,27

SWETT: Samuel,8

TAFT: Abigail,17

TARBELL: Betsey,47;John,76

TAYLOR: Ebenezer,59;Linda,96;William,82

TEMPLE: David,17

THOMAS: Mr.,170;Philip,32,47

THOMPSON: Jonathan,35

THORNTON: Debra,96

TIMM: Rita,88

TOLVA: Martha,175,176

TORRANCE: Thomas,153

TOWNE: Francis,31,47

TOWNSEND: Adam,98;Perry,98

TREADWELL: Sarah,16

TREAR: J.D.,158

TREDWELL: Hannah,7

TRUMBLE: John,24

TUCK: William,75

TYLOR: Lovicie,170

VIVION: Mary,73,74

WADE: Samuel,65

WADLEIGH: Ephraim,8

WAITE : Jonadab,7;Thomas,10

WALDER: Laurel,96

WALDRON: Hannah,75

WALKER: Edward,80;Elizabeth,49;Lovina,
    4,50,67,80,85

WALLACE: Brian,102;Kenneth,102;
    Michael,102

WARNER: Daniel,8;John,33;Mary,12;
    Priscilla,13,26,33

WARRINGTON: Patricia,135;Shirley,135

WATSON: Dorcas,7;John,7

WEBB: Christian,164,174;Colin,164,174;
    James,164,174;Ronald,164,174;
    Thomas,119,164,174

WEEKS: Amy,97;Jerry,97;Kenneth,97;
    Rettie,97;Rose,97

WETZ: Joseph,81

WHEELER: Josiah,32;Lydia,32;Nathan,
    32,47;William,16

WHIPPLE: Archelaus,7;Daniel,17;
    Elizabeth,7,17;James,16,29;
    Jemima,16;John,7,16,17,23;Joseph,
    7;Lucy,32;Mary,7;Priscilla,7;
    Sarah,7,32;Susannah,7;William,12

WHITE: Silas,154;William,10

WHITEHEAD: Ada,170;Ann,134;Anna,170;
    Brandi,173;Brian,173;Brookie,
    173;Candy,173;Catherine,170;
    Charles,171;Charles E.,4,103,
    119,162-165,167,169,174,175,177,
    184-186,190;Cindy,173;Edwin,171,
    178;Emma,119,164,165,170,174;
    Enoch,169-171;Eric,171;Harry,
    176;Henry(Ray),175,176,182,190;
    James,169-172,178-180;Jane,2,
    119,164,165,174;Jessica,173;
    John,170;Judy,119,164,165,175;
    Julia,171,178;Katie,171;Leroy,
    171;Linda,173;Lloyd,173;Lorea,
    176;Martha,169-171,178;Mary,170;
    Minnie,171,178;Ralph,171;Randy,
    173;Rollie,173,174,190;Ula,175;
    Walter,171,178;William,169,171-
    173,176-178,181,183,186,190

WHITING: Jonas,14,27

WHITTENMORE: Benjamin,58

WICKINGHAM: Thomas,9

WIGGLESWORTH: Samuel,29,35

WILKINSON: John,169,170;Martha,169,170

WILLIAMS: Elizabeth,58;Guy,81;Isaac,
    73,76,77;Sarah,73,75,76,77

WILLIS: Mary,78

WILSON: Albert,111;Arthur,110;
    Catherine,110;Chilon,111;Darby,
    110;Desdemona,111;Edith,110;
    Elizabeth,36,37,40;Hannah,110;
    James,154;Jane,110;John,85,110-
    112;Mahala,110;Milton,111;
    Nathaniel,65;Nancy,111;Olney,
    111;Rachel,110;Sarah J.,1,4,80,
    85,86,99,103-106,108-113,117,
    118,123;Serepta,111;Susan,136,
    137;Theophilus,37;William,110,
    111

WINN: Abiather,76

WINTERBERG: Deborah,69;Jody,69;Lynette,
    69;Robert,69

WINTHROP: Gov. John,5

WITT: Elizabeth,37

WOOD(S): George,119,164,175;Heather,
    164,175;Leora,67;Lucy,17

WOODBURY: Benjamin,14,27;Elizabeth,
    75;John,41;Peter,75

WOODMAN: John,13;Sarah,7

WOODIER: Grace,74

WOODWARD: Grace,100

WOOLCOTT: Emerson,14,27

WORDEN: Susan,77

WRIGHT:Dale,102;Elizabeth,121;Jason,
    102;John,58;Melissa,102

YEOMANS: Phoebe,78

YOUNG: Ione,87;Ira,49;Norman,87

ZIMMERMAN: Elsie,119

ZINK: Judith,89